BIBLE WOMEN

ALL THEIR WORDS AND WHY THEY MATTER

LINDSAY HARDIN FREEMAN

ABOUT THE COVER: "Spiritual Gifts," a watercolor painting by Kathy Eppick. An Episcopalian, Eppick sketched the idea during a retreat, which focused on women discovering their spiritual gifts. A member of the Episcopal Church Visual Arts community, she is also a teacher and figure skater and lives in Cerritos, California.

Library of Congress Cataloging-in-Publication Data
Freeman, Lindsay Hardin.
Bible women : all their words and why they matter / Lindsay Hardin Freeman.
pages cm
Includes bibliographical references and index.
ISBN 978-0-88028-391-5 (alk. paper)
1. Women in the Bible. 2. Rhetoric in the Bible. I. Title.

BS575.F75 2014
220.9'2082--dc23
2014026093

ISBN 978-088028-391-5
Library of Congress
Printed in USA

Forward Movement
www.forwardmovement.org

BIBLE WOMEN

ALL THEIR WORDS AND WHY THEY MATTER

LINDSAY HARDIN FREEMAN

Forward Movement

in partnership with the

Episcopal Church Women

Dedicated to all women and girls

who have been beaten, used, abused, raped, thrown away

who have died on street corners

in lonely fields

on their doorsteps

in refugee camps

in utero

who have spoken, screamed, or cried

whose words were not remembered or understood

and to those who could not speak

who were silenced, beaten back

their cries known to You alone.

Restore them, Lord

renew them

make them whole

on earth

as it is in heaven.

WITH SPECIAL THANKS TO:

Susan Webster
Christy Stang
Joyce White
Leonard Freeman
Richelle Thompson

WHAT READERS ARE SAYING

Author and visionary Lindsay Hardin Freeman brings us another great leap forward in comprehension of the realities of the female presentations in the Bible. Her diligent analysis of every line uttered by women in scripture delivers startling insights never before analyzed, nor understood, as parts of a deeper message regarding the female half of the human species. This gender, as we all know, is in desperate need of a healthier level of interaction and with *Bible Women: All Their Words and Why They Matter*, Lindsay Hardin Freeman offers us hope for a fresh platform of progress.

Barbara Forster
Human rights activist

Reading *Bible Women* is an opportunity to get reacquainted with not only the stories of biblical woman but also to reflect anew on their words and actions. Included here are some of the most familiar biblical women and, importantly, some of those not frequently the focus of study but introduced here with devotion and respect. An excellent resource for individual and group prayer and reflection.

The Rev. Dr. Sheryl A. Kujawa-Holbrook, PhD, EdD
Dean of the faculty
Professor of practical theology and religious education
Claremont School of Theology, Claremont, California

In *Bible Women: All Their Words and Why They Matter*, Lindsay Hardin Freeman brings to light an entirely new and in-depth understanding of the often unrecognized contribution women made in the overall biblical narrative. Freeman's very adept biblical scholarship provides what I believe to be groundbreaking work in providing greater awareness and appreciation of the importance Bible women play in our sacred story.

The Rt. Rev. Brian N. Prior
Bishop, Episcopal Church in Minnesota

Author Lindsay Hardin Freeman deftly coaxes into high relief the muffled voices of women in the Bible. We see ourselves in their anguish, estrangement, and life-giving passion and meet them in those very places in our lives. Each page calls us to be a daughter of God by stepping out of the past to share our own stories of transformation and learn the ways of God from one another.

Cynthia Carson
Vice president, Province VII Order of the Daughters of the King
Education for Ministry mentor, Sewanee School of Theology

Lindsay Hardin Freeman has provided a great gift to the women of our church, and to all people searching for relevance in even the smallest of words and action. As she writes in her introduction, "Their words are meant for us." Here is a fascinating offering for group study and personal reflection from this consummate storyteller and teacher.

The Rev. Nancy R. Crawford
National president, Episcopal Church Women
Eugene, Oregon

CONTENTS

The Women Who Speak in the Apocrypha

The Women Who Speak in the New Testament   355

PREFACE

This book is the result of thousands of individual research hours and old-fashioned, around-the-table Bible study.

Several years ago, I had the pleasure of serving as an interim rector at Trinity Episcopal Church in Excelsior, Minnesota. I'd just finished a book, *The Scarlet Cord: Conversation with God's Chosen Women*, telling the stories of twelve Bible women from a first-person perspective. Because women in the Bible tend not to say much, I filled in historical details where possible: why they took the actions they did, how they felt, whom they loved.

Writing that book always begged these questions: What did Bible women actually say? Who were those that talked (or rather, who were women whose words were written down)? How many were there? What were the broad themes among those who spoke? What are the surprises—those things that have been under our noses for centuries but largely dismissed until now? What might their words mean for us today? How might their actions increase our faith?

I asked who within the congregation would be interested in researching such topics, and three people stepped up: the head of the altar guild, our church librarian, and a bright, home-schooled, high school girl.

We got out colored markers and sticky notes and read the Bible cover to cover, marking the words said by women, hand-counting them, recording them on spreadsheets, and analyzing them in context of their larger stories. We met for two hours weekly, worked at home for endless hours, laughed at seemingly bizarre narratives, and felt our stomachs clench upon reading some of the more tragic stories.

This research was done using the New Revised Standard Version (NRSV) of the Bible, rather than working from the Bible's original Hebrew and Greek. Our choice was to work within a text that provides accessibility to contemporary readers. We believe that any group or individual can take a Bible off the shelf and get to work and that our effort proves this is possible.

We scoured seminary libraries, bookstores, bibliographies, and online articles. We sought out church leaders, scholars, and primary sources about Bible women who speak but found few leads. Our research led us to this conclusion: Until now, there has not been a systematic, reflective analysis of which Bible women talked, what they said, how much they said, and what their words might mean for contemporary Christians.

There are many reasons for this omission in scholarship. The Bible was composed in a patriarchal society; and it has been mostly men, over the centuries, who have studied the ancient writings and worked to make sense of them. Until the twentieth century, there was not a substantial body of work on women in the Bible in general. There are more male than female characters in the Bible and thus, perhaps more interest, and an analysis of women who spoke—or more accurately, had their words recorded—would automatically leave out the women who didn't speak (or whose words weren't included in the scriptures).

Are there exceptions? Of course—yet the predominantly male character of the Bible is unmistakable. Still, the Bible is larger than its parts. And more important than any analysis is this: as the inspired word of God, the Bible is our sacred treasury. From it, we learn about God and God's love for us, good and evil, atonement and redemption, and about our spiritual grandmothers and grandfathers.

Lindsay Hardin Freeman
Summer, 2014

INTRODUCTION

Fresh Water: Hearing from Bible Women Firsthand

Bible women are an endangered species. Trapped in dry and dusty literary caskets for centuries, they are easily dismissed because they, more than men, are often viewed as simply "good" or "bad." Mary, the mother of Jesus, is "good" (and usually wearing blue). Mary Magdalene, Jesus' companion, is "bad." (She was a prostitute, wasn't she?) Eve bad. Jezebel bad. Busy Martha of Bethany not so good, compared to her contemplative sister Mary (except Mary is presented as a bit of a complainer). Old Elizabeth is good; the inquisitive woman at the well is bad, because of her many marriages. So go the stereotypes.

Does it matter? Absolutely. Should we care? Without question. Would we be lesser people without these women and their stories? Totally.

Some of the most (alternately) courageous, funny, brave, and faithful women in history, Bible women speak through the centuries with their words and the witness of their lives to guide and instruct our hearts. Their words are part of God's word, the Bible, for a reason. Their words are meant for us.

Moments of Grace and Violence

Read this book and you will see moments of grace and high moral ground. You will also be horrified at intense brutality and violence: some of it by women, but most of it perpetrated against women.

Yet, repeatedly, God used their stories. Through these women God spoke, intervened, changed, illustrated, and proclaimed the story of redemption. Like a great reservoir of wisdom, a pond of undiscovered, deep nurturing waters, their stories are here for us.

Within-the-faith Perspective

This book is written from a Christian perspective. We see the sweep of religious history here: we see the foundation of our faith in our Jewish forebears, and we see Jesus as the fulfillment of many prophecies revealed in pre-Christian days. More, we come at this from a within-the-faith perspective. We hope we have used the best tools of scholarship—but not from an "outside" judging perspective. Our intent is not to stop at counting words—but to learn from, and be fed by, our sisters and our foremothers in the faith.

For that reason, we use the terms "Old Testament" and "New Testament" rather than "Hebrew Scriptures/the First Testament" or the "Christian Scriptures." The thirty-nine books of what we call the "Old Testament" reflect our Protestant Christian version of these texts. Hebrew scripture (the *Tanakh*) combines these texts differently, into twenty-four books.[1]

In Hebrew, the first language in which the Bible was developed, the word "testament" means "covenant" or "contract." That covenant was based on the Law, or the Ten Commandments. With the sacrificial death of Jesus on the cross, we have a new covenant, a new testament that promises eternal life to all who believe. We can never measure up. Yet God promises to love and redeem us.[2]

Women who speak in the Apocrypha are also included here. Accepted canonically as part of the biblical canon in Roman Catholic and Greek Orthodox communities, the Apocrypha is considered important teaching material that is edifying, but not doctrinal in the Protestant arms of the Christian faith (including The Episcopal Church). Yet the stories of women within it are essential to a comprehensive understanding of the Bible. Full of wisdom, drama, and horror, they jump off its pages like firecrackers.

Stories: A Way of Studying the Bible

Stories don't tell us what is true, they tell us what must be true.

Author Unknown

Real truth is eternal, pointing us to the heart of God. Truth cannot always be seen or recorded; sometimes it is beyond words. Sometimes it lies unspoken, expressed in actions or events. Sometimes we see only edges of the truth that point to a larger whole. We see the stars; we know they are there. We cannot see other universes, but we know they are there. And that knowledge leads us to a deeper, more reflective understanding of God.

That is the way with Bible stories as well: they point us to the heart of God and to our spiritual ancestors. Yet for some, the stories happened so long ago that they appear to be far from the truth—useless, easily dismissed, even stumbling blocks to faith.

Take the Garden of Eden, a somewhat troublesome story over the ages. People who believe in the biblical stories of creation stand accused of ignoring science. Those who believe in evolution are told they don't believe the Bible. We're in. You're out.

But not here.

Here we walk the *via media*—Latin for "the middle way." We look for the eternal truths, the ones that must be true. And we use the time-honored premise in the Anglican Communion of applying the three elements of scripture, tradition, and reason. In that context, the following truths can be learned, for example, from the creation story:

- Adam and Eve are the first man and the first woman because they realize they are different from other life forms, and that as humans, female and male, they are made in God's image;

- They find they are free to separate from God;

- They explore independence, free will, and failure;

- They discover their actions have consequences not only for them but also for their children;

- They discover work brings benefits, such as food and clothing;

- They experience grief and the beginning of faith;

- They find that they are only able to have children after they leave the garden (the place of innocence); and

- They learn about pain and death as part of maturing and being on their own.

Such are the truths of the creation story—and the process for discovering the truth in every Bible story. With such an understanding, the word of God is always alive, not a crusty document with its people buried under layers of dust and restrictions. It is, rather, a collection of life-giving stories of our spiritual ancestors and, more importantly, an exploration into the nature of God.

Use that frame of mind. Reach beyond the boundaries of time to explore the lives of our spiritual foremothers. And enjoy them for who they were: malicious, competent, faithful, murderous, funny, and endearing. Think of Bible women as relatives at a family reunion: you love some; you like some; you find some are mentally deficient or from *The Twilight Zone*; you can't stand others. But because they are all part of the family tree—because they are part of you—they are worth knowing.

Tools for Bible Study

The best book for Bible study is...the Bible! Get one if you don't have one. Get two if you have one; three if you have two. As noted, this book uses the New Revised Standard Version in its Bible quotations, spelling, punctuation, and numerological statistics. When needing fresh insight, we'll often turn to *The Message* by Eugene Peterson. Or, if we want lofty language and want to hear about "damsels" instead of girls, we'll go to the King James Version.

Just read the Bible, whatever the translation. Meditate on it. Leave it out on the coffee table. Read it in the daytime; read it when you can't sleep at night. Share it with your children, your grandchildren, your friends. Make it a lifelong habit. Join a group, preferably a women's Bible study group. Use this book to get started.

Definition of Terms

This is a user-friendly book, designed to be free of intimidating words and phrases, in the hopes that Bible women will be more accessible to more people. Each section highlights a specific woman and what she said. Her actual words are in boldface.

NAME AND DESCRIPTOR

Named or unnamed, if a woman or group of women spoke without a male voice accompanying them, they—and their words—are here.

PROFILE IN HISTORY

Each woman is given a "bracket" here, defining how well she is known. You might be surprised to discover how many new Bible women step out of the pages—and what new things you learn about the ones you thought you knew.

Bracket terms:

High: She is known in both religious and popular culture. Most people know Mary was Jesus' mother. Most know Delilah had something questionable going on with Samson, and that hair was involved. Most know Eve was the first woman in the Bible.

Moderately high: Fairly good name recognition, although specific life accomplishments may or may not be known. Example: Jezebel. While most people have a sense of Jezebel being wicked and seductive, they might not know why she acted the way she did, and how she was eventually murdered. Other examples in the "moderately high" group include Mary and Martha of Bethany. The names are familiar…but why?

Moderate: The name is familiar, but the action may not be. Example: Hannah, who begged God to give her a son. Or Miriam, Moses' sister, who stood on the banks of the Nile, watching baby Moses float away in a basket and praying that he not be put to death.

Moderately low: Should ring a bell, but doesn't always. Example: Herodias, who told her daughter, Salome, to ask for the head of John the Baptist. The beheading is known by most Christians, yet nine out of ten people do not know that this deadly conversation is the only full dialogue in the Bible solely between a mother and daughter.

Low: Bare visibility, as in a heavy fog. Try Rachel's midwife, who gave comfort in the midst of both life and death.

So low as to be crawling on the floor: They seem to be strangers, even for those who are well-studied in the Bible. Like the woman in 2 Kings who ate her son (tragic but true). Or Athaliah, who killed her grandchildren and then, when a surviving grandson was restored to the throne, shouted, "Treason! Treason!" You may not have heard of her. And there is little reason to hear from her again.

CLASSIC MOMENT

Here we name the main event for which the woman is known—for example, Eve took the fruit and ate it; Sarah gave birth at age ninety; Mary Magdalene was the first to see the risen Christ.

DATA

How many words does she speak? Where does she fit in the progression of Bible women in terms of words and message?

WHO WAS SHE?

Was the woman in question a prophet or a healer or a warrior or a mother? To whom was she related? Was she widowed? Never married? Did she have children? (While some of these questions may seem pejorative today, they determined much of a woman's life in biblical times.) What stands out about her? What could you keep in your heart about this woman to guide and comfort you?

WHAT DID SHE SAY?

Nuts and bolts. These women are in this book because their words are on record. What was it that they said? No misappropriation; no "he said, she said." If she said it, if she was a real person, and if her words were recorded, then she, and her words, are here, in bold text.

LIKELY CHARACTERISTICS

Was this Bible woman generous? Selfish? Animated? If she had been your neighbor, how would you describe her? Note that neighbors can be beautiful, smart, irritating, insulting, obnoxious—and adulterers or murderers as well. Bible women exhibit a variety of opinions and behaviors; our goal is to be honest about both strengths and faults.

HER STORY

What is her context? What brings her into the Bible? What is her background? Here we employ the five "Ws" of journalism: who, what, when, where, and why.

CONSIDER THIS

Why exactly did Jael slip a tent peg into the enemy's head? Did it have anything to do with a warrior, not her husband, being in her tent? And when King Solomon threatened to slice a baby in half, how did that determine the baby's real mother? And what about the prostitute thing that always shadows Mary Magdalene? Is there any truth to that? This section explains each woman's actions in her context, and provides additional thoughts, much like an op-ed piece.

WHAT MIGHT WE LEARN FROM HER?

Dust-balled for too long, these women have much to teach us. How might their experiences inform our lives? What rings true about their values (or lack thereof)?

For those of you using this book for Bible study, the questions are to help spark your discussions. If you are reading this book on your own, let the thoughts lead you as a spirit guide might.

Who's In? Who's Out?

In deciding which Bible women should be included in this book, here are the questions we asked:

Did the woman speak on her own?

She's here.

Did the woman speak in a group, with other women?

She's here.

Was the woman only quoted by someone else?

She's not here.

Did the woman speak only in a group with men, saying the same exact words?

She's not here.

Was the woman real or could she have been real—or was it an idea of a woman, such as in a vision or parable?

We kept with our rule of flesh-and-blood women. If she's in an image or parable, we did not count her.

If a woman said something twice, are those words counted twice?

She is counted once; her words twice.

CHAPTER 1

FOUNDATIONAL FINDINGS

What are the numbers? What do they mean?

By our count, using the New Revised Standard Version of the Bible in English, about 14,000 words are spoken by women. While the NRSV is, of course, translated from Hebrew and Greek, we used the ancient texts for occasional reference questions but kept our analysis consistent by using the NRSV for word counts.

Fourteen thousand words is not much. By comparison, the average novel (take *Brave New World* by Aldous Huxley) is about 64,000 words long. Barack Obama's annual State of the Union address averages about 7,000 words; George W. Bush's were about 5,100 words.[3] Using the average speaker's pace of about 120 words per minute, the words of Bible women could be uttered in less than two hours.

The Bible—including the Old Testament, New Testament, and Apocrypha—is about 1.1 million words long.[4] Ballpark total, then: about 1.2 percent of the words in the Bible are said by women. Obviously this is an incredibly small number. There are two ways to look at that sum. We could be angry and dismiss the whole thing, or we could pay more attention to what the verbal minority says. This book chooses the second option.

THE FORTY-NINE NAMED WOMEN WHO SPEAK IN SCRIPTURE

Eve, Sarah, Hagar, Rebekah, Leah, Rachel, Tamar, Shiphrah, Puah, Miriam, Zipporah, Mahlah, Noah, Hoglah, Milcah, Tirzah, Rahab, Achsah, Deborah, Jael, Delilah, Naomi, Ruth, Orpah, Hannah, Michal, Abigail, Bathsheba, (Young) Tamar, Jezebel, Athaliah, Huldah, Esther, Anna, Sarah (in Tobit), Edna, Judith, Susanna, Salome, Herodias (mother), Herodias (daughter), Mary Magdalene, Mary (mother of James), Elizabeth, Mary (mother of Jesus), Martha, Mary (of Bethany), Sapphira, and Lydia.

In the Bible, such words as "small" and "least of them" often mean, "Pay attention; something is happening here." Note these examples of biblical minimalism:

- Gideon says he is the least of his tribe, and therefore not worthy to be called as a judge or warrior in Israel—yet he goes on to be both (Judges 6:15).

- Hagar, a servant, is the only person in the Old Testament to name God and one of the few to talk directly with God (Genesis 16:13).

- King David, the youngest of eight brothers, is recognized by Samuel as the future king of Israel (1 Samuel 16:12).

- Mary, a young adolescent girl, is chosen by God to give birth to Jesus (Luke 1:31).

- Elizabeth, an older childless woman, is chosen by God to give birth to John the Baptist (Luke 1:13).

And from Jesus, the same:

- When two or three are together in his name he will be in the midst of them (Matthew 18:20).

- If his disciples have the faith of only a mustard seed, they could move a mountain (Matthew 17:20).

- The widow put into the treasure only two small coins yet was lauded by Jesus because it was all she had (Mark 12:42-44).

- We hear this theme from Judith as she prays to God in the Apocrypha: "For thy power depends not upon numbers, nor thy might upon men of strength; for thou art God of the lowly, helper of the oppressed, upholder of the weak, protector of the forlorn, savior of those without hope" (Judith 9:11).

Clearly, God's vision does not place high value on quantity, but on quality. And the quality of words spoken by Bible women—whether they were said out of love, fear, passion, or frustration—is strong indeed.

WOMEN WHO SPEAK: HOW MANY?

We can identify ninety-three specific women who speak in scripture. Seventy-eight of them do so individually, both named and unnamed. Of these, fifty-one are in the Old Testament, twenty in the New Testament, and seven in the Apocrypha. There are also fifteen who speak only in groups of women. Together, these ninety-three make a small group, one that could fit in a large bus, or a train car or two. (A full list of the women may be found on page 462).

Those are the ones who are counted. There are other women who speak in groups of unnamed women in the Old Testament. But they must remain uncounted, for who knows how many "women of Israel" lined the streets to cheer the victorious King David on his way home from slaying Goliath? Or how many women jeered at poor Jeremiah? No matter; the important thing is that their voices are here. Just maybe these uncountable ones stand in for the rest of us.

WORD COUNTS: WOMEN IN THE BIBLE

The ten women who talk the most in the Bible, in order (including the Apocrypha), are:

1. Judith	(Judith)	2,689 words
2. Shulammite woman[5]	(Song of Solomon)	1,425 words
3. Esther	(Esther & Greek additions)	1,207 words
4. Mother of seven sons	(2, 4 Maccabees)	616 words
5. Hannah	(1 Samuel)	474 words
6. The woman of Tekoa	(2 Samuel)	437 words
7. Huldah	(2 Kings, 2 Chronicles)	416 words
8. Naomi	(Ruth)	411 words
9. Abigail	(1 Samuel)	316 words
10. Rebekah	(Genesis)	293 words

The ten women who talk the most in the Bible, in order (not including the Apocrypha), are all in the Old Testament:

1. Shulammite woman	(Song of Solomon)	1,425 words
2. Hannah	(1 Samuel)	474 words
3. The woman of Tekoa	(2 Samuel)	437 words
4. Esther	(Book of Esther)	416 words
5. Huldah	(2 Kings, 2 Chronicles)	416 words
6. Naomi	(Ruth)	411 words
7. Abigail	(1 Samuel)	316 words
8. Rebekah	(Genesis)	293 words
9. Rahab	(Joshua)	255 words
10. The queen of Sheba	(1 Kings, 2 Chronicles)	228 words

Surprisingly, or not, given our present culture, a good number of the women who spoke in the Old Testament and the Apocrypha—including the two women with the most words—are not particularly well-known today. Judith, for example, may have a recognizable first name, but most people could not recount her deeds. Such is also true of the Shulammite woman of the Song of Solomon—and that is particularly tragic, for she is different from all other women in the Bible. Beautiful, erotic, and sensual language flows from her lips as she describes the search for her missing lover. That depth of physical and emotional passion has no equal in the rest of the Bible—and she speaks more than any other woman in the Old and New Testaments!

Some of the most well-known women speak very few words:

Ruth	(Ruth)	212 words
Mary, mother of Jesus	(Luke, John)	191 words
The Samaritan woman	(John)	151 words
Sarah	(Genesis)	141 words
Jezebel	(1 and 2 Kings)	108 words
Eve	(Genesis)	74 words
Mary Magdalene	(John)	61 words
The bleeding woman	(Matthew, Mark, Luke)	22 words
Mary of Bethany	(John)	12 words
Woman caught in adultery	(John)	3 words

Another surprise: Think of the impact that these women have had through their very few words. Knowing that most people speak an average of 120 words per minute, more than half of the people on this list would qualify for speaking less than a minute, overall. Less than a minute! And yet their words have changed the world, particularly Mary's. If she had not said, "Let it be to me according to your word" (Luke 1:38), the world would be very different.

Words can also name great and wonderful truths. Think of Mary Magdalene, sharing the extraordinary joy of Jesus' resurrection: "I have seen the Lord!" (John 20:18) The world was transformed by the greatest miracle of all—the resurrection of Christ. Once those simple few words were spoken, nothing would ever be the same.

CHAPTER 2

COMMON DENOMINATORS

From the individual study of each of these women, the following themes emerge:

BIBLE WOMEN, ESPECIALLY those who speak, are surprisingly bold.

Traditionally, the view of Bible women has been that they are subservient and passive—but that is as far from the truth as saying the earth is flat or that it's the center of the universe.

Shrinking violets they are not. Immoral or moral, most Bible women step up and say what they think, what they need, or what they want. Most take fearless actions and accept daunting risks. Women in the Bible do not shuffle onto its pages; they stride across, with their heads held high and their hearts full of passion.

Eve is an example when she does what God says not to do. Sarah, out of grief at her own infertility, sets Abraham up with Hagar so that a son of the covenant will be born. The Egyptian midwives, Shiphrah and Puah, risk their lives saving Hebrew babies. The woman of Bahurim hides two men in her well—and then lies. Pharaoh's daughter saves Moses. The wise woman of Abel arranges to have a man beheaded to save her town. Even Job's wife ("curse God and die!") was outspoken.

In the Apocrypha, Sarah (a different Sarah than the one in Genesis) loses seven husbands by the hands of a demon and prays for God to take her life. Judith chops off King Holofernes's head and tucks it in her bag.

In the New Testament, Mary agrees to bear God's son (an action largely taken for granted by the rest of us but a huge risk for her). Mary of Bethany pours extravagant oil on Jesus' feet and wipes them with her hair—a clearly outrageous act. Mary Magdalene and the other women witness the crucifixion, and by being present, they identify themselves with Jesus, the revolutionary.

Some of these women are well-known in history. Others have been largely ignored for two thousand years. But one thing is true: None are passive. None are quiet. And for that, thanks be to God.

START TO FINISH, women in the Bible push against restraints, using their God-given gift of free will.

From the first woman to speak in the Bible (Eve) to the last (the fortune-telling slave girl in Acts), Bible women knock on doors seeking healing, redemption, and freedom—or, in the case of some—control, revenge, and power (think Jezebel or Delilah). Sometimes the doors for moving ahead open graciously; other times they are locked and must be battered down. Thankfully, most—but not all—move themselves and the world ahead in God's name, although there are a few who seem to bang on the doors of Hades (and to be prime candidates for long-term residency there).

And within the two compass points of Eve and the fortune-telling slave girl, dozens of other women push on traditional boundaries to be healed, freed, heard, and redeemed. The daughters of Zelophehad battle Mosaic law. Pilate's wife sends a secret missive, trying to save Jesus from death. The bleeding woman fights her way through crowds to touch Jesus' garment, and Mary Magdalene and other women hit the road with Jesus, leaving their safe homes behind.

They are always pushing outward, not knowing what lies on the other side. Pushing outward, giving birth. Pushing outward, like the universe did from the moment of creation. The blueprint found in the heavens, that of the ever-expanding universe, is the same spirit women deploy in the Bible—and is a God-given gift.

THEY COME "OVER THE TRANSOM" as God's surprise agents. In the days before central heating and air-conditioning, hotel rooms sported a large pane of glass over each guest's doorway that could be opened for heat or fresh air.

Old movies were famous for showing thieves, con men and lovers propelling themselves up and over the transom, through the open space.

That sense of coming in over the top in surprising—and often, scandalous—ways is also true of many girls and women in the Bible.

Take for example the five women—the only women—listed in Matthew's genealogy of Jesus. Rahab, a prostitute, shelters Hebrew spies and helps their people cross into the Promised Land. Tamar seduces her father-in-law, exercising her right to have a child with "family" sperm. Ruth, a foreigner, helps set the stage for King David to be born. Bathsheba will always have a question mark hanging over her head for bathing in sight of David—yet their son, Solomon, becomes Israel's second-most important king. (For the record, this author believes Bathsheba was entitled to bathe on her roof without kingly interference.) And Mary, a young peasant girl, accepts the most challenging choice of all: to bear a son—God's son—without having known a man.

Yet it is not their actions alone that make such a difference. Clearly, the Holy Spirit, that same Spirit that moved over the murky depths of chaos at creation, was alive and at work in the souls and hearts of these women—delivering them from bondage and encouraging the light in their souls to grow brighter.

MOST ARE UNMARRIED. Most people might see the women who speak in the Bible as quiet, married women. Such an understanding might consciously or unconsciously be attributed to some New Testament passages such as "women should be silent in the churches," (1 Corinthians 14:34) or "wives, be subject to your husbands as you are to the Lord" (Ephesians 5:22-24).

While those passages tend to be widely quoted in some circles, they need to be examined in context, as does all scripture. There is also the amazingly efficient and productive "good wife" in Proverbs 31. She does not speak. Perhaps if she did, she might offer a slightly different view of her world.

Surprisingly, the majority of women, when called to a task by the Holy Spirit, are on their own, outside the bounds of a traditional marital relationship. Old Testament examples include Rahab, Ruth, the witch of Endor, the queen of Sheba and more. In the New Testament, consider Mary and Martha of

Bethany, or Mary Magdalene—all, as far as we know, were single. Take Lydia in Philippi—an affluent merchant on her own. The servant girls the night before Jesus was crucified were most likely single. Mary, Jesus' mother, was unmarried at the time Gabriel approached her about the birth of Jesus, and likely widowed when she stood at the foot of the cross.

The point is this: Bible women, especially those who were single, had much more power than is admitted in many religious circles today. And it wasn't a matter of being given power; it was a matter of finding and using the power they had.

BIBLE WOMEN SUFFER HORRIBLE LOSS, and at times are like pawns moved on a patriarchal chessboard, but they remain bright lights in sacred history.

Being a woman in ancient times, especially in the violent pre-monarchy years, was tough. Women were assigned marriage partners by their fathers or brothers for economic and political reasons. They were considered property and treated as such; love was not part of the equation.

Outside of the father/brother machine, other ways of obtaining women for marriage included taking a captive maiden or two as victory "spoils" in war or entering into a marriage contract with concubines (girls and women from lower-class families with little bargaining power) for the purpose of bearing children. A third way was raping a girl or woman, making her permanently "unfit" and undesirable for other men and, ironically, leaving the rapist as the best potential husband material.

While clearly a number of presumably solid relationships did exist (Sarah and Abraham, Rebekah and Isaac, Zechariah and Elizabeth, Deborah and Lappidoth), marriage was built on the social structures of the day, including the importance of having children. Without children, it was believed, an individual's life and worth would dissolve into the desert sands, leaving nothing for the future, or for God. As always, historical and social context must be noted. Concubines, for example, had some protection, in that they were given food and shelter and a family name for their children. Raping a girl and then marrying her, in those times, was seen as more beneficial than condemning her to a beggar's life or a life of prostitution, one of the few ways women could support themselves.

And there is the concubine in Judges 19, one of the most violently abused women in the Bible. She is not on record as having spoken. Thrown out the door by her master one horrible night to satisfy the demands of desert hospitality (which demanded that the head of a household must share everything with his "guests"), she is gang raped until daybreak by a group of men. As the sun rises, she is found clinging to the doorposts, but when her master says, unbelievably rudely, "Get up, let us be going," she does not move or speak. (Sadly but not surprisingly, she has died.) The master divides her body into twelve pieces and sends one piece to each of the twelve tribes of Israel for help in avenging her death.

This is a thoroughly sickening story, hard to stomach. We can only hope that God has granted this unnamed woman eternal peace. Even though her words were not recorded, she is remembered here because in our search for truth, we cannot ignore parts of the Bible that leave us cold.

Life in biblical times for women was emotionally, spiritually, and physically treacherous—and that makes their accomplishments even more extraordinary.

The women cover all the stations of power as men do in the Bible, just in fewer numbers. Examples:

- Women were not known as warriors or judges, yet Deborah was both.

- Women were not known as killers, yet Jael and Judith killed top enemy leaders.

- Women did not serve as priests, yet when they—including Hannah, Hagar, Rebekah, and Sarah (from Tobit)—cried out in prayer, God answered.

- Women were not known as diplomats, but the woman of Tekoa and the wise woman of Abel were two of the best, and the queen of Sheba was a skilled and prudent ambassador on behalf of her nation.

- Women were not named in the twelve-disciple group, but some of Jesus' closest allies were women, including Mary and Martha of Bethany, and Mary Magdalene.

- Women were not known as merchants, but the "good wife" of Proverbs 31 and Lydia in Acts were clearly successful in business.

- Women were not seen as political advisors, but King Saul sought out the witch of Endor (who told him, correctly, that he would die in battle the following day), and King Josiah's assistants sought out Huldah to explain the spiritual and political meaning of scrolls, newly found in the temple at Jerusalem.

- Women were not seen as prophets, yet it was Anna who recognized Jesus as the long-awaited Messiah when he was only eight days old.

- Women were not seen as negotiators, yet Abigail negotiated with King David not to slay her household, and the wise woman of Abel negotiated with Joab to save her town. Both were successful.

- Women were not seen as poets, but some of the oldest and most beautiful poetry is found with women's names attached (the Song of Miriam, the Song of Deborah, the Song of Hannah, and Mary's *Magnificat*).

- Girls were not seen as particularly useful, but Jesus' mother was probably about fourteen when she bore him; the servant girl of Naaman's wife suggested a cure for Naaman's leprosy; Pharaoh's daughter saved little Moses while young Miriam stood guard; and Rebekah was just a girl when she greeted Abraham's servant and married Isaac within a few days, sight unseen.

- And finally, women were not seen as reliable witnesses, but there is the whole Resurrection story, where Jesus did not appear to his disciples first, but met the women at the tomb.

THESE WOMEN WERE the primary social media of their day.

Today a substantial part of the world has access to Twitter, Facebook, and Google. Obviously this was not the case in biblical days, when women were often the ones who shared the news. Consider the women who lined the streets after David slew Goliath, intensifying their growing dislike of Saul in favor of the young and vibrant David. "Saul has killed his thousands...David his ten thousands" (1 Samuel 18:7).

Women and girls met each other at the town well, a particularly welcome chance to get out of the house. The seven daughters of the priests of Midian drew water for their flocks there. They were so excited when they reached home, talking about the young Egyptian they met at the well that their father had them ask the man to dinner—and he turned out to be Moses, who married Zipporah, one of the sisters.

Consider the girls who were also on their way to draw water when young Saul walked through town, head and shoulders above the crowd, and very handsome. Asking for how he might find Samuel, the prophet and judge, the girls seemed quite responsible in answering, and no doubt enjoyed sharing the news.

And in Jesus' time, the word about the young healer and his miracles spread quickly, most often via women. Picture the five-times married woman at the well in John 4, running back to town, saying that this man told her everything about herself! Could he be the Messiah? Or Jesus telling the women at the empty tomb (Mark 16) to "go tell his disciples and Peter" that he had risen. Jesus knew they would make sure that the word was known.

Whether they took actual steps to claim and build the kingdom of God, or whether they supported others in this work, women of the Bible gave endlessly of themselves and their resources to engage the world with God's love—much like women of faith today.

Step now into God's sacred circle of mothers, grandmothers, warriors, prophets, witches, prostitutes, and murderers. You won't come out the same.

THE WOMEN WHO SPEAK IN THE OLD TESTAMENT

"The serpent tricked me, and I ate." —Eve

Have you ever harbored any notions that Old Testament women are weak? Passive? Unworthy? Put those ideas in concrete shoes and deep-six 'em. Now.

Old Testament women are powerful and compelling examples of what it means to live in exceedingly challenging days—historically, spiritually, and emotionally. They express emotions in a way that men do not, solve problems behind the scenes, and use their intuitive and intellectual skills to be God's people—all despite the fact that they live in a world where they are seen as property, and it is rare to be loved, truly loved.

Without exception, they are purpose-driven, their goals ranging from saving a nation to scavenging a last meal. Most are faithful. Most are bold. Some, with due cause, are irritating. A few are evil.

We must know their stories to know our own. Let's get started.

CHAPTER 3

WOMEN WHO SPEAK IN GENESIS

Of the eleven women who are on record as having spoken in the Book of Genesis, there's not a spineless one among them. Some are skeptical and defiant. Others make somewhat unbelievable sexual decisions. One laughs in God's presence. Eight of the eleven are fiercely committed to bearing children, or bringing them safely into the world (six become mothers and two are midwives).

Women say more in the Book of Genesis (some 1,100 words) than in any other book in the Old and New Testaments, save one, and most of their comments have to do with life: helping to make it happen, sustaining it, protecting it, and grieving it.

In reading their narratives, remember the old saying that stories don't tell us what is true, they tell us what must be true. Look for deep truths, the meaning behind the actions.

By the numbers

Words spoken by women in Genesis: 1,117

Number of women who speak: 11 (Eve, Sarah, Hagar, Lot's older daughter, Rebekah, Leah, Rachel, Rachel's midwife, Tamar, Tamar's midwife, Potiphar's wife)

EVE

*Over the line,
Out the gate*

PROFILE: HIGH

▷ **READ HER STORY:** Genesis 3-4

▷ **CLASSIC MOMENT:**
Eating the fruit which God forbade her
and Adam to consume

▷ **LIKELY CHARACTERISTICS:**
Curious, Non-compliant, Gullible, Lonely,
Intelligent, Subversive, Willful

▷ **DATA:** 74 words

Who was Eve?

The first woman and the first mother // The first person to sin and the first person to walk away from God // The first mother to experience the murder of her child (and this by the hand of her firstborn son) // The only woman in the Bible to talk with an animal // The only person other than Jesus to talk with both God and Satan

What did Eve say?

The woman said to the serpent, "**We may eat of the fruit of the trees in the garden; but God said, 'You shall not eat of the fruit of the tree that is in the middle of the garden, nor shall you touch it, or you shall die.'**" *Genesis 3:2-3*

Then the LORD God said to the woman, "What is this that you have done?" The woman said, "**The serpent tricked me, and I ate.**" *Genesis 3:13*

Now the man knew his wife Eve, and she conceived and bore Cain, saying, "I **have produced a man with the help of the Lord.**" *Genesis 4:1*

Adam knew his wife again, and she bore a son and named him Seth, for she said, **"God has appointed for me another child instead of Abel, because Cain killed him.**" *Genesis 4:25*

Eve's story

A dam and Eve are in the garden of Eden: a place with no evidence of death, demise, or even bad weather. Adam often walks in the garden with God in the late-day sun; the animals are friends; all live peaceably. Eden appears to be a place where all is perfect…forever.

God has, however, placed a fruit-laden "tree of knowledge" in the midst of Eden—and warns Adam not to touch it or he and Eve will die. Note that God speaks directly to Adam regarding the tree, although Eve clearly knows the mandate. Alone with a crafty serpent one day, Eve is lured by the serpent's words: "You will not die…your eyes will be opened, and you will be like God, knowing good and evil" (Genesis 3:4-5).

She sees that the fruit looks delightful, and it would be good for food. She thinks it will make her wise. Reaching out and snagging a piece of fruit from the forbidden tree, she eats it, offers some to Adam…and all goes downhill. God is angry and expels them from the garden, Adam is sentenced to hard labor, and Eve is told that Adam will rule over her and she will experience pain in childbirth. Fleeing the garden, the exiled companions come to "know" each other and have children. The older, Cain, murders his brother, Abel.

Consider this

Let's enter Eve's story, at least initially, as people who walk beside her without judgment. She knew the boundaries that God had set and rejected them, allowing herself to be duped as the serpent broke through her defenses.

Eve had questions and the capacity, yet in many ways, she, like Adam, was a child: innocent, trusting, curious. Somehow the serpent gained Eve's confidence—perhaps like child molesters who move slowly toward that day when trust will be forever abused.

Into what vulnerability of Eve's did the serpent tap? Eve speaks of the desire for knowledge. Loneliness is another possibility. Was life infinite at that point for human beings? Did Eve know anything of death? Had she even seen it? Did plants and animal compatriots die, or did life seem to stretch out endlessly? Was boredom a factor? In the midst of such questions stood the tree of knowledge. The serpent, apparently drawing from some invisible well of authority, convinced Eve that she would be wise—just like God—if she ate the fruit. And so it happened.

Some see Eve as a mythical figure. Others see her as the first woman on earth. Either way, Eve seems to get the blame for leading humankind astray, forever.

But how valuable is Eve for the twenty-first century? Believe her story and you can't possibly believe in evolution. Believe in evolution and she remains an entertaining, almost fairy-tale like character.

Remember that stories don't tell us what is true; they tell us what must be true. Look for the deep truths here, as with any Bible story. Live into it. Trust your instincts, intellect, and reason as you descend deeper into its many levels.

What about sin? Did Eve sin? Yes, because she walked away from God and separated herself from God. In fact, the word "sin" in its root means "separation." She did what God had forbidden her to do, and tempted Adam to do the same. Interestingly, however, the word "sin" is not used in the Genesis story.

Should she have stayed away from the fruit, the serpent? Yes, because doing so was God's desire. But without her, we'd still be in the garden. Actually, "we" probably wouldn't be here at all. Adam and Eve did not have children until they left the garden; it was only after their exit that they became parents. Yet despite their sins, and perhaps because of them, Christians also see in this passage the first clue of a redeemer, the presence of evil, and the meaning of maturity.

Did God expect Eve to take the fruit? Did God design things so she would be tempted? Most likely. Either way, Eve used the divinely given gift of free will to reach out, press on, experiment, and grow—as do most women in the Bible. Keep an eye out, in the pages to come, for ways in which both God and women work toward restoring that circle of love and trust.

Good and evil. God and Satan. (Some would say that the serpent was only an agent of Satan, but Wisdom 2:24 implies they are the same being.) These are truths we need to come to terms with on our own, after we've left our own childhood gardens, sorted our beliefs, reached maturity, come to know God. It is not an easy thing to do. Yet even when we fall, God is there for us as he was for Eve—seeking reconciliation, setting boundaries, encouraging healing, providing companionship, introducing love.

What might we learn from Eve?

▷ Stay away from those who tempt you, even if the temptation seems innocent. Ask God for support.

▷ Do not take a crafty snake's word for things, even if said figure does not appear in snake attire. Most snakes don't.

▷ You may be forced out of the garden, but perhaps it wasn't the best place for you.

▷ Decisions, healthy or unhealthy, may affect generations.

Eve is the only person in biblical history,
other than Jesus, to talk with both God and Satan.
That's an impressive resume.

For reflection

1. The garden is described as a stress-free, protected environment. What might have been missing for Eve? Why did she take the fruit?

2. Eve became a mother only after leaving the garden (Genesis 4:1). What does that imply about motherhood and maturity?

3. Do you share any of Eve's traits? How have they helped you? How have they hindered you?

4. What would our world be like if Eve had not eaten of the forbidden fruit?

5. Eve acted before she spoke with God. What temptations are you struggling with today? How might you ask God for help?

6. If you are moving out of what has been your comfort zone, what would the angels advise? Continue or turn back? Retreat or forge ahead?

SARAH

Proud and powerful

PROFILE: HIGH

▷ **READ HER STORY:** Genesis 16-21

▷ **CLASSIC MOMENT:** Laughing to herself behind a tent wall when three desert travelers tell Abraham that she will bear a child within a year

▷ **LIKELY CHARACTERISTICS:** Faithful, Blunt, Enterprising, Cantankerous, Loyal, Tenacious, Jealous, Loving

▷ **DATA:** 141 words

Who was Sarah?

At age ninety, the oldest woman in scripture—and possibly in human history—to bear a child // The first woman in the Bible to send her husband into the arms of another woman // The only woman in the Bible to be on record as laughing // The first Israelite to be buried in the Promised Land // The spiritual foremother of Judaism // The only woman in the Bible to talk of the "pleasure" of sex in later life

What did Sarah say?

Now Sarai, Abram's wife, bore him no children. She had an Egyptian slave-girl whose name was Hagar, and Sarai said to Abram, "**You see that the LORD has prevented me from bearing children; go in to my slave-girl; it may be that I shall obtain children by her.**" *Genesis 16:1-2*

31

Then Sarai said to Abram, "**May the wrong done to me be on you! I gave my slave-girl to your embrace, and when she saw that she had conceived, she looked on me with contempt. May the** LORD **judge between you and me!**" *Genesis 16:5*

So Sarah laughed to herself, saying, "**After I have grown old, and my husband is old, shall I have pleasure?**" *Genesis 18:12*

But Sarah denied, saying, "**I did not laugh**"; for she was afraid. *Genesis 18:15*

Now Sarah said, "**God has brought laughter for me; everyone who hears will laugh with me.**" And she said, "**Who would ever have said to Abraham that Sarah would nurse children? Yet I have borne him a son in his old age.**" *Genesis 21:6-7*

So she said to Abraham, "**Cast out this slave woman with her son; for the son of this slave woman shall not inherit along with my son Isaac.**" *Genesis 21:10*

Sarah's story

Picture Abraham and Sarah about the time that God intervenes in their lives. She is sixty-five; he is seventy-five. Despite their long marriage, they have no children—and that would have been heartbreaking for both, but especially for Sarah.

Then, one night at Mount Haran in present-day Turkey (some four hundred miles northeast of Aleppo, Syria), history changes. God calls Abraham aside, telling him that he will make of him a great nation, providing him with many descendants and much land, blessing those who bless him and cursing those who curse him (Genesis 12:1-2*).*

Abraham and Sarah head out with their relatives, servants, and sheep. They spend years in the wilderness and cover hundreds of miles. Not knowing their destination, they trust God to reveal the Promised Land. Dangers and isolation surround them. Survival becomes all-important.

Yet despite God's promise, no child arrives. And then, like one who walks into a lake with weights tied around her neck, Sarah perceives a terrible possibility: that God has promised descendants to Abraham, but not necessarily to her.

She takes action (Genesis 16:1-2). Believing deeply in the covenant God has made with Abraham, she sends Abraham into the arms of her exotic servant, Hagar—for any child born to a servant would, under ancient law, belong to the slave's master and mistress.

Who knows how much time it took Hagar to conceive? It could have occurred with one liaison or taken several years. Once Hagar becomes pregnant, Genesis says that she "looked with contempt upon her mistress" (Genesis 16:4). Sarah dealt harshly with her, and Hagar fled into the wilderness, where God told her to return to Sarah. Hagar did—and gave birth to Ishmael.

Only after the birth of Ishmael does God tell Abraham that Sarah will conceive—and that Sarah's child, not Hagar's, will be heir to God's covenant. Yet God also tells him that Hagar's descendants, starting with Ishmael, will be blessed and will multiply, becoming a great nation (Genesis 17:20).

Finally, when Sarah is ninety, she overhears (while listening through a tent wall) three strangers tell Abraham that she will give birth to a son the following year. In one of the most endearing moments in the Old Testament, Sarah laughs to herself, not believing that at her age, pleasure—both sexual and maternal—will come her way.

It turns out that the strangers were angels—and one was God. As predicted, Sarah gives birth. She names her son Isaac (which means "laughter"), and all is quiet...until Ishmael is about fourteen and Isaac is about three. Sarah becomes increasingly agitated with Ishmael, banishing the boy and his mother to the wilderness. They do not return.

Consider this

Sarah was strong-willed, felt matters of the heart deeply, and spoke seven times (seven is a fortuitous number in biblical language). Like most biblical women, she was a survivor.

Here is where many contemporary Christians miss an important key to understanding Sarah's actions: she was fully dedicated, actively committed, to helping God's plan happen. She did not shirk from her calling to produce a child who would, in turn, produce as many descendants as there were stars in the sky. She would risk all to make that God-given promise happen.

Although Sarah was legally within her rights to suggest a child from an Abraham/Hagar union, many readers may find her actions immoral. But in her mind, her intervention was divinely inspired in response to God's word. And without this feisty woman, there would have been no Isaac, no Jacob, no Mary, no Deborah, no Jesus. We'd have no great example of a woman laughing in the Bible. We'd be short one tough old woman.

Despite the dramatic moments and perhaps because of them, Sarah and Abraham represent a "vivid and enduring love story"[6] in the Bible. Their bond was unbreakable, their lives forever entwined.

What might we learn from Sarah?

▷ You're never too old to serve God—or to enjoy intimate relationships (and in this story, they go hand in hand).

▷ If you don't laugh, you might as well be dead.

▷ Maturity, wisdom, and perseverance are powerful tools.

▷ Stay strong despite difficult circumstances. It will all make sense one day, even though that day may be beyond your lifetime.

For reflection

1. Why did God choose Sarah to be the spiritual matriarch of the Jewish people? What gifts did she have that helped bring God's covenant to fulfillment?

2. The spiritual roots of Judaism, Christianity, and Islam spring from this story, with angst and despair going back to the very conceptions of Ishmael and Isaac. What does that say about world religions today?

3. Sarah overheard the angel and found that she was to have a baby late in life—and laughed. How would you have responded? What does her laugh mean to you? How might you find holy laughter in at least one event today?

4. What does Sarah's story say about the range of gifts that older people bring to the faith community?

5. Read Genesis 17:17, where Abraham laughs when God says that Sarah will bear a son. Has your spouse or partner ever lost faith in you? What was your response?

HAGAR

Lost and then found

PROFILE: MODERATE

▷ **READ HER STORY:** Genesis 16 and 21:9-20

▷ **CLASSIC MOMENT:** After being banished to the wilderness—basically a death sentence—Hagar weeps, and God saves her and her son

▷ **LIKELY CHARACTERISTICS:** Independent, Emotive, Resourceful, Taunting, Protective, Maternal

▷ **DATA:** 33 words

Who was Hagar?

The first person in the Bible to cry // The mother of Abraham's first son // Sarah's servant // A woman who fled abuse //The only person in the Hebrew Bible to name God (El-Roi: "O God of Seeing")[7] // One of three women in the Old Testament to talk individually with God—and hear God answer[8] // A woman who, unwisely, taunted another over an inability to bear children // A revered figure in Islam; some call her Islam's spiritual foremother

What did Hagar say?

The angel of the LORD found [Hagar] by a spring of water in the wilderness, the spring on the way to Shur. And he said, "Hagar, slave-girl of Sarai, where have you come from and where are you going?" She said, "**I am running away from my mistress Sarai.**" *Genesis 16:7-8*

So [Hagar] named the Lord who spoke to her, "**You are El-roi,**" for she said, "**Have I really seen God and remained alive after seeing him?**" *Genesis 16:13*

Then she went and sat down opposite him a good way off, about the distance of a bowshot; for she said, "**Do not let me look on the death of the child.**" And as she sat opposite him, she lifted up her voice and wept.[9] *Genesis 21:16*

Hagar's story

Hagar, of Egyptian origin, is Sarah's servant. After many years in the wilderness, Sarah has given up all hope of becoming pregnant and turns to Hagar for help. Under ancient laws, any child born to a servant would, by rights, belong to her and Abraham.

Perhaps it took one visit; likely it took more; perhaps it took years. We assume Hagar was willing—for it would have been an honor to bear the child of the tribe's leader—but perhaps she was not. Consensual sex? When one is ordered to have sex with the most powerful man in the tribe, the term "consensual" is questionable.

When Abraham banishes Hagar to the wilderness upon Sarah's mandate, thirst almost kills both mother and son. Excruciatingly more painful, however, is the looming death of Ishmael, whom she has hidden under the shade of a bush. Hagar weeps, and upon hearing the voice of the youth, God acts to save him (Genesis 21:17).

"Come, lift up the boy," says God, "for I will make a great nation of him." Thus was born a key building block of Islam, with God having heard a woman in distress and saving her child.

With God's help, Hagar finds Ishmael a wife of Egyptian descent; Ishmael marries and produces twelve tribes. Through Sarah and Hagar, then, come stories of origin for all three Abrahamic faiths: Jewish, Christian, and Muslim.

Consider this

Hagar is truly one of the overlooked and underappreciated women of the Hebrew Bible.

Her dialogue with God is a story of relationship and action. God finds Hagar when Sarah (and Abraham) banished her; Hagar does what God tells her to do; Hagar recognizes that she is in the presence of the divine and names God, who protects both mother and son (Genesis 21:20-21).

A true survivor, Hagar is a striking example of the line from the hymn "Amazing Grace": "I once was lost and now am found." She serves as a childbearing vessel and is criticized for being haughty. She flees from abuse, comes to know God, obeys God's word, gives birth, is banished, yet survives—and passes on her faith to her descendants.

What might we learn from Hagar?

▷ If we are lost, abused, or abandoned, God will hear us when we call out.

▷ Sometimes we need to travel through the wilderness to reach home.

▷ Taunting is not a good idea.

▷ It is good to prepare our children to be self-sufficient, as Ishmael was when he hunted so that he and his mother could survive.

For reflection

1. How would it have felt to be Hagar before, during, and after her pregnancy with Ishmael?

2. God heard Hagar's cries and acted, even though Hagar had not mentioned God's name until that moment. What does that say about the presence of God?

3. Consider the issue of slavery. What might we learn from Hagar's story? Where is redemption?

4. How does one discern the best time to leave a painful situation? What part do faith and prayer play in that process?

5. Although Hagar and Sarah never find reconciliation, throughout the centuries many women have dedicated their lives to establishing peace—whether it be in family, national, or international systems. What women do you see taking a lead role in peacemaking? Is there a situation now in your faith community or family where women are establishing peace?

LOT'S OLDER DAUGHTER

Creating hope from horror

PROFILE:
SO LOW AS TO BE
CRAWLING ON
THE FLOOR

▷ READ HER STORY: Genesis 19

▷ CLASSIC MOMENT: Initiating sex with her father

▷ LIKELY CHARACTERISTICS:
Purposeful, Determined, Resolute, Tough, Resilient, Manipulative

▷ DATA: 80 words

Who was Lot's older daughter?

One of two women[10] in scripture to have sexual intercourse with her father // A survivor of kidnapping // The observer of a terrifying night, where her father offered to send her and her sister out to a mob to be gang-raped // A woman left motherless when her mother turned into a pillar of salt // Abraham's great-niece

What did Lot's older daughter say?

And the firstborn said to the younger, "**Our father is old, and there is not a man on earth to come in to us after the manner of all the world. Come, let us make our father drink wine, and we will lie with him, so that we may preserve offspring through our father.**" *Genesis 19: 31-32*

On the next day, the firstborn said to the younger, "**Look, I lay last night with my father; let us make him drink wine tonight also; then you go in and lie with him, so that we may preserve offspring through our father.**" *Genesis 19:34*

Lot's older daughter's story

To give some context, Lot is Abraham's nephew. He and his family have been traveling with Abraham and Sarah. When the group finally reaches Canaan, the ever-generous Abraham takes Lot up to a high spot (the Hill of Benjamin) and offers him first choice of the land. Selfishly, Lot chooses the entire Jordan basin, including the evil towns of Sodom and Gomorrah. Alas, the land is already settled. Lot and his family do not get dinner invitations or friendly waves from neighbors. What they get is kidnapping.

Held hostage by four tribal chiefs, Lot and his family are doomed until Abraham provides an army of 318 soldiers (note the specificity in that number; they were probably family members) and arrives to rescue Lot.

Abraham is over a hundred years old, but his backbone seems made of steel. Using both his warrior and diplomat personas, developed from years in the wilderness among hostile clans, he disperses the enemy and bargains with God. When God says that the evil town of Sodom will be destroyed, Abraham persuades God to send two angels there, masquerading as male travelers, to see if there are any righteous men left. The angels—although biblical tradition says that Lot understands them to be humans, not angels—stay overnight with Lot. At night, a mob surrounds the house, demanding that the men be sent out so that the crowd may "know" them—"know" as in rape.

Lot refuses, instead volunteering his two virgin daughters: "Look, I have two daughters who have not known a man; let me bring them out to you, and do to them as you please; only do nothing to these men, for they have come under the shelter of my roof" (Genesis 19:8).

What seems cruel and unbelievable is just that. Yet Lot is doing what ancient custom demands, protecting visitors with all he has—or, in this case, with the souls of his daughters.

> Wait a minute. This girl's father offers
> to send her out to be gang-raped;
> her mother is turned into a pillar of salt;
> God destroys her town and her fiancé;
> and she gets her father drunk to have sex with him?
> Are we in still in the Bible?
> How did we miss this in Sunday School?!

Consider this

Many of the stories in the Bible are beautiful and easy to read. This is not one of them. Narratives such as these demonstrate that the Bible is a living, breathing document with stories of real people. Genesis 19 is not something one would make up.

The key to understanding the daughters' actions is that they believed the world was imploding, heading for destruction. They had good reason to feel this way. Their fiancés[11] were dead, killed in the destruction of Sodom. Their mother was dead, turned into a pillar of salt. The human race would end with them.

In what seems a terrible environment, Lot's older daughter (who is never named) carves a path of sustainability, of redemption, of life. She creates a future from destruction, ensuring the future of the human race as she understands it. She and her sister act to fulfill God's covenant, helping the family of Abraham and Sarah to number more than all the stars in the sky.

Life does not often turn out the way we had expected or desired. Lot's older daughter would have preferred a normal life, out of harm's way. As uncomfortable as her choice seems to us, she found a way to higher ground and helped her sister to get there as well. With God's help, and in fulfillment of God's covenant, she created life from destruction and love from devastation.

What might we learn from Lot's older daughter?

▷ You can get destroyed if you look behind you when it is time to move forward.

▷ A faith context will help you make decisions.

▷ Horrendous circumstances may offer no good choices, but may demand that you choose one of them anyway.

▷ Values may change in times of war or perceived end times.

For reflection

1. Was Lot's older daughter's act one of faith or despair?

2. Why have generations avoided this story? Is it that the sexual aspect is difficult to ingest? By not talking about it, what do we miss?

3. The daughters were, presumably, spared embarrassment and humiliation because their father was not aware of what was happening. What does that say about them? What does that say about him?

4. Values may change in times of stress or war. Have you ever made a decision that you thought you never would—that had something to do with ensuring your own or another's emotional or physical survival?

5. "Date rape" drugs are illegal and immoral. How does this story compare to the contemporary use of such drugs?

REBEKAH

Love and loss

PROFILE:
MODERATELY
HIGH

▷ READ HER STORY: Genesis 24-27

▷ CLASSIC MOMENT: Intervening so that Jacob, her younger son, would receive his father's blessing over fraternal twin Esau

▷ LIKELY CHARACTERISTICS:
Adventuresome, Hospitable, Sly, Decisive, Duplicitous, Strategic, Protective

▷ DATA: 293 words

Who was Rebekah?

The woman who spoke the most words in the Book of Genesis // The wife of Isaac, the daughter-in-law of Sarah and Abraham, the sister of Laban, and the mother of Jacob and Esau // A kind, enthusiastic, and adventurous girl // A girl who left home to marry a man she had yet to meet // One of only two girls in the Bible to have a recorded conversation with her mother (although here, her brother was present and mother and brother spoke as one)[12] // One of the few women who converses with God // A woman who famously tricks her husband

What did Rebekah say?

"**Drink, my lord**," she said, and quickly lowered her jar upon her hand and gave him a drink. When she had finished giving him a drink, she said, "**I will draw for your camels also, until they have finished drinking.**" *Genesis 24:18-19*

She said to him [Abraham's servant], "**I am the daughter of Bethuel, son of Milcah, whom she bore to Nahor.**" She added, "**We have plenty of straw and fodder and a place to spend the night.**" *Genesis 24:24-25*

Then the girl ran and told her mother's household about these things...As soon as [Laban] had seen the nose-ring, and the bracelets on his sister's arms, and when he heard the words of his sister Rebekah, "**Thus the man spoke to me,**" he went to the man and there he was standing by the camels at the spring. *Genesis 24:28-30*

And they called Rebekah, and said to her, "Will you go with this man?" She said, "**I will.**" *Genesis 24:58*

And Rebekah looked up, and when she saw Isaac, she slipped quickly from the camel, and said to the servant, "**Who is the man over there, walking in the field to meet us?**" *Genesis 24:64-65*

The children struggled together within her; and she said, "**If it is to be this way, why do I live?**" *Genesis 25:22*

Rebekah said to her son Jacob, "**I heard your father say to your brother Esau, 'Bring me game, and prepare for me savory food to eat, that I may bless you before the** LORD **before I die.' Now therefore, my son, obey my word as I command you. Go to the flock, and get me two choice kids, so that I may prepare from them savory food for your father, such as he likes; and you shall take it to your father to eat, so that he may bless you before he dies.**" *Genesis 27:6-10*

But Jacob said to his mother Rebekah, "Look, my brother Esau is a hairy man, and I am a man of smooth skin. Perhaps my father will feel me, and I shall seem to be mocking him, and bring a curse on myself and not a blessing." His mother said to him, "**Let your curse be on me, my son; only obey my word and go, get them for me.**" *Genesis 27:11-13*

Now Esau hated Jacob because of the blessing...But the words of her elder son Esau were told to Rebekah; so she sent and called her younger son Jacob and said to him, "**Your brother Esau is consoling himself by planning to kill you.**

Now therefore, my son, obey my voice; flee at once to my brother Laban in Haran, and stay with him a while, until your brother's fury turns away— until your brother's anger against you turns away, and he forgets what you have done to him; then I will send, and bring you back from there. Why should I lose both of you in one day?" *Genesis 27:41-45*

Then Rebekah said to Isaac, "I am weary of my life because of the Hittite women. If Jacob marries one of the Hittite women such as these, one of the women of the land, what good will my life be to me?" *Genesis 27:46*

Rebekah's story

Picture an apple on the kitchen counter, next to a free-trade, organic dark chocolate bar, made with caramel and sea salt. Like Bible stories about women, Rebekah often comes up as that apple—left sitting on the counter while the less disciplined of us grab chocolate, the more compelling choice.

Similarly, Bible readers pass by Rebekah, concentrating instead on Jacob and Esau, her conflicted sons. She is often tossed aside, seen as manipulative and cunning. (She is, a bit.) There is, however, much more to this girl-woman than it seems—and at almost three hundred words, she has more to say than any other woman in Genesis.

Visualize her as she first appears: a joyful and beautiful young girl, generous of heart and spirit, drawing water at the town well. An old man—hot, dusty, and careworn—approaches her.

"May I have some water?"

"Yes, of course! Here. And might I water your camels?"

Bingo.

What Rebekah does not know is this: the thirsty man is Abraham's servant, looking for a wife for Isaac among Abraham's relatives, now living hundreds of miles away. On a mission from Abraham, he has asked God for divine guidance: the right woman, he prays, will offer water to both him and his camels.

And Rebekah does.

He is elated, adorning her with jewelry and other gifts (the Bible specifically says a gold nose-ring, along with other expensive presents). She takes him home to meet her family; he asks them for permission to take her to wed Isaac. They agree. Upon rising the next morning, the family is stunned to find the servant anxious to be on his way, as they had hoped for at least ten days to say goodbye. Rebekah's mother and brother Laban ask her if she is willing to go with the servant (unusual because most girls were never asked if or when they wanted to marry). "I am willing," she consents. And she is on her way to a new life.

Surely she wonders about the man to whom she has just promised herself. Will he treat her well? Will he be a good father? When the caravan pulls up, she spots a man in the fields. Told it is Isaac, she dons a veil and runs to him. Isaac takes her into the tent of his mother, Sarah, who had died by then, and Rebekah becomes Isaac's wife.

Despite this apparently love-filled relationship (Genesis 24:67), Rebekah does not become pregnant. To his credit, Isaac does not take another wife (perhaps he had come to believe the circumstances of his own birth were far too troublesome), and they remain childless for almost two decades. One wonders how much pressure Rebekah experienced during those years, for God had promised that Sarah would "give rise to nations; kings of peoples shall come from her" (Genesis 17:16). So far, Sarah's descendants number just one: Isaac.

Finally, after twenty years, Rebekah conceives. But what would normally be nine months of anticipation soon backfires. Fraternal male twins Esau and Jacob battle in utero so much that she cries out to God—and God responds.

Despondent, Rebekah asks, "If it is to be this way, why do I live?"

God answers, "Two nations are in your womb, and two peoples born of you shall be divided; the one shall be stronger than the other, the elder shall serve the younger" (Genesis 25:23).

Such a two-way street between God and individual women in the Old Testament is extraordinarily rare. God spoke with Eve, Hagar, and Rebekah. Not just to them, but with them, back and forth. In dialogue.

Over the ages, many Bible readers have thought of Rebekah as one who was full of deceit and cunning. But take another look. She knows something of divine destiny, having heard directly from God that the older twin will serve the younger. As a woman of the covenant, and like her mother-in-law before her, Rebekah will intervene to ensure that God's promise takes precedence.

In his old age, Isaac goes blind. One day, knowing he will soon die, he tells his older son Esau, the family hunter, to kill some game, and then make him "savory food, such as I like, and bring it to me so that I may bless you before I die" (Genesis 27:4). Like Sarah before her, Rebekah is listening.

Ordering their other son Jacob to take two choice goats from the family's flock, she makes Isaac the meal he has requested—but not before draping Esau's garments over Jacob and covering his arms and neck with soft animal fur so as to convince the old man that Jacob is indeed the older brother. Jacob presents the food, Isaac is sated, and while Esau is still occupied in the fields, the patriarch gives Jacob his eternal blessing (Genesis 27:27-29).

When Esau discovers how his mother and brother have tricked him and Isaac, he threatens to kill Jacob. Rebekah hustles Jacob out of town, sending him in the direction of her brother Laban and his clan.

Sadly, she never sees her younger son again. Twenty years later, Jacob returns with two wives and a large family, but in his absence, his mother has died.

Consider this

Helping God's world to emerge takes a huge toll on the woman who had once been a gentle, spirited girl at the well, the girl who had made a decision to leave home and not look back. Her favorite son was out of her sight forever; she would never see nor hold his children in her arms.

Yet without her actions of taking on and letting go, the story of God's people would not have been the same. She took on the adventure of leaving home; she bid farewell to her original family members to marry a stranger in a faraway place; and in resolving the conflict between her sons, she let go of her favorite one so that God's word might be fulfilled.

Without her courage to marry a man she had not met (as was common in those days), sons Esau and Jacob would not have been born. Without her courage, grandson Joseph, the last of the patriarchs, would have been only a dream.

Like Mary, Jesus' mother, the future of God's people was in a young woman's hands. Like Mary, she answered God's call and loved her son dearly, only to see him depart from her life much too soon.

What might we learn from Rebekah?

▷ Choices made in youth will influence our old age.

▷ The knowledge and love of God is a two-edged sword.

▷ Actions of mothers will influence generations.

▷ Love for children and their growth may mean difficult times of sacrifice.

For reflection

1. Some say that Rebekah was a woman of deceit, yet God had told her that Jacob would be the stronger twin and the older would serve the younger (Genesis 25:22-23). Given that knowledge, and knowing she was a daughter of the covenant, did she interfere with God's work or help it along?

2. Like Mary, most mothers ponder things in their hearts. By the time Jacob and Esau were grown, Rebekah had, no doubt, pondered God's words many times. If she helped God's plan to emerge, why has she been accused of lying and interference over the years? Would the same have been true of a man?

3. What qualities did Rebekah possess in her youth that helped her in mid-life? What are the gifts you've always had that help you?

4. By acting to fulfill Jacob's destiny, Rebekah alienates her husband and other son. In that environment, life for her must have been particularly difficult. Have there been times in your life when you have put someone else's interests ahead of yours and then faced painful consequences?

LEAH

*Workin'
for love*

▷ **READ HER STORY:** Genesis 29-31

▷ **CLASSIC MOMENT:** Bait and switch: when their father, Laban, shuffles Leah into the wedding tent instead of Rachel

▷ **LIKELY CHARACTERISTICS:** Sturdy, Fertile, Reliable, Tenacious, Heartbroken, Yearning

▷ **DATA:** 137 words

Who was Leah?

The direct ancestor of many key people in scripture, including Moses, Miriam, Aaron, King David, and Jesus // Laban's daughter, a daughter-in-law of Isaac and Rebekah, Rachel's sister, Rebekah's niece, and Jacob's first wife // The biological mother of six sons and one daughter // The wife who would grow into old age with Jacob, and be buried alongside him

What did Leah say?

When the LORD saw that Leah was unloved, he opened her womb; but Rachel was barren. Leah conceived and bore a son, and she named him Reuben; for she said, "**Because the LORD has looked on my affliction; surely now my husband will love me.**" *Genesis 29:32*

She conceived again and bore a son, and said, "**Because the LORD has heard that I am hated, he has given me this son also**"; and she named him Simeon. *Genesis 29:33*

Again she conceived and bore a son, and said, "**Now this time my husband will be joined to me, because I have borne him three sons**"; therefore he was named Levi. *Genesis 29:34*

She conceived again and bore a son, and said, "**This time I will praise the** LORD"; therefore she named him Judah; then she ceased bearing. *Genesis 29:35*

And Leah said, "**Good fortune!**" so she named him Gad. *Genesis 30:11*

Leah's maid Zilpah bore Jacob a second son. And Leah said, "**Happy am I! For the women will call me happy**"; so she named him Asher. *Genesis 30:13*

In the days of wheat harvest Reuben went and found mandrakes in the field, and brought them to his mother Leah. Then Rachel said to Leah, "Please give me some of your son's mandrakes." But she said to her, "**Is it a small matter that you have taken away my husband? Would you take away my son's mandrakes also?**" *Genesis 30:15*

Rachel said, "Then he may lie with you tonight for your son's mandrakes." When Jacob came from the field in the evening, Leah went out to meet him, and said, "**You must come in to me; for I have hired you with my son's mandrakes.**" *Genesis 30:16*

So he lay with her that night. And God heeded Leah, and she conceived and bore Jacob a fifth son. Leah said, "**God has given me my hire because I gave my maid to my husband**"; so she named him Issachar. *Genesis 30:18*

And Leah conceived again, and she bore Jacob a sixth son. Then Leah said, "**God has endowed me with a good dowry; now my husband will honor me, because I have borne him six sons**"; so she named him Zebulun. *Genesis 30:20*

Here Rachel and Leah speak together:

Then Rachel and Leah answered him, "**Is there any portion or inheritance left to us in our father's house? Are we not regarded by him as foreigners? For he has sold us, and he has been using up the money given for us. All the property that God has taken away from our father belongs to us and to our children; now then, do whatever God has said to you.**" *Genesis 31:14-16*

Leah's story

In fear for his life after deceiving Esau, Jacob flees to his mother's family, where he falls in love with the beautiful Rachel. He works for seven years to earn the right to marry Rachel, but on his wedding night, father-in-law Laban shuffles Leah, the elder daughter, into the bridal chamber instead. When the sun rises the next morning, there is no going back.

As far as Laban is concerned, it is the perfect arrangement. For Jacob and Rachel (for whom Jacob must work another seven years), it is not. Laban's rationale is that the older sister must marry first—and more wives will produce more children, which will increase the clan's worth.

Sharing a husband between two sisters is never a good idea, especially when said husband continues to favor the one he wished he had made love to on his wedding night. As a complicating factor, Rachel seems to be infertile and Leah produces babies like water going over Niagara Falls.

Leah bears Jacob six sons before Rachel gets pregnant for the first time with her son Joseph. Leah's maid has also borne Jacob two sons, as has Rachel's maid. Rachel gives birth to one more son, Benjamin, then dies just after childbirth. From the offspring of the twelve sons develop the twelve tribes of Israel. Leah also gives birth to a daughter, Dinah.

Trace Leah's emotional state through this process, remembering that she is also responsible for naming her servant's children. Initially, she seems to work for Jacob's love through the offering of sons; as time goes on, she seems to find more of an emotional balance, even lightheartedness.

The Origins of the Twelve Tribes of Israel, in order of birth

FROM LEAH AND JACOB

#1 Reuben (Look-It's-a-Boy!): "God has granted me children; now Jacob will love me."

#2 Simeon (God Heard): "God knows that I am hated, so he has given me this child in consolation."

#3 Levi (Connect): "Now Jacob will connect with me."

#4 Judah (Praise God): "This time I will praise the Lord!"

#5 Issachar (Bartered): "Because I gave my maid to Jacob, God has honored me."

#6 Zebulun (Honor): "This time my husband will honor me with gifts because I gave him many sons!"

(Daughter: Dinah. No recorded statement. Dinah is a silent victim of rape, whom several brothers avenge.)

FROM RACHEL'S MAID BILHAH AND JACOB

#7 Dan (Vindication)

#8 Naphtali (Fight)

FROM LEAH'S MAID ZILPHAH AND JACOB

#9 Gad (Lucky)

#10 Asher (Happy)

FROM RACHEL AND JACOB

#11 Joseph (Add, as in "add another son for me")

#12 Benjamin (Rachel named him Ben-oni (Son of my Pain) but Jacob changed his name to Benjamin (Son of Good Fortune).

Consider this

Thousands of years have passed since the story of Rachel and Leah. Yet many families experience the same dynamics: love, passion, jealousy, scheming, grief, duty, and yearning.

Leah knows, firsthand, the love and passion of which Jacob is capable—for she experienced it in his tent when he thought it was Rachel in his arms. From that point on, she sees what real love is, yet she does not receive it. By the time of son number five, she must barter with Rachel for a night with Jacob—indicating that Rachel is in charge of Jacob's sex life. Leah's comments indicate that she yearned for Jacob's love and respect, enduring great emotional and physical labor.

After Rachel dies giving birth to Benjamin, the air seems to clear. Leah and Jacob grow old together, and there is a sense, finally, that they enjoy mutual respect, companionship, and perhaps even love. After all, they share a common story, chiseled from blood, persistence, and faith. How sweet those years must have been for Leah. Most of the "big names" in scripture are descended from her, including Moses, David, and Jesus. Let's trust she knows that; let's hope she has some happiness at last.

Who doesn't want to be loved, genuinely loved? Who wants to be forever competing for love? Even though love was not the engine for marriage in ancient times, it must have been painful to be known as second-best for so long.

What might we learn from Leah?

▷ Our contributions to life may make an impact long after we are gone.

▷ Love isn't something that can be forced.

▷ Smaller goals may be in reach, even if your main goal is out of your control.

▷ Make the best of what you have, even if it isn't exactly what you want.

▷ Find worth in yourself, not in another's perception of you.

For reflection

1. Love takes different forms, especially during a long marriage. Do you think Leah received her heart's desire during her lifetime? If so, how? If not, how did she find fulfillment?

2. Imagine the heartbreak that Leah felt when Jacob expressed rage after having been deceived by Laban. What would it have been like to be her?

3. Can you imagine bartering with your sister for a chance to be loved by your husband? Do you think Leah's perseverance paid off?

4. Are there lessons to be learned here about dysfunctional family systems in contemporary families? If so, what might they be?

RACHEL

Betwixt, between and beloved

▷ **READ HER STORY:** Genesis 29-31

▷ **CLASSIC MOMENT:** Being switched for her sister on what should have been her wedding night

▷ **LIKELY CHARACTERISTICS:**
Beautiful, Emotive, Dramatic, Spirited, Possessive, Jealous, Demanding

▷ **DATA:** 112 words

Who was Rachel?

The beloved wife and first cousin of her husband Jacob, the mother of Joseph and Benjamin, the younger sister of Leah, the daughter-in-law of Isaac and Rebekah, the daughter of Laban, and the niece of Rebekah // The victim of a switch by her father so that her sister Leah would be Jacob's first wife // The first woman in the Bible to die in childbirth // The occupant of the oldest single memorial to a woman mentioned in the Bible, located just outside Bethlehem

What did Rachel say?

When Rachel saw that she bore Jacob no children, she envied her sister; and she said to Jacob, **"Give me children, or I shall die!"** Jacob became very angry with Rachel and said, "Am I in the place of God, who has withheld from you the fruit of the womb?" *Genesis 30:1-2*

Then she said, **"Here is my maid Bilhah; go in to her, that she may bear upon my knees and that I too may have children through her."** *Genesis 30:3*

Then Rachel said, "**God has judged me, and has also heard my voice and given me a son**"; therefore she named him Dan. Rachel's maid Bilhah conceived again and bore Jacob a second son. Then Rachel said, "**With mighty wrestlings I have wrestled with my sister, and have prevailed**"; so she named him Naphtali. *Genesis 30:6-8*

Then Rachel said to Leah, "**Please give me some of your son's mandrakes.**" But [Leah] said to her, "Is it a small matter that you have taken away my husband? Would you take away my son's mandrakes also?" Rachel said, "**Then he may lie with you tonight for your son's mandrakes.**" *Genesis 30:14-15*

[Rachel] conceived and bore a son, and said, "**God has taken away my reproach**"; and she named him Joseph, saying, "**May the LORD add to me another son!**" *Genesis 30:23-24*

Here Rachel and Leah speak together (64 words):

Then Rachel and Leah answered him, "**Is there any portion or inheritance left to us in our father's house? Are we not regarded by him as foreigners? For he has sold us, and he has been using up the money given for us. All the property that God has taken away from our father belongs to us and to our children; now then, do whatever God has said to you.**" *Genesis 31:14-16*

And she said to her father, "**Let not my lord be angry that I cannot rise before you, for the way of women is upon me.**" *Genesis 31:35*

WHAT THE HECK IS A MANDRAKE?

Not your normal vegetable. A plant of the nightshade family, it has white or purple flowers and sports large yellow berries. Forked, its fleshy root apparently resembles the human form with a torso and two legs. Widely used in medicine, magic, and for aphrodisiac purposes over the centuries, folklore says that the tuber shrieks when pulled from the ground. Rachel saw mandrakes as a way to enhance her fertility; thus the request.

Rachel's story

Jacob, on the run from Esau, reaches his Uncle Laban's home and begins work as a shepherd. As fate would have it, Laban has two daughters, and Jacob falls in love with Rachel, the younger and more beautiful of the two girls.

When Jacob asks Laban for Rachel's hand in marriage, Laban says he must "earn" her by working first for seven years. Yet after seven years—and there had to be much anticipation and excitement after waiting that long—Laban slips Leah, instead of Rachel, into the wedding tent.

As one writer, Miki Raver, says, "How could Jacob have been fooled? Was he that drunk?"[13] Couldn't he tell the woman in his bed was the wrong one? Apparently not. There were no light switches to flip, just candles. There must have been plenty of wine. Women dressed to cover themselves completely, especially at weddings...and it would seem that Leah was rather quiet.

Come morning, Jacob demands his bride of choice. Laban meets Jacob's fury with another demand: seven more years of work from Jacob in order to "earn" Rachel.

Once Rachel and Jacob are finally married, she experiences a common Old Testament theme: Rachel finds herself unable to bear children. What multiplies her emotional pain is watching Leah produce one son after another for Jacob. In fact, the first thing she says in the Bible is, "Give me children or I will die!" Like Sarah, Rachel offers her maid to Jacob, so she might legally provide children. Leah follows suit.

When Rachel finally does give birth to Joseph, both parents are besotted with him, and his father adores him more than his other children. (Joseph grows into a difficult and spoiled teenager...but turns out well as an adult.) Years later, Rachel bears Benjamin but dies in childbirth, putting a sad punctuation point on a poignant life.

Consider this

In the Old Testament, we see time and again that historically significant women (Sarah, Rebekah, Hannah, etc.) who bear historically significant children (Isaac, Jacob, Samuel) have trouble getting pregnant. Implication: God's intervention is necessary for the fulfillment of the sacred story. And so it is with this story. By the time Rachel gives birth, she has waited an extraordinarily long time and has seen her sister bear six sons and a daughter.

Polygamy was common in ancient days; some would claim that the situation didn't bother Rachel. Not a chance. And no doubt she was in great emotional and physical pain when she died in childbirth, sensing the life drain from her and knowing she would not be the one to raise her younger son.

Passion. Love. Children. Grief. Rachel's love and agony have not been forgotten, inspiring God's children to remember her in times of deep grief.

From her torment comes the famous cry in Matthew (2:18), quoting the prophet Jeremiah (31:15): "A voice is heard in Ramah, lamentation and bitter weeping. Rachel is weeping for her children; she refuses to be comforted for her children, because they are no more." Centuries later, during the second Babylonian exile (circa 587 to 538 B.C.E.), Jeremiah envisioned Rachel as rising from her grave, grieving for Israel's children in exile. Matthew reiterated her grief in the New Testament as he recounted Herod's slaying of the Holy Innocents—all Bethlehem boys under two years of age at the time of Jesus' birth.

Haunting and yet somehow comforting, Rachel's story reminds us that God's people are no strangers to grief and tragedy—yet in the life of faith, no tear goes unnoticed.

What might we learn from Rachel?

  ▷ Life is short, but what we do with our lives may make a difference for all humanity.

  ▷ Loved ones bring both joy and trouble.

  ▷ Faith and prayer are essential when all seems broken.

  ▷ The pieces of our lives may seem fragmented and nonsensical, but God uses all for good.

For reflection

1. Rachel was Jacob's first choice as a bride, but her father switched her for her sister Leah. However, without that move, the twelve tribes of Israel would, likely, not have come into being. Have there been painful parts of your life that have made more sense when viewed in later years?

2. Perhaps Joseph understood the emotional pain that his mother had felt, for while imprisoned in Egypt (after his brothers sold him as a slave to Egyptian travelers), he articulated a visionary approach to suffering. Note his words in Genesis toward his brothers: "Even though you intended to do harm to me, God intended it for good..." *Genesis* 50:20). How might such an understanding be helpful today when facing suffering?

3. Have you experienced the kind of emotional pain that Rachel did, thinking that the thing you wanted the most would never happen? What have you learned that you might pass on to others?

4. Have you wept over infertility issues, the lack of a child, or the death of a child? How did you find peace?

RACHEL'S MIDWIFE

"Do not be afraid"

PROFILE: LOW

▷ **READ HER STORY:** Genesis 35:16-21

▷ **CLASSIC MOMENT:** Delivering Rachel's second son, Benjamin, and comforting her as she dies

▷ **LIKELY CHARACTERISTICS:** Attentive, Compassionate, Skilled, Decisive, Practical

▷ **DATA:** 11 words

Who was Rachel's midwife?

The first midwife mentioned in biblical history // A proclaimer of the classic biblical words: "Do not be afraid" // The witness to the death of a highly significant biblical woman // One who proclaims both birth and death

---

What did Rachel's midwife say?

When [Rachel] was in her hard labor, the midwife said to her, "**Do not be afraid, for now you will have another son.**" *Genesis 35:17*

Rachel's midwife's story

Picture this: outside Bethlehem, the cries of a woman in childbirth ring out full of pain. Throughout the night and the next day they continue—but soon become drowned out by primitive, grasping tears of grief, sorrow, and fear.

"Do not be afraid," says the midwife. "Do not be afraid, for soon you will give birth to another son."

Moaning, more incoherent moaning. But then a lusty cry bursts forth from a tiny, red-faced, screaming baby boy. The mother, now bleeding uncontrollably, catches only a glimpse of her new son before darkness washes over her and she is gone.

Cradling the newborn in her arms as he roots for milk, the midwife reaches over to close the dead woman's eyes.

Consider this

"Do not be afraid, for soon you will give birth to another son."

Was the midwife telling Rachel to not be afraid because she would have a son and not a daughter? Was she trying to distract Rachel from a grave medical situation? Was she saying Rachel's main work on earth was done and that she should not be afraid of death?

In those days, bearing sons was the goal. Daughters were necessary for society but a burden for families. Most likely, the midwife could see the end was near and wanted to give Rachel some good news in the midst of her despair.

A woman in labor. A woman who is traveling. A woman in distress. A woman of God who is told, "Do not be afraid."

Bells should be ringing. Think of this story and the similarities to Jesus' birth. Mary, the mother of Jesus, was also on the road in labor, near Bethlehem. She is also told, "Do not be afraid."

What might we learn from Rachel's midwife?

▷ Childbirth is dangerous.

▷ It is a sacred honor to walk with those in transition, whether helping women give birth or preparing a loved one for burial.

▷ Providing comfort is a holy endeavor.

▷ The words "Do not be afraid" never go out of style.

Come, labor on.
Claim the high calling angels cannot share—
to young and old the Gospel gladness bear; redeem the
time; its hours too swiftly fly; the night draws nigh.[14]

For reflection

1. How does the role of midwife speak to the role of women in the Bible?

2. Do you think the midwife's words in Genesis 35:17 were meant to comfort or distract Rachel from her impending death? Recall a situation when another woman provided great comfort to you. What made her actions memorable?

3. Visualize how you have walked with another who was in transition. What did you learn? How did it feel? What do you most need from others when you have been the one in transition?

4. What are some of the most comforting words you have ever heard?

TAMAR

One smokin' hot ancestor

PROFILE:
MODERATELY LOW

▷ **READ HER STORY:** Genesis 38

▷ **CLASSIC MOMENT:** Seducing her father-in-law

▷ **LIKELY CHARACTERISTICS:** Scandalous, Determined, Brave, Clever, Purposeful, Knowledgeable, Persistent, Deceptive

▷ **DATA:** 60 words

Who was Tamar?

A woman who fought for her right to bear children in the face of great odds // The only woman in biblical history to seduce her father-in-law // The only woman in the Bible to be sentenced to death by fire for her presumed crime of adultery // The second biblical woman to give birth to twin sons whose birth order was conflictual // A rather scandalous ancestor of Jesus, yet listed in Matthew's genealogy of Jesus

What did Tamar say?

When Judah saw her, he thought her to be a prostitute, for she had covered her face. He went over to her at the road side, and said, "Come, let me come in to you" for he did not know that she was his daughter-in-law. She said, "**What will you give me, that you may come in to me?**" He answered, "I will send you a kid from the flock." And she said, "**Only if you give me a pledge, until you send it.**" He said, "What pledge shall I give you?" She replied, "**Your signet** and your cord, and the staff that is in your hand." So he gave them to her, and went in to her, and she conceived by him. *Genesis 38:15-18*

As she was being brought out, she sent word to her father-in-law, "It was the owner of these who made me pregnant." And she said, "Take note, please, whose these are, the signet and the cord and the staff." *Genesis 38:25*

Tamar's story

Tamar (Tay-mar) makes Calamity Jane look like Mary Poppins.

To give you some back story, Judah (this would be Leah and Jacob's fourth son and the half-brother of Joseph) had several sons. The oldest of them, Er, married Tamar, and then died by the hand of God, for he was "wicked in God's sight" (Genesis 38:7). We do not know the specific wickedness that encouraged God to strike down Er, other than that Tamar was not a Jew.

Upon the death of a husband, ancient Hebrew law dictated that it was the duty of the next brother in line to marry the widow and impregnate her so that the older brother's name and inheritance rights might be carried on in the name of the deceased male. Don't be shocked here, but widows and daughters did not inherit.

Up steps Onan, the second brother, who "spills his seed" (an early form of birth control, now called "Onanism"), instead of impregnating Tamar. Such an action ensured that Onan would receive Judah's inheritance, for no grandson would be born in Er's

News Bulletin

Tamar, a widow, is pregnant. Judah, her former father-in-law, is furious.

"Burn her at the stake!" says the old man.

"Wait!" she cries. "Take this ring, staff, and seal to Judah and tell him I am pregnant by the man who owns them."

In shock, Judah is silenced.

"They are mine," he finally says. "She is more right than I. Set her free."

name. Tamar must have been humiliated, but God was angered—and struck Onan dead.

Only one brother, Shelah, is left. Hmmm, thinks Judah. Two of my sons have died while married to this woman; do I want to risk the last one?

He shuns Tamar but does not release her from her vow of marriage within the family. Had he done so, she would have been free to remarry. In sending her back to her father's house without such freedom, however, he condemns her, giving her no chance to have children or a future.

But Tamar will not go "gentle into that good night." It's not her fault that her husbands have died; she wants to claim and act on her right to bear children. Since Judah will not give her the vehicle for those children—his third son—she designs a plan. She will seduce the newly widowed Judah, claiming the family sperm as her due.

Dressing as a prostitute, she plants herself in Judah's path as he walks to a neighboring town. The fish is hooked: they have sex. Short of money, Judah says he will send a goat for payment. She insists that he lend her his staff, signet, and cord for collateral.

Judah keeps his word—or at least, he tries. When he attempts to send the promised goat by way of a servant, the prostitute cannot be found.

Months pass. When word reaches Judah that his daughter-in-law is pregnant and has "played the whore," he mandates that she burn to death. But calm, non-anxious Tamar has great presence of mind. In a different century, she would make a fine lawyer. She holds up the cord, ring, and signet. "It was the owner of these who made me pregnant" (Genesis 38:25).

Boom! Judah acknowledges the new life in her womb as his own—and even admits he was wrong. "She is more in the right than I, since I did not give her to my son Shelah" (Genesis 38:26).

Case closed. The Bible says that "he did not lie with her again." Good call.

Consider this

Like several women before her, Tamar found herself unable to conceive. But unlike the others, she took matters into her own hands to make conception possible.

When Judah refused to give her his third son, as mandated by Jewish law, she seduced him to get her due: a child of her own. Throughout the Old Testament, men most often saw women as vessels to bear children. Here that order is reversed: Tamar uses Judah as a family vessel to deliver sperm.

Tamar was within her rights to proceed in this fashion; however, Judah could still have called for her death. Contemporary readers will balk, and deservedly so, but ancient Jewish law provided an option called the levirate,[15] which allowed for the closest male relative to act as sperm donor. Such an action trumped incest laws normally in force.

Clearly, Tamar, by producing her twins, increased her worth in the cultural and economic system of the time. But she has also accomplished the following:

- She has children to love and to love her, who will care for her as she grows old;

- She leaves her mark on history;

- She has triumphed when marked for life in the shadows;

- She has given Judah two new sons.

Through the birth of one of her twins, Perez, the line of Judah (and Tamar) continues through Boaz, Obed, King David, and eventually, to Jesus (Matthew 1). The lion of Judah, a symbol of Judah and his tribe, would be used as a Jewish symbol for centuries, as Jerusalem was located in Judah.

What might we learn from Tamar?

▷ Stay singular with your goal. Think creatively.

▷ Sometimes we have to make ourselves count when no one else will.

▷ Assess the cost before taking action.

▷ Actions by our ancestors help make us who we are today.

▷ Life is not over until it's over.

For reflection

1. Even though it was Tamar's right to marry Judah's younger son, she was denied that option. Considering this refusal, evaluate her actions with Judah.

2. Tamar's actions may not have been as far-fetched as they appear. What ancestors of yours might have similar stories to tell? Would you be who you are today without such actions?

3. Who were Tamar's descendants? Would they have been born had Tamar not seduced Judah? How would that have affected history?

4. Like so many other Bible women, Tamar risked her life to reach her goal. What are the things for which you would risk your life?

TAMAR'S MIDWIFE

"What a breach!"

▷ **READ HER STORY:** Genesis 38: 27-30

▷ **CLASSIC MOMENT:** Identifying conflict as she delivers Tamar's twin boys

▷ **LIKELY CHARACTERISTICS:** Skilled, Wise, Discerning, Prophetic

▷ **DATA:** 13 words

Who was Tamar's midwife?

The second midwife in biblical history to have her words recorded // A healer who tried to bring comfort // A woman who predicted fraternal conflict at birth and in future years

What did Tamar's midwife say?

When the time of Tamar's delivery came, there were twins in her womb. While she was in labor, one put out a hand; and the midwife took and bound on his hand a crimson thread, saying, "**This one came out first.**" But just then he drew back his hand, and out came his brother, and she said, "**What a breach you have made for yourself!**" Therefore, he was named Perez. Afterward his brother came out with the crimson thread on his hand; and he was named Zerah. *Genesis 38:27-30*

Tamar's midwife's story

Inhabitants of the twenty-first century would see the conditions surrounding childbirth in Tamar's time as primitive. No drugs, or at least no modern ones. No C-sections. No doctors with advanced degrees. Death in childbirth was common. Yet, in those difficult days, as in some contemporary births, there was a shining light for mothers-to-be: midwives.

Skilled in the art of delivering newborns and soothing women in the pain of childbirth, midwives were an essential link to both present and future. Their professional skills included both medical competence and—as Tamar's midwife so aptly demonstrated—wisdom. She was able to save both the mother and her twin sons and predict future conflict because of the unusual birth order of Perez and Zerah.

Consider this

Here's the key to this unusual story. Tamar sought what was hers by right: a child. She found a way to stay within the system and claim that right. God blessed her doubly with twin sons, a grand prize in those days. (The sons were no doubt also a consolation for Grandpa/Dad Judah, whose first two sons had died.) The bloodline would stay secure.

When the twins began to emerge from the birth canal, a tiny hand first appeared. Thinking quickly, the midwife tied a scarlet cord around that baby's wrist, only to have that baby draw back and the other twin fully emerge. Thus Perez was the first son. Again the apparent underdog, as confirmed by the midwife, has emerged victorious.

Perez, like his mother Tamar, broke new ground, realigning the normal way things were done. He brought happiness to Tamar and Judah and served as a model for the marriage of Boaz and Ruth: "Then all the people who were in the gate, along with the elders, said, "...may your house be like the house of Perez, whom Tamar bore to Judah" (Ruth 4:11-12).

One final clue to this story: Tamar's midwife uses a scarlet cord to mark the identity of Zerah, whom she assumes will be the firstborn. Alert readers will see that Rahab, a prostitute, (Joshua 2:17-21) also uses a scarlet cord to mark her identity so that she might be delivered from the destruction of Jericho. Tamar and Rahab are two of four women outside the Jewish circle. Through their inclusion into Jesus' bloodlines, both new genes and new personalities come into play.

Tamar's midwife, then, is one of several women who help open doors to new life. She delivers the babies safely and in doing so, joins the ranks of women in the Bible who are there when needed, who keep the lifeblood flowing, and who pave the road for the birth of Christ.

What might we learn from Tamar's midwife?

▷ You never know the implications your work will have thousands of years later.

▷ Clarity is important when practicing one's profession.

▷ Naming potential conflict is part of the healing arts.

For reflection

1. Why was the action taken by Tamar's midwife important?

2. This woman is the second individual midwife to have her words recorded in the Bible. What did she say? Why did it matter?

3. Imagine the hardships of having a baby in Old Testament times: no drugs, a high mortality rate of both mother and child, no advanced medical care, and (at times) no choice. Many mothers in biblical times were only girls themselves, forced into marriage and not emotionally prepared for motherhood. What parts of the world today have similar dynamics?

4. Women help others bring new life into the world, whether it is a new baby, a new idea, or a new ministry. List some of the ways you help to birth new life in God's name.

POTIPHAR'S WIFE

A lusty liar

PROFILE: MODERATE

▷ **READ HER STORY:** Genesis 39

▷ **CLASSIC MOMENT:** Trying to seduce Joseph, failing, and then screaming rape

▷ **LIKELY CHARACTERISTICS:** Selfish, Bored, Disloyal, Demanding, Duplicitous, Vengeful, Vicious

▷ **DATA:** 99 words

Who was Potiphar's wife?

The only woman in the Bible who sets out to seduce her husband's employee // The only woman in the Bible to falsely accuse a man of attempted rape // The woman who lands Joseph in jail

What did Potiphar's wife say?

Now Joseph was handsome and good-looking. And after a time his master's wife cast her eyes on Joseph and said, "**Lie with me.**" But he refused... *Genesis 39:6-8*

One day...while no one else was in the house, she caught hold of his garment, saying, "**Lie with me!**" *Genesis 39:11-12*

When she saw that he had left his garment in her hand and had fled outside, she called out to the members household and said to them, "**See, my husband has brought among us a Hebrew to insult us! He came in to me to lie with me,** and I cried out with a loud voice; and when he heard me raise my voice and cry out, he left his garment beside me, and fled outside." *Genesis 39:13-15*

When his master heard the words that his wife spoke to him, saying, "**This is the way your servant treated me**," he become enraged. And Joseph's master took him and put him into the prison. *Genesis 39:19-20*

Potiphar's wife's story

Married to one of the most powerful men in Egypt, she wants more. She wants Joseph, her husband's handsome top aide—and the overseer of their home. His sad brown eyes, his outstanding physique, his remote nature… and most of all, his hard body pressed against hers; she wants it all.

Relentlessly, she whispers, "Lie with me." And each time, the young upstart refuses, citing her husband's trust. "How could I do this to Potiphar—and, most of all, to God?"

Enough! One morning, when no one else is in the house, she reaches for his shirt, trying to pull it off.

"Lie with me!"

Joseph flees, leaving the garment in her hands.

Scorned and humiliated, she shouts: "Rape! My husband hired a Hebrew, and he tried to rape me! Look—here is his shirt. Here is the proof!

When Potiphar comes home, she repeats her story. Joseph is jailed, and Potiphar's wife is not heard from again.

Consider this

Potiphar's wife has the power to destroy Joseph's life, and she almost does. There is no concern for Joseph, just a focus on what she wants. While sexual opportunity presents itself here, this is not just a story about sex—but also, power dynamics.

Guiding himself with morals and faith, Joseph takes the high road, even when smacked in the face by temptation. He does the right thing; his conscience is clear, even though his employer does not believe him. While it's not fair that Joseph is jailed, he is a man of such deep faith that he stays optimistic, concentrates on what he can do well (interpret dreams), and is eventually freed.

Potiphar's wife, on the other hand, is morally corrupt. Most of the time in the Bible, it is men who are blamed for immoral behavior. Not here. Not even close.

Ironically the words, "Lie with me," have a double meaning: the physical act of intercourse, and the calling of another into a life of deception and falsehoods. By refusing, Joseph shows real moral courage.

Bravo for Joseph! And Potiphar's wife? She's a loser.

What might we learn from Potiphar's wife?

▷ Power and affluence can be corrupting.

▷ Boredom can be a trap; find some rewarding activities.

▷ Stay within the bounds of marriage.

▷ Lashing out in rage when desires are not met is destructive.

▷ Do not use other people.

For reflection

1. What were Potiphar's wife's motives in trying to seduce Joseph?

2. The story of Potiphar's wife reads like a soap opera...or an occasional work setting. Name some similarities in contemporary society.

3. How is this story more about power than sex? How does it resemble or not resemble contemporary instances of abuse?

4. Why might this be a good story to share with young men and young women? What does it have to say about values and about situations in which there seems to be no way to avoid trouble?

CHAPTER 4

WOMEN WHO SPEAK IN EXODUS

On its surface, the Book of Exodus is about God, Moses, the Hebrew people, and their exodus from Egypt.

Behind the scenes, however, exist some surprises, of which the largest is this: twelve women in a row protect Moses and help his journey through birth, life, boyhood, and young adulthood in just the first two chapters of Exodus.[16] What? Twelve tribes of Israel, twelve apostles of Jesus...yet this all-female cast of twelve is often overlooked. Shocking.

Exodus is a great book. Especially when you have the whole story.

By the numbers

Words spoken by women in Exodus: 123

Number of women who speak: Three individuals (Pharaoh's daughter, Miriam, and Zipporah) plus two groups (Shiphrah and Puah, priest of Midian's daughters)

SHIPHRAH AND PUAH

Truth to power

PROFILE: LOW

▷ **READ THEIR STORY:** Exodus 1

▷ **CLASSIC MOMENT:** Choosing the dictates of their conscience, they refused to kill the babies in their care

▷ **LIKELY CHARACTERISTICS:** Nurturing, Bold, Brave, Steely, Quick-witted, Purposeful

▷ **DATA:** 23 words

Who were Shiphrah and Puah?

Midwives who risked their lives to save Hebrew babies // The first people in the Bible to practice civil disobedience

What did Shiphrah and Puah say?

So the king of Egypt summoned the midwives and said to them, "Why have you done this, and allowed the boys to live?" The midwives said to Pharaoh, **"Because the Hebrew women are not like the Egyptian women; for they are vigorous and give birth before the midwife comes to them."** *Exodus 1:18-19*

Shiphrah and Puah's story

Exodus brings a new era, for the bones of Sarah, Rachel, Leah, Rebekah, and Tamar have turned to dust. No longer is there a son (descendant) of Abraham and Sarah in a position of authority in Egypt, as Joseph had been.

Instead the Hebrew people are forced to toil daily as slaves, roasting in the hot Mediterranean sun while building temples, roads, and tombs year after year.

In typical Egyptian-ruler fashion, Pharaoh (like Herod, around the time Jesus was born), is threatened by both their numbers and their muscle. And he's not the only one, the Bible says: "the more they were oppressed, the more they multiplied and spread...The Egyptians became ruthless in imposing tasks on the Israelites..." (Exodus 1:12-13).

Worried that the Hebrew people will overthrow the country, Pharaoh decrees a horrible edict: the slaughter of all male Hebrew babies under two years old to destabilize the slaves' growth and demoralize the people.

Midwives, however, are in the business of facilitating birth, bringing children into the world—not destroying them. And on that fateful day, when Shiphrah and Puah are called before Pharaoh and told they must destroy new life, they are horrified. Chances are they would have been killed on the spot had they resisted then and there. Somehow they manage instead to stay alive and return home.

Back at work, exercising their vocation, they know they cannot kill; the power to do so is just not within their souls. They are healers, life-givers, not murderers. Continuing to help babies draw their first breath, they simply go about their work, their holy calling.

Soon they are hauled back to face the Pharaoh, who demands to know why the boys have been allowed to live.

"Because the Hebrew women are not like the Egyptian women; for they are vigorous and give birth before the midwife comes to them" (Exodus 1:19). Although the midwives are filled with fear, the king is satisfied with their answer and releases them.

Evil, however, knows no bounds. Raising the stakes, the king orders all newborn Hebrew boys to be thrown into the Nile River, for death will be certain there. But that is, as Uncle Wiggily would say,[17] a story for another day.

Consider this

Shiphrah and Puah are moral women committed to life, not death. Saying no to power in favor of the greater good, they are the first to practice civil disobedience in the Bible. Their knees may have been knocking together as they faced the king, but they chose life in the midst of death: they took the right path, the moral path, instead of following an unjust mandate.

Fighting unjust laws often begins with small steps. Think of Rosa Parks, refusing to give up her seat on the bus. Think of young Malala Yousafzai, shot by the Taliban in Pakistan for simply seeking an education. Think of Saudi Arabian women slipping behind the wheel and driving, even though they do not have the legal right to do so.

What might we learn from Shiphrah and Puah?

▷ There are principles worth fighting and dying for.

▷ Our vocations, whether at home, at the office, or on the battlefield, are worthy of all we can give.

▷ Our actions may reverberate for generations.

For reflection

1. There were many midwives in biblical times, but only Shiphrah and Puah are remembered by name. How did their act of civil disobedience set the tone for Moses' accomplishments?

2. If ordered to kill a newborn—and refusal meant your own death, how might you react?

3. Have you ever acted on the principle of civil disobedience? To what extent did your faith help you with the process and what was the result?

PHAROAH'S DAUGHTER

"More than just a bath"

PROFILE: MODERATE

▷ **READ HER STORY:** Exodus 2

▷ **CLASSIC MOMENT:** Lifting baby Moses out of the Nile River and decreeing that he will live

▷ **LIKELY CHARACTERISTICS:** Innocent, Playful, Warm-hearted, Caring, Privileged

▷ **DATA:** 32 words

Who was Pharoah's daughter?

A young woman who, unknowingly, changed the direction of history // The daughter of the Pharaoh // A girl who arranged for Moses to be raised and educated in the top tier of Egyptian society

What did Pharoah's daughter say?

"This must be one of the Hebrews' children," she said. Then [Moses'] sister said to Pharoah's daughter, "Shall I go and get you a nurse from the Hebrew women to nurse the child for you?"

Pharaoh's daughter said to her, "Yes." *Exodus 2:6-8*

Pharaoh's daughter said to her, "Take this child and nurse it for me, and I will give you your wages."...She named him Moses, "because," she said, "I drew him out of the water." *Exodus 2:9-10*

Pharoah's daughter's story

Back story: After his plan to have the midwives murder all newborn baby boys is thwarted, Pharaoh mandates that all male babies under two be thrown into the Nile River and drowned. Imagine the heartbreak. But Moses' mother (Jochobed) finds a way to set him free and save his life.

After somehow keeping the little guy quiet for several months following his birth, she obtains or weaves a sturdy basket, coats it with pitch and sets it in the bulrushes that line the river's edge. She must know this is the spot where Pharaoh's daughter bathes. Posting her daughter as a sentry, she walks away, leaving her firstborn son in God's hands.

The beautiful young woman (well, she was beautiful—she saved a baby's life—what more proof do you need?) finds Moses and decrees he shall be raised in the palace. Sister Miriam emerges from the bulrushes, volunteers her mother as a nurse and hears the lovely word, "Yes." She fetches Jochobed, who brings Moses home.

Knowing that her son must leave home so much earlier than most, those few years must have been full of love, teaching—and suppressed tears. At the age of seven, Moses is brought back to the palace and educated in Egyptian ways. In a way, he has two mothers: the first who gives him birth, and the second who gives him new life.

Consider this

When Moses' mother floated her son's basket in the Nile, it could have worked out really badly.

Pharaoh's daughter or his guards could have had Moses' head bashed against the rocks (Psalm 137:9). No doubt her father would have been pleased. Or she could have tossed the little boy out deeper—where crocodiles lurked, hunting their next meal.

Yet she does none of that. Rather, she seems to fall in love. Imagine her in the sunlight, her bare feet in the water. Her servants stand with her, their arms filled with towels, scented oils, and soap. Tossed over her shoulders, as she leans over to lift the basket's lid, is her shining black hair. Perhaps Moses grabbed that hair with his tiny fist; perhaps he looked into her eyes and smiled.

Somewhere she has learned compassion.

Pharaoh's daughter names the child Moses, which means "I drew him out of the water." Like the midwives before her, she too has saved a life. Because of her kind nature, she prepares the way for Moses, who goes on to be a kind of midwife himself, delivering his people from the bonds of slavery into a life of freedom and wholeness.

We should also note that her act will eventually bring pain and suffering to her people. When Pharaoh refuses to heed Moses' request and let the Israelites leave Egypt, God strikes them with ten plagues, including the deaths of their own firstborn sons.

What might we learn from Pharoah's daughter?

- ▷ The future is unseen—what matters is doing the right thing today.

- ▷ Advocacy for the vulnerable is a holy gift.

- ▷ Our vocations are worthy of all we can give.

- ▷ God works across cultural divides.

For reflection

1. When Pharaoh's daughter lifted baby Moses out of the water and then saved his life, what went through her mind?

2. Given that callous indifference to child mortality still exists around the world today, how might we draw from the big picture of our faith to alleviate such violations?

3. As a mother, it must have been hard for Jochobed to see her boy raised in a different culture, yet most likely, she considered herself blessed for having at least several initial years with him. She could have rejoiced in that time and used it well, or she could have squandered it. How do you think she handled that time?

4. Name any situations troubling you. Visualize putting them in a basket, closing the lid, and setting them afloat to rest in God's hands.

MIRIAM

Big sister par excellence

**PROFILE:
MODERATELY
HIGH**

▷ **READ HER STORY:** Exodus 2, Exodus 15, Numbers 12, Numbers 20:1, 26:59, Deuteronomy 24:9, 1 Chronicles 6:3, Micah 6:4

▷ **CLASSIC MOMENT:** Watching over little Moses in the Nile River and suggesting that their mother nurse him until he is old enough to live in Pharaoh's palace

▷ **LIKELY CHARACTERISTICS:** Faithful, Joyous, Protective, Supportive, Musical, Critical, Tribal

▷ **DATA:** 36 words

Who was Miriam?

The older sister of Moses and Aaron // A woman who appeared in more books of the Bible than any other // The woman who spoke the most in Exodus // The first woman to be called a prophet // The first biblical woman to sing and to lead other women in song and dance // A sentry and protector of Moses

What did Miriam say?

Then his sister said to Pharaoh's daughter, **"Shall I go and get you a nurse from the Hebrew women to nurse the child for you?"** *Exodus 2:7*

Then the prophet Miriam, Aaron's sister, took a tambourine in her hand; and all the women went out after her with tambourines and with dancing. And Miriam sang to them: **"Sing to the Lord, for he has triumphed gloriously; horse and rider he has thrown into the sea."** *Exodus 15:20-21*

What did Miriam (and Aaron) say?[18]

While they were at Hazeroth, Miriam and Aaron spoke against Moses because of the Cushite woman whom he had married (for he had indeed married a Cushite woman); and they said, "**Has the** Lord **spoken only through Moses? Has he not spoken through us also?**" *Numbers 12:1-2*

Miriam's story

Miriam steps out of hiding on the banks of the Nile when baby Moses' life hangs in the balance. Suggesting her mother as a nurse for the child, she enables Moses to stay at home until he reaches the age of reason. Later, she accompanies both brothers on the Exodus from Egypt, when Moses triumphantly leads the Israelites to freedom.

It is that freedom that Miriam raises in song, leading the other women in chorus and dance after the Exodus. Such vitality is the upside of Miriam. Unfortunately, there is also a downside. Years later, as the Jews are still on their journey to find the Promised Land, Moses' wife, Zipporah, dies, and he remarries a "Cushite" (Egyptian) woman. Miriam and Aaron rebuke Moses. The tables are turned; God is now the furious one. He upbraids both siblings, telling them that Moses is the primary leader in the wilderness, and that he needs their support.

God then punishes Miriam, inflicting a horrible skin disease (like leprosy or similar to it) that causes her to turn white, presumably covered with lesions. God then throws her out of camp for a week, further indicating his anger and displeasure.

Consider this

Miriam and Aaron both criticized Moses, yet God did not banish Aaron or inflict skin sores on him. Was Miriam singled out for punishment because she was female? Or because she, as the oldest, should have known better? Whatever the reason, God needed her to be supportive of Moses, even though, in the past, laws regarding social purity had reigned supreme. Perhaps there were bigger fish for God to fry here. God needed unity as he readied the Hebrew people for nationhood and needed primary family members to work together. God needed Miriam fully on board.

Contemporary readers often take the Exodus for granted. Try substituting the themes of slavery, genocide, sex-trafficking or life in a refugee camp today. Consider the meaning of freedom—especially for those caught in seemingly inescapable chains.

Power. Abuse. God. Theological developments. Sibling rivalry, authority issues, freedom, the demands of leadership, male-female dynamics. It's all here.

What might we learn from Miriam?

▷ Never give up.

▷ Sometimes being a non-threatening presence works best.

▷ It is hard to watch loved ones in danger, but harder still to watch them die. Do what you can to save their lives. Step up. Pray. Act.

▷ Sometimes young people are the best problem-solvers.

For reflection

1. Along with watching over Moses at the Nile, Miriam is remembered for leading the women in song and dance after they had escaped from Egypt (Exodus 15:20-21), and for being castigated by God for criticizing Moses. What ups and downs did she experience in her life and how did she survive them?

2. What caused the disagreement between Miriam and Moses? See Numbers 12:2. How does this kind of disagreement happen in families today?

3. Women led challenging lives in the days of Exodus. How were they punished differently from men? Reflect on Numbers 5:11—12:2. Do you think Miriam deserved this punishment? What happened to Aaron? What were the power dynamics at work?

THE PRIEST OF MIDIAN'S DAUGHTERS

Guess who's coming to dinner?

▷ READ THEIR STORY: Exodus 2

▷ CLASSIC MOMENT:
Meeting Moses at the well

▷ LIKELY CHARACTERISTICS:
Fun-loving, Protective, Chatty

▷ DATA: 17 words

Who were the priest of Midian's daughters?

Seven unmarried girls // Daughters of Jethro // Water fetchers // Descendants from the tribe of Levi, living in Midian[19] // Eyewitnesses to the life of Moses

What did the priest of Midian's daughters say?

They said, "**An Egyptian helped us against the shepherds; he even drew water for us and watered the flock.**" *Exodus 2:19*

The priest of Midian's daughters' story

Little do these innocent girls know that this day is different, that a killer is watching them as they work and cavort around the well. Little do they know that he will share their dinner table that night—and the bed of one of the girls for a lifetime.

The man is Moses, who has settled in Midian after fleeing Egypt for killing an Egyptian overseer. He watches quietly some distance from the well, not wanting to draw attention. As local men begin to taunt and harass the girls, his internal temperature rises. Just as he did in Egypt, he throws himself into the fight on the side of the underdogs. He chases the bullies away—and then fills the girls' jugs so they can water their sheep.

Scampering home, the girls are questioned by their curious father.

"Why are you home early? What's happened?"

"An Egyptian helped us at the well today. He rescued us from savages!"

Hmmm, thinks the father of seven daughters, knowing that he must find husbands for all of them. "Why did you leave him? Why didn't you bring him home for dinner?"

Moses is found and brought back for dinner. In gratitude for saving his girls, their father gives one daughter, Zipporah, to Moses in marriage. (Note: "Giving" a daughter to a man as his wife was standard practice in ancient times—and this father was no fool, as the "Egyptian man" appeared single, well-educated, kind, and robust.)

Consider this

Think of yourself as a code-breaker in the Bible, noticing patterns and numerical precedence. When you see the numbers three or seven or twelve, slow down—for they are spotlights, pointing the way to a significant event. "Over here," they say, "look over here!"

And so it was for Moses that day that he entered the presence of seven young women. Good fortune was his, as on that day he met both his future wife and found temporary work tending sheep.

By the numbers

THE NUMBER THREE:

- Jonah spent three days in the belly of the whale

- Jesus' ministry lasted three years, according to Luke (Luke 13:7)

- The Trinity: God the Father, God the Son, God the Holy Spirit; God the Creator, Sustainer, and Redeemer

THE NUMBER SEVEN:

- The seven demons Jesus cast out from Mary Magdalene

- The seven days of creation

- A sabbatical year every seventh year (Leviticus 25:4)

THE NUMBER TWELVE:

- The twelve apostles

- The twelve tribes of Israel

- The twelve women shepherding Moses through life

What might we learn from the priest of Midian's daughters?

▷   You never know what a day will bring.

▷   Stay close to your siblings.

▷   Be kind to your in-laws, for they may one day determine your future.

For reflection

1. Action around water is a common theme in both the Old and New Testaments. Think of Rebekah, meeting Jacob's servant at the well. Consider the woman at the well in John 4. What it is about a well—or water—that inspires important events?

2. Name the clues in this story that indicate an important event is about to happen.

3. What would it have meant to be the parent of seven daughters?

4. Do you think the girls noticed Moses' potential as much as their father did?

5. Where is God in this story?

ZIPPORAH

A flinty woman

PROFILE: LOW

▷ **READ HER STORY:** Exodus 4

▷ **CLASSIC MOMENT:**
When she circumcises her son

▷ **LIKELY CHARACTERISTICS:**
Fearless, Brave, Angry, Dexterous, Decisive

▷ **DATA:** 15 words

Who was Zipporah?

The only woman in the Bible to circumcise a child // One of seven sisters // Moses' first wife // A woman who ameliorated God's anger toward Moses // The mother of two sons

What did Zipporah say?

But Zipporah took a flint and cut off her son's foreskin, and touched Moses' feet[20] with it, and said, **"Truly you are a bridegroom of blood to me!"** So she let him alone. It was then she said, **"A bridegroom of blood by circumcision."**
Exodus 4:25-26

Zipporah's story

Zipporah, one of seven sisters, marries Moses. Over the next several years, the young couple lives with her family while Moses tends to her father's sheep. Two sons, Gershom and Eliezer, are born. Days turn into nights, months into years…until several life-changing events occur.

One day, when Moses is out with the flock, he comes across a sight never before seen: a burning bush, red-hot in flames…burning yet not consumed.

"Take off your shoes!" says a voice. Moses complies. "Moses! Return to Egypt and tell Pharaoh to set my people free!"

Taking off his shoes was the easy command. After more demonstrations of God's power, Moses, Zipporah, and the boys head toward Egypt.

Yet trouble awaits—major trouble, for God is not a pastoral counselor, nor an accommodating travel agent. Attacking Moses, God tries to kill him. (No reason is given for this.)

It seems Moses is doomed—until Zipporah jumps in with a sharp piece of flint, probably the one she would have used to kindle fires. She cuts off Gershom's foreskin and throws it at Moses' "feet," saying, "Truly you are a bridegroom of blood to me!"

Only after the Exodus do we see Zipporah again, for Moses sends his family back home shortly after this incident. Understandably.

Consider this

Zipporah is mentioned three times in the Bible: as a bride for Moses, as the only female circumciser, and as a relative onlooker when her father Jethro reunites with Moses.

Reviews on Zipporah herself are mixed. Scholar Edith Dean says she was "rebellious and prejudiced," and that she was one of several "undistinguished Bible wives."[21] This is a bit hard to understand, as her action was unlike that of any other Bible woman. Jewish scholar Tikva Frymer-Kensky[22] states that Zipporah and Moses did not have a fulfilling relationship and that his "neglect of Zipporah is obvious."

Did Moses neglect her? Possibly, given the time it took to live through the ten plagues of Egypt, talk with God, negotiate with Pharaoh, and lead the people across the Red Sea. Here's another option, and one that seems a bit more viable: Moses was trying to protect Zipporah by sending her and the boys home until the Hebrew people had been set free.

Speaking of neglect, Moses had apparently neglected a key requirement of fatherhood: to circumcise his son on the eighth day of his life, thus failing to mark him as a child of God under the covenant that God had established with Abraham (Genesis 17:10-14.) Given his Hebrew roots, this indifference to circumcision is surprising, but may also indicate 1) that his Egyptian upbringing temporarily overshadowed his Hebrew heritage or 2) Zipporah and Moses had different faiths (Zipporah was most likely a polytheist) and that as a young couple, the rituals of faith were easily dismissed.

Perhaps on that dark night, however, her intuition told her that unless she took on the customs of her spouse—and helped him recover the fundamentals of his religion—there would always be conflict.

With God chasing Moses down, she had a choice, unlike the day that she was married. In taking the knife to her son, she chose Moses and God—and marked that pact with blood. Far from being one of the playful seven sisters at the well, she was now a grown woman, fiercely protecting her family.

A night of passion, for both God and Zipporah. A night of horror for Moses, for usually God was a trustworthy companion. A night unlike all others.

What might we learn from Zipporah?

▷   It is best to resolve large differences, such as faith, before marriage.

▷   God is unpredictable and sometimes strikes without warning.

▷   Marital harmony may be strained because of a spouse's work.

▷   Core beliefs will always make a difference.

For reflection

1. Zipporah was the only woman in the Bible to circumcise a child. Does that act change your opinion of her at all, given that she seemed fairly nondescript beforehand? Describe what comes to your mind (besides horror movies) when you hear: "You are a bridegroom of blood!"

2. Faith development in families occurs over time. To what extent have different faith backgrounds affected your family? Has there been any resolution? What have you learned?

3. The Bible says that God "tried to kill Moses." If God is all-powerful, why was it a matter of "trying?" And why might God have wanted to kill him?

CHAPTER 5

WOMEN WHO SPEAK IN NUMBERS

In many books of the Bible, families appear dysfunctional or at the least, highly complex. In the one story where women talk in the Book of Numbers, that is blessedly not the case. Here we find a group of named sisters who act bravely and cooperatively to protect their interests, collectively demanding a change in the legal system. If they win their case, their name and heritage will remain intact. Lose it and they will be swallowed up, their land and property going to the closest male relative.

By the numbers

Words spoken by women in Numbers: 64

Number of women who speak: five named women in a group (the daughters of Zelophehad)

THE DAUGHTERS OF ZELOPHEHAD

Legal warriors: Mahlah, Noah, Hoglah, Milcah, and Tirzah

PROFILE: LOW

▷ **READ THEIR STORY:** Numbers 27

▷ **CLASSIC MOMENT:** Presenting a case to Moses to inherit the family name and property—and winning

▷ **LIKELY CHARACTERISTICS:** Articulate, Strong, Well-spoken, United, Confident, Purposeful

▷ **DATA:** 64 words

Who were the daughters of Zelophehad?

The largest group of sisters in scripture to have their names recorded // Five sisters who had no brother // The first women (on record) to propose a change to Mosaic law // The first women (on record) to challenge their inheritance rights

What did the daughters of Zelophehad say?

They stood before Moses, Eleazar the priest, the leaders, and all the congregation, at the entrance of the tent of meeting, and they said, **"Our father died in the wilderness; he was not among the company of those who gathered themselves together against the LORD in the company of Korah, but died for his own sin; and he had no sons. Why should the name of our father** be taken away from his clan because he had no son? Give to us a possession among our father's brothers." *Numbers 27:2-4*

The daughters of Zelophehad's story

Picture these five young women with their heads held high. Their father, a good man, has died. Even though they are troubled, they are not overtaken by grief. They, are, however, facing the cliff of poverty and anonymity; in those days, women had no rights of inheritance. The property that had belonged to their father would legally pass into the hands of male relatives, and their father's name would vanish.

This is no theoretical discussion—for at the time their father died, census takers were counting faithful Jewish men and their descendants. From that count would come land assignments after the group crossed into the Promised Land. (Yes, the land did belong to other people, but the Israelites saw it as their own, based on God's promise to Abraham.)

The girls debate the inequity of it all, then go to the halls of power: the Tent of Meeting. There, in one strong and united voice, they ask for their due.

It is not fair, they say. It is not fair for our father's name and lineage to fade away because he has no sons. It is not fair that his property be given to some distant male relative. He is our father; we are his daughters.

And God bless Moses, who takes them seriously, appealing to God, the author of all laws and the foundation-builder of Mosaic law. God sides with the daughters, who inherit the property.

As a footnote to this story, the new law was amended several years later to say that if a woman were to inherit her father's property, she must marry a man of the same tribe, thus preserving religious as well as legal ties. That was not a problem for these five daughters, who all married men of the covenant. However, it may have affected others down the road.

Consider this

These five young women were ahead of their time. At a time when women were considered property, they confronted a profoundly unfair law and took it to the hall of power. Working together, they saved their family name and established their own financial security.

Moses deserves credit here for not dismissing the girls out of hand. He could have turned them away with just a shake of his head. Instead, he listened and consulted God. This dilemma describes the balance of a policy request versus an everyday decision. Moses understood this was big stuff; this was one for the Boss to decide.

Some may think of this story as an arcane biblical detail. Not so. Computer data searches find the case referred to as recently as June of 2013, when Edie Winsor used it to inspire her argument to the Supreme Court, speaking against the Defense of Marriage Act.[23] Zelophehad's daughters were also cited in an article by Henry C. Clark in the American Bar Association Journal of February 1934. There, Clark calls it an "early declaratory judgment in which the property rights of women marrying outside of their tribe are clearly set forth."[24]

What might we learn from the daughters of Zelophehad?

▷ Stand up for yourself.

▷ If possible, present your case with others.

▷ Speak to the right people.

▷ Give just cause for why things should change.

For reflection

1. These women were instrumental in changing Mosaic law. What makes their witness so strong? How did they combine purpose with faith?

2. Consider your family. Was there a situation where you stood united for the right principle? As adults or children? Is that sense of unity still there?

3. Have you known families who have been torn apart after the death of the matriarch and/or patriarch? What steps are best taken to avoid that kind of conflict?

4. How might the dynamics of this story inspire you to right an injustice?

NUMBERS

CHAPTER 6

WOMEN WHO SPEAK IN JOSHUA

Although only two women have their words on record in the Book of Joshua, they are both assertive, bright, and strategic survivors. One is a prostitute, the other a bride-prize. Both thrive...after taking matters into their own hands. Rahab gets credit for most of the words spoken here, as some 255 out of 277 are hers.

JOSHUA

By the numbers

Words spoken by women in Joshua: 277

Number of women who speak: Two (Rahab, Achsah)

RAHAB

Harlot and hero

▷ **READ HER STORY:** Joshua 2, 6; Matthew 1:5; Hebrews 11:31; James 2:25

▷ **CLASSIC MOMENT:** Hiding two Hebrew spies on her roof and lying to the king's guards

▷ **LIKELY CHARACTERISTICS:** Brave, Protective, Defiant, Duplicitous, Sensual, Faithful, Decisive

▷ **DATA:** 255 words

Who was Rahab?

A prostitute // A resident of Jericho // A protector of the Hebrew people // A guardian of her family // An ancestor of Jesus

What did Rahab say?

Then she said, "True, the men came to me, but I did not know where they came from. And when it was time to close the gate at dark, the men went out. Where the men went I do not know. Pursue them quickly, for you can overtake them." *Joshua 2:4-5*

Before they went to sleep, she came up to them on the roof and said to the men: "I know that the LORD has given you the land, and that dread of you has fallen on us, and that all the inhabitants of the land melt in fear before you. For we have heard how the LORD dried up the water of the Red Sea before you when you came out of Egypt, and what you did to the two kings of the Amorites that were beyond the Jordan, to Sihon and Og, whom you utterly destroyed. As soon as we heard it, our hearts melted, and there was no courage left in any of us because of you. The LORD your God is indeed God in heaven above and on earth below. Now then, since I have dealt kindly with you, swear to me by the LORD that you in turn will deal kindly with my family. Give me a sign of good faith that you will spare my father and mother, my brothers and sisters, and all who belong to them, and deliver our lives from death." *Joshua 2:8-13*

She said to them, "**Go toward the hill country, so that the pursuers may not come upon you. Hide yourselves there three days, until the pursuers have returned; then afterward you may go your way.**" *Joshua 2:16*

She said, "**According to your words, so be it.**" She sent them away and they departed. Then she tied the crimson cord in the window. *Joshua 2:21*

Rahab's story

Rahab was a prostitute—and is identified as such five times in the Bible, in Joshua 2:1, Joshua 6:17, Joshua 6:25, Hebrews 11:31, and James 2:25. Bible records indicate that she lived about 1250 BCE in the city of Jericho. One of the longest inhabited cities in the history of the world, Jericho is also one of the lowest towns on the face of the earth, about nine hundred feet below sea level. Rahab's home, about ten by twelve feet, was built into the wall of the city, a wall that was several stories high, with a rooftop area. Jericho had these walls for good reason, having been the site of much conflict over the years.

At this point in history, the Hebrew people, tens of thousands of them,[25] are gathering around the hills of Jericho, preparing to invade, for Jericho is the first city in the Promised Land. This is the second time the Israelite people have reached the edge of the land; the first time was forty years before, when Moses had asked his tribal leaders to evaluate potential entrance into the land. All except Joshua and Caleb were horrified at the prospect.[26] "Why is the Lord bringing us into this land to die by the sword? Our wives and little ones will become booty—let us start now and go back to Egypt!"[27]

Until this point God had been patient. No longer! Banishing his people to the wilderness for forty years, God encourages them to develop new traits, including trust, courage, faith, and unity.

By the time they have matured spiritually, Moses has died and Joshua is their new leader. It is time, again, to spy out the Promised Land. And where better to stay than the home of a prostitute? Foreign men come and go; no one pays attention. Easy in, easy out.

They spend the afternoon. Talking, most likely.[28] And then comes a knock on the door: the king's men.

"Let us in! We know you've got spies in there!"

Rahab faces a dilemma. Turn the men in and she's off the hook; lie and she could die.

She lies...but only after she has run the men up to her rooftop and hidden them under bales of flax. Then she yanks open the door, pointing to the hills: "They're not here! They went that way! If you hurry, you can catch them!"

"Whew," say the spies when the danger has passed. "Nice going. See you around."

"Not so fast!" says Rahab. "I saved your life—now you save mine!"

She can still turn the men in. One scream would do it. Instead she bargains for her family to be spared in the coming attack.

"Dang," says one. "She's got us," says the other.

Shrugging, they give her a scarlet cord to throw out of her window, so they can recognize her home in the midst of chaos. Lowering them out of her window by a rope, Rahab gathers family members and stays indoors.

Bloody mayhem erupts several weeks later. The Israelites kill everyone—men, women, children, even the animals, as they follow the rules of holy war in conquering Jericho.[29] But Rahab and her family are safe, carried off by the spies to a new life. She marries into the Jewish faith (in Matthew's genealogy of Jesus, she is listed as having married Salmon, the Jewish tribal leader) and gives birth to Boaz—bringing her genes and identity into the blood of many future descendants, including Jesus.

Consider this

Because of Rahab, the Judeo/Christian story would never be the same. An outsider and a sinner saves God's people. A woman of questionable standards has literally opened the door for the Israelites to enter the Promised Land. Using her survival skills and her faith, Rahab has helped to secure a nation.

In helping the spies, she has found personal redemption as well. Men who use her body and drain her spirit are no longer a concern, for she marries and has a child of her own and a place in history.

What might we learn from Rahab?

▷ Our days are numbered.

▷ God gives us courage when we need it.

▷ We do what we have to do to survive.

▷ Redemption may involve giving up our lives.

▷ Sometimes deception is necessary for a greater good.

For reflection

1. Why do you think Rahab acted to protect the spies? Because a) she was scared of them, b) she found herself believing in their God, or c) they offered her the best chance of protection?

2. The writer of the Letter to the Hebrews includes Rahab on a list of heroes of the faith. What might this story teach us about girls and women caught in the web of prostitution and sex trafficking?

3. How might God have been active in Rahab's life before the spies knocked on her door? Today we would call such an encounter a God-moment, the work of the Holy Spirit, or simply "grace." What would you call it?

4. Throughout history, God comes down on the side of marginalized and oppressed people. Who else in scripture experienced some of the same redemptive dynamics as Rahab?

ACHSAH

Speaking up, speaking out

PROFILE: LOW

▷ **READ HER STORY:** Joshua 15:15-19, Judges 1:12-15

▷ **CLASSIC MOMENT:** Requests property from her father after being given away as a bride-prize

▷ **LIKELY CHARACTERISTICS:** Intelligent, Obedient, Practical, Outspoken, Self-determined

▷ **DATA:** 41 words (22 in Joshua, 19 in Judges)

Who was Achsah?

The daughter of Maacah (known only as Caleb's concubine) and Caleb[30] // A bridal gift for Othniel for defeating the enemy in battle // A landowner // A woman of strategy and foresight

What did Achsah say?

"Give me a present; since you have set me in the land of the Negeb, give me springs of water as well." *Joshua 15:19*

"Give me a present; since you have set me in the land of the Negeb, give me also Gulloth-mayim." *Judges 1:15*

Achsah's story

Achsah (pronounced Axa) is one brave young woman. She is usually overlooked in scripture, as few are familiar with her. Her bravery and willingness to speak up for herself are traits she shares with her father, Caleb.

The name "Caleb" may ring a bell, and this is why: Shortly after Moses led the Hebrew people through the Red Sea and across the wilderness, he sent Caleb, Joshua, and ten others to "spy out" the Promised Land. Upon their return, Caleb and Joshua were ready to help lead the invasion—but the others were scared, saying the Hebrew people were "like grasshoppers,"[31] not up to the challenge. Because of such intransigence and fear, God became enraged, sentencing the people to forty years in the wilderness.

After those four decades, Moses and others have died, but Joshua and Caleb, because of their bravery, are allowed to cross over into the Promised Land.[32]

Even in that holy land, there are many battles to fight, for it is already inhabited. When Achsah grows old enough to marry, her father, then 85, offers her as the prize for the man who defeats the Canaanites in battle. The winner is Othniel, Caleb's nephew: a man of strong lineage, character and physique. As is the custom, Caleb gives Othniel land—unfortunately, it is mostly desert.

And then Achsah does the thing for which she is remembered, approaching her father with the intent of acquiring land with water, because land is no good without it. She first asks her husband to request it from Caleb, then, upon prompting from her adoring father, she asks for it herself—and receives more of each resource than she had requested.

Consider this

By biblical standards, this girl and her father had a good relationship with each other. In the twenty-first century, it would be an anathema to be named the prize for the best warrior in battle. But in Caleb and Achsah's days, if a man emerged as the victor in war, he was (most likely) a strong warrior, a leader of men, a good strategist, intelligent, and brave. Such qualities would be attractive in a spouse.

It's all about context. When hopeful parents seek a sperm donor in current days, they page through records and pictures of potential fathers, looking for signs of intelligence, good health, strong genes, and attractive physical attributes. Some prospective parents go so far as to request certain eye and hair tones.

DNA sampling and father-to-be catalogs were not available some twelve centuries before Christ. Rather, seeing a man in action would say a great deal.

Contemporary readers may miss the apparent love between father and daughter here; they cared deeply for each other. Likewise, we may miss the logic and planning of a brave young woman as well. She has practically and strategically worked within the system to assure a bright future.

An important thread is developing here. Women are speaking up and using the power they have, albeit limited, to secure their futures. Cast against the dominant male power structures of the times, that thread is more like a strong cord, linking such figures as Achsah, the daughters of Zelophehad, and Rahab.

Ah, that's it! It is a cord—a scarlet cord, just like the one Rahab used to mark her window so that her life would be spared. Tying these women, and others, together is a scarlet cord: a sign of feminine strength, of bravery, of survival. That cord symbolizes what is needed to thrive, whether it be water, land, or lasting love.

What might we learn from Achsah?

- ▷ Assess what we have.

- ▷ Ask for what we need.

- ▷ Draw on the positive traits of ancestors past.

- ▷ Plan well for the future.

For reflection

1. Achsah was offered as a prize to a warrior for winning a key battle. What were the pros and cons of that action, in that time?

2. Achsah gives proof to the statement, "Ask and you shall receive." Think about your life this past year. Were there times that you could have stepped forth and asked for something and didn't? Do you now wish you had?

3. What makes Achsah important in the history of Bible women? What characteristics did she show? What might her actions teach us?

CHAPTER 7

WOMEN WHO SPEAK IN JUDGES

A gold mine for rich material, the Book of Judges features extraordinary stories of Bible women: a warrior on horseback, a murderer, a martyr, a spy, and more. Find a favorite female character in these pages. It won't be hard.

JUDGES

By the numbers

Words spoken by women in Judges: 526

Number of women who speak: Eight (Achsah, Deborah, Jael, Jephthah's daughter, Samson's mother, Samson's wife, Delilah, Micah's mother)

DEBORAH

Ten thousand men and me

PROFILE:
MODERATE

▷ READ HER STORY: Judges 4-5

▷ CLASSIC MOMENT: Leading ten thousand soldiers into battle with Barak

▷ LIKELY CHARACTERISTICS:
Courageous, Wise, Powerful, Diplomatic, Prophetic, Decisive, Strong

▷ DATA: 114 words

Who was Deborah?

A judge and prophetess // A woman of strong faith // A brave activist // The first female warrior in the Bible // Wife of Lappidoth

What did Deborah say?

At that time Deborah, a prophet, wife of Lappidoth, was judging Israel. She used to sit under the palm of Deborah...and the Israelites came up to her for judgment. [Deborah] sent and summoned Barak son of Abinoam from Kedesh in Naphtali, and said to him, "**The LORD, the God of Israel, commands you, 'Go, take position at Mount Tabor, bringing ten thousand from the tribe of Naphtali and the tribe of Zebulun. I will draw out Sisera, the general of Jabin's army, to meet you by the Wadi Kishon with his chariots and his troops; and I will give him into your hand.'"** *Judges 4:4-7*

Barak said to her, "If you will go with me, I will go; but if you will not go with me, I will not go." And she said, "**I will surely go with you; nevertheless, the road on which you are going will not lead to your glory, for the LORD will sell**

Sisera into the hand of a woman." Then Deborah got up and went with Barak to Kedesh. *Judges 4:8-9*

Then Deborah said to Barak, **"Up! For this is the day on which the LORD has given Sisera into your hand. The LORD is indeed going out before you."** So Barak went down from Mount Tabor with ten thousand warriors following him. *Judges 4:14*

Deborah's story

Deborah is no "Judge Judy" here. Being a judge in Deborah's day was not just about resolving disputes. Rather, a judge was a top political leader; people trusted Deborah because of her intelligence, diplomacy, faith, and foresight.

And it was that foresight that sparked her story. Towns near and far are being attacked by the Canaanites, a tough and cruel people. Girls are carried off as spoils of war, towns looted, young men killed, and widows left to fend for themselves. Knowing that waiting to wage war will most likely cause the annihilation of her people, Deborah meets with Barak, the local general.

Ride out, she tells the general, for the Lord says it is time. Go to the top of Mount Tabor and take ten thousand of our best men with you. God will call out Sisera, the Canaanite general, and he will meet you there.

For the Lord says it is time. In these words, Deborah confirms her role both as God's prophet and servant. No more waiting, no more hesitation; the future of Israel is at stake.

Stunned, Barak offers a rather surprising response, unusual for a male leader of his time: "I will go, but only if you go with me." He and Deborah ride out together, wait until God tells her it is the right time to attack, and then watch as God causes a huge flood to destroy their enemies, save one man. And that man will make a deadly mistake, stepping into the tent of a mysterious—and deadly—woman. (See the next story.)

JUDGES

Consider this

Deborah holds more political and military power than any other woman in the Bible. Warrior, prophet, and judge, she is essential to a comprehensive understanding of Judeo-Christian history. Using God as her strength and shield, Deborah was indeed "mother in Israel" (Judges 5:7). She loved her people, forecast the looming danger, took steps to fight it, and was on the front line, ready to lay down her life if need be.

There are still some people who do not trust women in leadership positions, yet this story challenges that belief. One would think that if God recognizes the leadership strengths of women, others might as well—especially over three thousand years later.

What might we learn from Deborah?

▷ A woman of faith can lead her people to victory—and spiritual health.

▷ Within the heat of battle we can find God's voice.

▷ Sometimes leadership means leading from the front lines; sometimes it means listening.

For reflection

1. Deborah is referred to as a "mother in Israel." Why might that term have been used to describe her?

2. Reread the Song of Deborah, known as one of the oldest parts of the Bible (Judges 5). (It is not included here because she sings with Barak, a man). How does their song compare to the Song of Hannah? (1 Samuel 2:1-10) The Song of Mary? (Luke 1:46-55)

3. Deborah, with God's guidance, knew the right time to attack the enemy. What does that mean for modern warfare? Is God's hand involved in global violence today? If so, to what extent?

4. Collaborative leadership describes the relationship and actions of Deborah and Barak. How were they ahead of their time? Given that such a model of leadership is found in the Bible, what ramifications might that have today?

JUDGES

JAEL

"I'll nail your head to the floor!"

PROFILE: UNFORTUNATELY LOW

▷ **READ HER STORY:**
Judges 4:17-22; Judges 5

▷ **CLASSIC MOMENT:** Luring the enemy into her tent and killing him

▷ **LIKELY CHARACTERISTICS:**
Quick-thinking, Brave, Calm, Deadly

▷ **DATA:** 23 words

Who was Jael?

A murderer with a tent peg // A married woman with the enemy at her door // A quick thinker // Possibly a rape victim

What did Jael say?

Jael came out to meet Sisera, and said to him, **"Turn aside, my lord, turn aside to me; have no fear."** So he turned aside to her into the tent, and she covered him with a rug. *Judges 4:18*

Then, as Barak came in pursuit of Sisera, Jael went out to meet him, and said to him, **"Come, and I will show you the man whom you are seeking."** So he went into her tent; and there was Sisera lying dead, with the tent peg in his temple. *Judges 4:22*

Jael's story

Although rarely discussed, this story presents an extraordinary moment: a woman commits murder—and puts an exclamation point on a battle already full of intrigue and daring.

On that fateful day of battle between the Hebrew people and the Canaanites, Jael finds herself at home, alone. She has likely heard that God's mighty flood has swept away the enemy, that the battle is over, but she is not an Israelite, so she stands apart from the fray.

From the doorway of her tent, she sees a massive, bruised figure struggling up the hillside. It is Sisera, the Canaanite general and the only survivor of the bloody war. Making a decision on the spot, she says, "Turn in here, my lord. Have no fear."

Why the familiarity? Does she know him? And even if she knows him, women did not invite unrelated men into their tents. Jael has more on her mind than would appear.

Exhausted from battle, he staggers inside, asking for water. Jael gives him goat's milk and cheese and covers him. No one will think to look for him in an enemy tent. At his request, she guards the door…until he falls asleep.

And then she creeps up behind the sleeping warrior, grasping a tent peg and mallet. Two-fisted, she slams it deep into his brain, shattering his skull and nailing his head to the floor, killing him where he lies.

Consider this

Women both start this fight and finish it.

Judges 4:18 says that weary Sisera gladly accepted Jael's offer to enter her tent. And perhaps they were familiar with each other. Her husband Heber might well have been one of the men hired to create iron chariot wheels, as that was the primary trade of Heber's people. Conjecture: Sisera may have been on the property before.

While it is (remotely) possible that Jael invited Sisera in to rest because she felt sorry for him, or lured him inside, planning to kill him, it is more likely that he ordered her inside, intending to rape and possibly kill her.

A final thought: Heber's clan came from the tribe of Midian, the clan to which Jethro, Moses' father-in-law, belonged. The Midianites were not practicing Levites (one of the twelve tribes of Israel), for they had broken away over the years in the wilderness. However, Hebrew blood ran in Heber's veins and likely in Jael's.[33] Although we will never know her exact motives, Jael may have been acting out of loyalty and love for her husband's original family (or her own) in raising the lethal peg to Sisera's head.

What might we learn from Jael?

▷ Be aware of tools in your surroundings that you could use to defend yourself and your family.

▷ Know where God is in your life.

▷ Be aware of those who may have an evil intent.

▷ Realize there are times when you might have to do something horrible for the good of your people.

▷ Keep your tent pegs sharp.

For reflection

1. Rabbinical studies tend to proclaim the innocence of Jael, and lean toward her either protecting herself before sexual violence or taking revenge after it.[34] What do you think might have happened inside the tent?

2. Would you be able to kill someone in self-defense? In other conditions? Describe.

3. Jael used a tent peg as the murder weapon because, most likely, it was nearby. What ways do you have to protect yourself should you be in a similar situation? Have you ever had to defend yourself?

4. Sisera's mother plays a small but haunting role in this story. Deborah and Barak sing of her worry that her son is so late coming home from battle. (Judges 5:28-30). To what extent are her actions and thoughts typical or atypical of most mothers?

JEPHTHAH'S DAUGHTER

A candle in the wind

PROFILE: LOW

▷ **READ HER STORY:** Judges 11:29-40

▷ **CLASSIC MOMENT:** Accepting her father's bargain—which means she will die

▷ **LIKELY CHARACTERISTICS:** Joyful, Loving, Obedient, Brave, Forgiving, Selfless, Practical

▷ **DATA:** 65 words

Who was Jephthah's daughter?

A girl between the ages of ten and fourteen // The only child of Jephthah // The granddaughter of a prostitute // A girl who consented to being sacrificed // A girl whose bravery was honored by generations

What did Jephthah's daughter say?

She said to him, "**My father, if you have opened your mouth to the LORD, do to me according to what has gone out of your mouth, now that the LORD has given you vengeance against your enemies, the Ammonites.**" And she said to her father, "**Let this thing be done for me: Grant me two months, so that I may go and wander on the mountains, and bewail my virginity, my companions and I.**" *Judges 11:36-37*

Jephthah's daughter's story

Jephthah (pronounced Jep-thah) was the son of a "marginal woman," a prostitute. After his father dies, he is ejected from his father's house by his half-brothers. Although this action is against the law, there is no recourse for Jephthah. Fleeing his home in Gilead, he establishes himself as a credible warrior across the land. Soon the people of Gilead ask him to return and lead them in war.

Knowing that battle success and survival depend on God, he initiates a covenant with God—promising that he will sacrifice the first living thing that comes out of his home upon his return.

Upon the war's successful conclusion, it is his daughter—his beautiful only child, shaking tambourines and dancing—who first runs to greet him. When he tearfully recounts his vow, she understands she must be sacrificed and asks for but one thing: that she might have two months to mourn "her virginity." In other words, she asks to grieve the loss of the highest aim of a woman in that time—becoming a mother.

Although there is no description of how the girl's life was ended, the Bible says of Jephthah that, "He did with her according to the vow he had made."

Consider this

Think as a forensic scientist. A girl has been killed at the hands of her father. Those sad facts cannot be changed, but we can try to understand why it happened, honoring her in the process.

Several issues pertain here. Calling on God while fighting, as Jephthah did, signals a deeply religious man. Promising God something in exchange for divine support is a straightforward gesture, and one that has been practiced throughout time in most cultures.

Most likely, Jephthah owned animals as part of his household, and may have assumed he would see an animal first and sacrifice it. He likely didn't dream the first thing he saw would be his beloved daughter. Still, however, looms the specter of Jephthah consciously thinking through the possibilities of who might be the victim, including the girl.

What good father would make such a vow? Girls and women were property then, so it was legally possible. But to his credit, Jephthah seems as stunned by the outcome as is his daughter. Jephthah would have known that the Hebrew people condemned child sacrifice, unlike many of their neighbors (Leviticus 18:21, Deuteronomy 12:31, Leviticus 20:1-5, 2 Kings 17:17-18).

His daughter knows that he cannot go back on his sacred vow, for God has indeed caused a victory. Even to the end (although details are not given), she remains faithful, seeing in her father's vow a promise to God that she must uphold. His word becomes her word, and she will die rather than see it broken.

During the reign of the Judges, lawlessness reigns. Values fall away. Authority shifts to the strongest warrior, and the door begins to open for a new kind of leadership: monarchy. Yet even in the midst of this profoundly serious story, we note a request that makes Jephthah's daughter even more real: the one thing she wants more than anything else is time with her girlfriends.

What might we learn from Jephthah's daughter?

▷ Discern which challenges we should accept and which ones we should not.

▷ Seek for negotiation when all seems lost.

▷ Handle all situations bravely while keeping our cool.

▷ Do not lose hope.

▷ Spend time with those we love.

For reflection

1. What would you have done if you were Jephthah's daughter? If you were Jephthah?

2. Are vows made to God more valuable than ones made to human beings?

3. Is there such a thing as being too obedient?

4. Have you ever experienced great joy only to suddenly face sorrow?

5. How does this compare to Abraham's act of (almost) sacrificing Isaac (Genesis 22:1-19)? There God intervened at the last moment. Where was God here?

JUDGES

▷ **READ HER STORY:** Judges 13-16 (These three chapters cover both mother and son; read all three to get the full challenge of parenting Samson)

▷ **CLASSIC MOMENT:** Hearing an angel tell her she would give birth to a son

▷ **LIKELY CHARACTERISTICS:**
Steady, Practical, Diplomatic, Obedient, Faithful, Calm, Positive

▷ **DATA:** 129 words

Who was Samson's mother?

The woman who spoke the most in Judges // An Israelite // A peasant // The initially barren wife of Manoah // A mother to a difficult but brave son // One of few women in scripture to be told by an angel that she would bear a son who would serve God

What did Samson's mother say?

Then the woman came and told her husband, **"A man of God came to me, and his appearance was like that of an angel of God, most awe-inspiring; I did not ask him where he came from, and he did not tell me his name; but he said to me, 'You shall conceive and bear a son. So then drink no wine or strong drink, and eat nothing unclean, for the boy shall be a nazirite to God from birth to the day of his death.'"** *Judges 13:6-7*

Then Manoah entreated the Lord, and said, "O Lord, I pray, let the man of God whom you sent come to us again and teach us what we are to do concerning the boy who will be born." God listened to Manoah, and the angel of God came again to the woman as she sat in the field; but her husband Manoah was not with her. So the woman ran quickly and told her husband, **"The man who came to me the other day has appeared to me."** *Judges 13:8-10*

And Manoah said to his wife, "We shall surely die, for we have seen God." But his wife said to him, **"If the Lord had meant to kill us, he would not have accepted a burnt offering and a grain offering at our hands, or shown us all these things, or now announced to us such things as these."** *Judges 13:22-23*

But his father and mother said to him, "Is there not a woman among your kin, or among all our people, that you must go to take a wife from the uncircumcised Philistines?" But Samson said to his father, "Get her for me, because she pleases me."[35] *Judges 14:3*

Samson's mother's story

This poor woman has no idea of the man her son will become: a primal, brutal, riddle-telling, Olympian-strong, unlucky-in-love, demanding...hero.

As a young man, Samson engages in behavior that must have been excruciating for his parents:

▷ He sees a foreign woman and demands his father "get her for him";

▷ He rips apart a lion with his bare hands;

▷ He kills two hundred Philistines and collects their foreskins;

▷ He ties three hundred foxes together by their tails and sets each pair of tails on fire;

- ▷ He slays a thousand Philistines with the jawbone of a donkey;

- ▷ He tells riddles instead of clearly communicating;

- ▷ He lets himself be tempted by Delilah.

Finally, after leading Israel for twenty years, he is blinded by the enemy. While put on display for ridicule at the temple in Gaza, he pulls the roof down in a show of dedicated brute force. Samson is killed; around him lay the bodies of some three thousand Philistines.

No wonder God spoke to his mother through a divine messenger before his birth—for Samson would not be a normal son. From the start, his mother was calm, practical, and optimistic. She knew her son would be essential to God's mission.

Consider this

In northern Minnesota's backwoods, hikers often find small rocks stacked one on top of another as a type of map. If they know how to read that ancient language, all will be clear as to which path to take. If not, one or more lost nights under the stars may result.

In the same way, think of this story as brimming with clues about this woman and her calling to be Samson's mother:

FIRST CLUE: "...a barren woman." No pregnancy test kit is needed here. Words pertaining to "a barren woman" usually mean that a son, important to God's unfolding story, will be born to a worthy woman. (Daughters are clearly important to God's story, but in the Bible none were born under the barren-mother scenario.)

SECOND CLUE: A divine messenger representing God talks to the woman (initially) instead of the man. Perhaps God trusted her more to hear the message; perhaps God knew that Samson's mother would be tested often by her somewhat odd son and wanted to give her confidence in the midst of challenging and tearful years. The key line, which only the woman had been told, is, "It is he who shall begin to deliver Israel from the hand of the Philistines." *Judges 13:5.*

THIRD CLUE: Samson's mother and father were "working in the field." Peasants and commoners are the salt-of-the-earth kind of people God consistently chooses for important deeds.

FOURTH CLUE: Samson's mother was to keep herself healthy during pregnancy, abstaining from alcohol and unclean food, and not cut Samson's hair. This passage also begins to build Samson's identity as wholly dedicated to God, yet eccentric.

FIFTH CLUE: The angel disappears in flames at the end of the conversation with Samson's parents—confirming that he is a divine messenger.

There is much going on here. Dynamics of marriage and power rise to the top. It is Samson's mother who first sees the messenger of God and tells her husband the news. He believes her and prays that God will come again—and elaborate. The messenger does return, but the husband is not there. Finally, on the third holy visit, Manoah's questions are answered, albeit briefly.

God clearly wanted to talk primarily with Samson's mother. The angel could have picked a time when husband and wife would have been together, or spoken just with Manoah, or been more communicative when the father was present. It is no wonder, then, that Samson's mother speaks more than any other woman in Judges, for she has much to say.

What might we learn from Samson's mother?

    ▷   God shows up in mysterious ways.

    ▷   A call to motherhood is holy.

    ▷   Anything can happen with God.

    ▷   God's line of communication extends from God to messenger to mother.

    ▷   Sometimes children do not act as parents hope they will, but love, human and divine, most often wins out.

For reflection

1. Samson's mother was awed by her encounter with God. Have you ever found yourself in a situation where you were afraid to believe, and yet you did—and amazing things happened? Discuss.

2. Why did God choose Samson's mother to receive the news about Samson's birth rather than his father?

3. The father seemed to want to hear the news directly, yet when he accompanied his wife to where she had seen the angel, he was largely dismissed. What were the power dynamics in this situation?

4. Samson's parents seem like good, sensible people. How can it be, then, that their son was so different? Has that happened in your family? Was there any redemption, as there was for Samson at the end of his life?

SAMSON'S WIFE

"What was I thinking?"

PROFILE: LOW

▷ **READ HER STORY:** Judges 14-15

▷ **CLASSIC MOMENT:** Not being Delilah. Who knew Samson had a wife?

▷ **LIKELY CHARACTERISTICS:** Weepy, Inconsistent, Beautiful, Manipulative, Scared

▷ **DATA:** 25 words

Who was Samson's wife?

A Philistine (the enemy) // Young and attractive // A scared but faithful daughter // A woman caught between dominant male forces // Most likely a polytheist

What did Samson's wife say?

So Samson's wife wept before him, saying, **"You hate me; you do not really love me. You have asked a riddle of my people, but you have not explained it to me."** *Judges 14:16*

Samson's wife's story

She is no more than a teenager, it seems, compelling and magnetic, at least to hormone-driven Samson. And she is exactly the opposite of what Samson's parents want for their son, for she is a Philistine. Yet Samson is determined to marry her and demands that his parents "get her for him."

On the way to obtain her, he kills a lion. During the wedding feast, which lasts seven days, he makes a bet with thirty Philistine men, asking his famous riddle (Judges 14:14). When they are unable to answer correctly, they seek out the young bride, threatening to kill her and destroy her family in a fire. For seven days, she begs and wheedles Samson for the answer. Finally he gives in and tells her; she is quick to relay the answer to the Philistines. Enraged, Samson kills thirty men, abandons her, and goes home. Her father then gives her to Samson's best friend.

Eventually Samson demands her return. Her father refuses and volunteers his younger daughter in her stead. Incensed, Samson ties the tails of three hundred foxes together (to match the number of men tenfold at the wedding ceremony), lights them on fire, and burns down the grain fields.

In retaliation, the Philistines capture Samson's wife and her father, and then burn them to death. More crimes are sparked between the Philistines and the Israelites; thousands are killed...and yet Samson remains a strong and popular leader of Israel for twenty years.

Consider this

Let's start here: it all depends on your POV—i.e. your point of view.

Gruesome and horrible, the story of Samson has captured imaginations for thousands of years. However, most people know only about him, his long hair, and Delilah—not his unfortunate wife. (Delilah was not his wife.)

Some might feel the details of Judges 14-15 are too brutal for children, too bizarre for adults, too meaningless for the twenty-first century. Better to turn our heads, they feel. Yet when we breeze past Samson's wife or mother, we diminish our knowledge base, thus diminishing our heritage. We disregard women and girls who lived in brutally hard times, had little control over their lives, and died tragic, painful deaths.

Perhaps the young unnamed woman here had eyes for Samson or even loved him; unfortunately, it did not matter, for she had no choice in marrying him. Like other women at the time, she was "given" by her father to the man of his choice, not hers. And like Delilah years later, she wheedled information from Samson because of outside pressures. Even though she complied, she was murdered—by the hands of her own people.

Where is God in all of this? Some believe the marriage was part of a divine strategy[36] to fully enrage Samson so that he might use his brute strength to avenge Israel. Yet God does not use innocent girls as bait and then have them killed to make others angry. All that is clear is that life during this era of the Judges was brutal, and that Samson's wife was caught in a terrible triangle of her father, husband, and people.

What might we learn from Samson's wife?

▷ Less complicated men might make better spouses.

▷ Sometimes there is no good choice.

▷ We do not always have control over outside forces.

▷ Sometimes answers come only after death, if then.

For reflection

1. Samson's wife used her wits—and some would say, emotional manipulation—to get the answer to a riddle from Samson. Yet she herself was a victim of emotional blackmail from her own people. Did she have options? If so, what were they? What would you have done in her situation?

2. Do the experiences of this young bride resemble women who are beaten or murdered in contemporary domestic violence or wartime situations? If so, where is God? Where is hope to be found?

3. Review Judges 14-15. Find the places where the numbers seven or thirty are used. What does that signal?

DELILAH

"Get me those scissors!"

PROFILE: HIGH

▷ **READ HER STORY:** Judges 16

▷ **CLASSIC MOMENT:** Cutting Samson's hair and thus robbing him of his strength

▷ **LIKELY CHARACTERISTICS:** Persistent, Cunning, Winsome, Seductive, Manipulative, Shrewd

▷ **DATA:** 123 words

Who was Delilah?

Samson's seducer and betrayer // The woman who cut his hair // Most likely, an Israelite

What did Delilah say?

So Delilah said to Samson, **"Please tell me what makes your strength so great, and how you could be bound, so that one could subdue you."** *Judges 16:6*

While men were lying in wait in an inner chamber, she said to him, **"The Philistines are upon you, Samson!"** *Judges 16:9*

Then Delilah said to Samson, **"You have mocked me and told me lies; please tell me how you could be bound."** *Judges 16:10*

"The Philistines are upon you, Samson!" *Judges 16:12*

"Until now you have mocked me and told me lies; tell me how you could be bound." *Judges 16:13*

"The Philistines are upon you, Samson!" *Judges 16:14*

"How can you say, 'I love you,' when your heart is not with me? You have mocked me three times now and have not told me what makes your strength so great.'" *Judges 16:15*

When Delilah realized that he had told her his whole secret, she sent and called the lords of the Philistines, saying, "This time come up, for he has told his whole secret to me." *Judges 16:18*

"The Philistines are upon you, Samson!" *Judges 16:20*

Delilah's story

Delilah uses the power of sex to entrap Samson into telling her his greatest secret—that his strength will be sapped if his hair is cut. The closest the Bible comes to admitting this sexual liaison is to say that Samson lay with his head in her lap. Such a position is not a normal conversation starter, especially with a woman from the enemy camp, so a sexual relationship is a logical conclusion.

Imagine the dialogue as Delilah visualizes the 1,100 pieces of silver she has been promised for finding the key to Samson's strength. "Tell me the secret of your, oh-so-strong arms," she might have said, running her fingers lightly along his biceps. Or this: "Your legs are as muscular as a lion's!" Or even this: "Other women just like your body, Samson. I love your mind as well. Please tell me everything, everything about you."

And so the net was cast for one of the biggest catches of the Old Testament: a weakened and vulnerable Samson. Weak enough to allow the Philistines to gouge out his eyes. Weak enough to be jailed. Vulnerable enough to know he had been betrayed.

Delilah disappears by name from the story at this point. We can imagine her, though, watching—and perhaps joining in—the ridicule on the final day of Samson's life. Hauled out to the temple steps like a puppet, he is surrounded by men and women of high standing, including top political leaders. An additional three thousand Philistines are on the roof, flinging insults down like tomatoes.

"Let me feel the pillars," he says to a guard. "I need to lean against them."

What harm could a blind, shackled man do?

A great deal. With a hand wrapped around each pillar, Samson jerks the mighty columns down. Everyone below is crushed, including Samson; most on the roof are killed as well.

A final, profound victory for Samson. A chilling defeat, and most likely death, for Delilah...unless she had left town immediately, her bags bulging with silver.

Consider this

Clearly, Samson was prone to share his secrets with the wrong woman. (Interestingly, the only woman whom Samson could trust in this triad of mother-wife-tempter stories was his mother.)

Over the waves of cruelty in both Philistine and Israelite sides, a key comparison rises up between Samson's wife and Delilah: the former was young and fairly innocent. She may have hoped for a good life with the massive man. In contrast, Delilah was a grown woman, seeking from the start to betray the long-haired giant.

Delilah could have been a Philistine, yet based on where she lived, there are some who believe she was an Israelite[37], thus deepening the betrayal. Either way, she was a traitor.

Stories like these are meant to raise emotions, engage minds, and bolster hearts, especially when learning one's story meant building a stronger identity and passing the faith to the next generation. Such stories were important building blocks for the emerging Jewish nation, and influenced many of the heroes of the New Testament, including Jesus.

What might we learn from Delilah?

▷ Men use women at times sexually, yet clearly it is a two-way street here.

▷ Persistence is often unjustly rewarded.

▷ Manipulation is a difficult tool to control—Delilah lets it drive her.

▷ The difference between being a traitor and a hero depends on which side you are working.

▷ Make sure to do a proper cost-benefit analysis before signing onto any evil Philistine schemes.

For reflection

1. How did Delilah get Samson to give up his secret? What vulnerabilities of his did she play to?

2. When have you known backstabbers like Delilah? What was your response?

3. Samson's last act of heroism must have been astounding to witness. What might have been Delilah's last thoughts, if she was there?

4. Where is God working in this story?

MICAH'S MOTHER

Odd but caring

PROFILE:
SO LOW AS TO BE
CRAWLING ON
THE FLOOR

▷ **READ HER STORY:** Judges 17:2-3

▷ **CLASSIC MOMENT:** Asking God to bless her son after he returns her stolen money

▷ **LIKELY CHARACTERISTICS:** Affluent, Polytheistic, Maternal, Forgiving, Tribal

▷ **DATA:** 28 words

Who was Micah's mother?

A wealthy woman // A mother who loved her son, a repentant thief, but wanted more for him // A mother who was ready to forgive // A woman with mixed values

What did Micah's mother say?

He said to his mother, "The eleven hundred pieces of silver that were taken from you, about which you uttered a curse, and even spoke it in my hearing, —that silver is in my possession; I took it; but now I will return it to you." And his mother said, "**May my son be blessed by the LORD!**" *Judges 17:2*

"**I consecrate the silver to the LORD from my hand for my son, to make an idol of cast metal.**" *Judges 17:3*

Micah's mother's story

As the scene opens, Micah's mother has discovered the theft of eleven hundred pieces of silver from her home—a significant sum. Perhaps she knows who stole it, perhaps not. When her son confesses, she asks the Lord to bless him. Then she spends two hundred of the coins to make a silver idol of God and sets it in her son's house as a shrine. Micah hires a young Levite to be his priest. (Levites were the priestly caste.) Eventually, though, Micah's priest joins with a marauding band of Israelites from the tribe of Dan; the idol is carried off by the tribe. When Micah gives chase, he is turned back.

Consider this

This is an odd story, particularly because the Ten Commandments forbid the making of idols and images, even God's image. It's odder still that the story appears to sit isolated, with no clear meaning jumping off the page. Yet have another look. Visualize this story as a piece of real estate. Out the back window into the past is the mother-wife-Delilah triad. Out the front window, the next story is one of the most gruesome tales in the Bible: the gang rape and dissection of a concubine.

Violence and political instability scamper across the pages of the Book of Judges like a tarantula: poisonous, out of control, and multi-limbed. Much like America's Wild West of the 1800s, power belongs to those who wrest it from their neighbor. Yet here are a mother and son who, after some early mistakes (stealing money, keeping an idol) try to do the right thing. Although flawed, they search for God, respect each other, value family, and manage to stay alive through dangerous times.

And one more curious thing: Delilah was paid eleven hundred pieces of silver to betray Samson. Micah's mother happened to have that exact amount of money stashed away. Could Delilah and Micah's mother have been the same person? Is this woman a slightly older Delilah? Bible scholars say no, because the timing is not quite right. Only a corner of Jewish midrash suggests there is a connection...but still, there are eleven hundred pieces of silver and two stories about slightly odd women, one following the other in the Bible. What do you think?

What might we learn from Micah's mother?

▷ Forgiveness is essential between family members.

▷ Worshiping God and spending money on idols is not a good partnership.

▷ What you teach children when they are young remains in their souls.

▷ Good parents want the best for their children.

For reflection

1. In what ways did this mother love her son? Did she express that love in a positive way? What, if any, were the negatives?

2. Like all mothers, she wanted a good life for her boy. How does the idol compare to ways we try to guarantee protection of our children?

3. Why, if the Ten Commandments prohibit the making of idols (Exodus 20:4), do you think she had one made? What idols have you made for yourself, and how have they affected your family?

4. Had the son not stolen her money, this would not have been an event, and therefore not recorded in the Bible. Why is it significant? What can we learn from it?

CHAPTER 8

WOMEN WHO SPEAK IN RUTH

This book is one of the greatest love stories of all time. Yet it is not a classic romance. Rather, two tough women take center stage initially—one rather cranky, the other kind—long before the groom appears on the scene. Scratch the surface here and you will discover that the main characters were people of deep and sacred values. Between the kindness and loyalty of Ruth, the stubbornness of Naomi, and the protection of Boaz, Naomi and Ruth come to a place where they indeed change the course of history—and become two of Jesus' most compelling spiritual foremothers.

RUTH

By the numbers

Words spoken by women in the Book of Ruth: 696

Number of women who speak: Two individuals (Naomi and Ruth) and four groups (Ruth and Orpah together, and three groups of the women of Bethlehem)

NAOMI

"Oy vey!"

PROFILE: HIGH

▷ READ HER STORY: The Book of Ruth

▷ CLASSIC MOMENT: Advising Ruth to curl up at Boaz's "feet"

▷ LIKELY CHARACTERISTICS: Sad, Bitter, Morose, Resourceful, Cranky, Purposeful, Meddling, Shrewd

▷ DATA: 411 words

RUTH

Who was Naomi?

A displaced Israelite living in a strange and alien land // A widow who was determined to return home to die // A mother who had lost both her sons // A woman with an intensely loyal daughter-in-law // A sad woman who eventually finds happiness and meaning // The great-great-grandmother of King David

What did Naomi say?

"Go back each of you to your mother's house. May the LORD deal kindly with you, as you have dealt with the dead and with me. The LORD grant that you may find security, each of you in the house of your husband." *Ruth 1:8-9*

"Turn back, my daughters, why will you go with me? Do I still have sons in my womb that they may become your husbands? Turn back, my daughters, go your way, for I am too old to have a husband. Even if I thought there was hope for me, even if I should have a husband tonight and bear sons, would you then wait until they were grown? Would you then refrain from marrying? No, my daughters, it has been far more bitter for me than for you, because the hand of the LORD has turned against me." *Ruth 1:11-13*

"See, your sister-in-law has gone back to her people and to her gods; return after your sister-in-law." *Ruth 1:15*

"Call me no longer Naomi, call me Mara, for the Almighty has dealt bitterly with me. I went away full, but the LORD has brought me back empty; why call me Naomi when the LORD has dealt harshly with me, and the Almighty has brought calamity upon me?" *Ruth 1:20-21*

"Go, my daughter." *Ruth 2:2*

"Where did you glean today? And where have you worked? Blessed be the man who took notice of you." *Ruth 2:19*

"Blessed be he by the LORD, whose kindness has not forsaken the living or the dead!" Naomi also said to her, "The man is a relative of ours, one of our nearest kin." *Ruth 2:20*

"It is better, my daughter, that you go out with his young women, otherwise you might be bothered in another field." *Ruth 2:22*

"My daughter, I need to seek some security for you, so that it may be well with you. Now here is our kinsman Boaz, with whose young women you have been working. See, he is winnowing barley tonight at the threshing-floor. Now wash and anoint yourself, and put on your best clothes and go down to the threshing floor; but do not make yourself known to the man until he has finished eating and drinking. When he lies down, observe the place where he lies; then, go and uncover his feet and lie down; and he will tell you what to do." *Ruth 3:1-4*

"How did things go with you, my daughter?" *Ruth 3:16*

"Wait, my daughter, until you learn how the matter turns out, for the man will not rest, but will settle the matter today." *Ruth 3:18*

RUTH

Naomi's story

Acantankerous stance toward life defines Naomi—and with good reason. Ten years before her recorded story begins, she and her family had fled Bethlehem for the neighboring territory of Moab, because of famine in Israel. There, in that hostile territory—for the Moabites and Israelites were longtime enemies—her two sons grew to adulthood and married Moabite women. Sadly, tragedy struck, killing both sons and Naomi's husband. She is left with two daughters-in-law, Ruth and Orpah, both childless young widows.

Stubborn as hell, she is determined to get back home to Bethlehem, some fifty wild and dangerous miles away, before she dies. Both Ruth and Orpah set out with her; but Orpah, at Naomi's urging, soon returns home where she might have a better chance of finding a husband. Even though Naomi urges Ruth to return as well, she has found her match: Ruth would rather be torn apart by lions than give up.

When they finally reach Bethlehem, Naomi is taunted by women friends from long ago. Heckling, they ask, "Is that Naomi?" Having outlasted the famine, they are now financially comfortable while she is a poor and homeless old woman.

"Call me Mara," she replies, "call me Mara." Her chosen name means "bitter." Picture her also as gaunt, sad, hungry, and depressed.

But Naomi had something her friends did not: Ruth.

Foraging in a field for gleanings (bits of grain deliberately left over from the harvest which the poor were allowed to gather), Ruth ensures the women's survival, at least temporarily. They may have been living in a corner of the city with other homeless women. Or, perhaps Naomi had saved enough pennies to rent a hardscrabble room. As food begins to relax the old woman's stomach muscles, she discovers that the field in which Ruth has been gleaning belongs to Boaz, a distant relative—and the old woman strategizes.

On harvest night, knowing that both food and spirits will flow freely, she takes the bull by the horns. Actually, she encourages Ruth to take Boaz by the hand: specifically, sneaking up and lying next to him when he is asleep on the granary floor, sated with wine and the joy of the harvest.

When decent, hardworking Ruth asks for more details, Naomi says only, "He will tell you what to do."

Ruth follows Naomi's advice. Boaz treats Ruth with honor and does not molest her or take advantage of her[38], and sends her home with six large bags of grain. They marry; a year later they have a son. Ironically, it is the women of the neighborhood who name the boy Obed. This time, the neighborhood women celebrate with her: "Naomi has a son! Naomi has a son!"

Naomi has more than a son, for she has a true daughter, a son-in-law, and a grandson. Her journey is complete; her heart is full.

Consider this

Stubbornness and faith on Naomi's part are the key themes here—and so is the fact that Naomi talked twice as much as her daughter-in-law. Despite great hardship, she secures new life for Ruth, adds the blood of outsiders to the pedigree of David and Jesus, and, just perhaps, reminds the Judeo/Christian world to look more kindly on the plight of immigrants and migrant workers.

On a lighter note, consider the humor here. Naomi was the ultimate matchmaker.

Naomi: "Go curl up beside Boaz when he's a bit drunk on the threshing room floor, after his work his done."

Ruth: "Say what??"

What might we learn from Naomi?

▷ Kindness is a great gift in times of sorrow; stubbornness is a sign of strength.

▷ Sometimes we need others to stay alive.

▷ We may think God has abandoned us but we should always have hope.

▷ Sometimes our real children are not the ones we birthed.

▷ We find the way home only after time in the wilderness.

For reflection

1. Naomi's great journey began with one small footstep, then another. What adventures have you had that began with one small step? Did you end up at your planned destination or did God point you another way?

2. Naomi tried to discourage Ruth and Orpah from accompanying her. What does this say about her?

3. In contemporary society, Naomi might have been tucked away in a nursing home so "she wouldn't wander." After all, trekking from Moab to Bethlehem might be considered wandering by those who don't understand. What are the implications here?

4. Naomi told Ruth to go to the threshing house floor, wait until Boaz was done drinking, lie down beside him, and "uncover his feet." While this ended well, it was a huge gamble. Why would she suggest such a risky action?

5. Like contemporary parents, Naomi was probably dismayed when her son married Ruth, given that she was not a Jew. Yet without Ruth's love, Naomi might have died in the desert, or staggered into Bethlehem and withered away. How might this marriage have been inspired by the Holy Spirit? And what might that mean for young people you know and love?

RUTH AND ORPAH

Sisters at heart

PROFILE: MODERATE

▷ **READ THEIR STORY:** Ruth 1:1-14[39]

▷ **CLASSIC MOMENT:** When they separated, Orpah going home and Ruth forging ahead

▷ **LIKELY CHARACTERISTICS:** Strong-willed, Loyal, Resolute, Loving, Protective

▷ **DATA:** 9 words

Who were Ruth and Orpah?

Naomi's daughters-in-law; each had married a son of Naomi's // Natives of Moab // Childless widows // Women who were young enough to still give birth // Like sisters; they had been in the same clan for ten years

What did Ruth and Orpah say?

They said to her, **"No, we will return with you to your people."** *Ruth 1:10*

Ruth and Orpah's story

See the previous account of Naomi and the next section about Ruth to learn their story, as well as reading the Bible text itself.

Consider this

What seemed the dangerous route to take was the one that brought Naomi home—and endowed a life for Ruth, who so loyally followed her. What happened to Orpah? Ruth gets the attention in the Bible, but it is possible that Orpah returned home to a fine life. We will never know.

What might we learn from Ruth and Orpah?

▷   Going backward or going forward, God is there.

▷   Change is part of life; going back is not always an option.

▷   New life often comes from death.

▷   Not everyone's solution is the same.

RUTH

For reflection

1. There on that wilderness trail, what do you think went through Orpah's mind? Ruth's?

2. When is it best to turn back? When is it best to press forward, and how do you know the difference?

3. How do you find God's hand in the decision-making process?

4. Have there been similar splits in your family?

RUTH

"Your people will be my people"

▷ **READ HER STORY:** The Book of Ruth

▷ **CLASSIC MOMENT:** When she insists on accompanying Naomi to Bethlehem

▷ **LIKELY CHARACTERISTICS:**
Loyal, Obedient, Loving, Courageous, Self-sacrificing, Kind, Hardworking, Resilient

▷ **DATA:** 212 words

Who was Ruth?

A loving, loyal daughter-in-law // A widow // A native of Moab; a foreigner in Bethlehem // An unselfish, hard-working, obedient woman // A woman filled with "chesed"—i.e., sacred kindness // The daughter-in-law of Rahab, great-grandmother of King David, and ancestor of Jesus

What did Ruth say?

"Do not press me to leave you
or to turn back from following you!
Where you go, I will go;
where you lodge, I will lodge;
your people shall be my people,
and your God my God.
Where you die, I will die—
there will I be buried.

May the Lord do thus and so to me,
and more as well,
if even death parts me from you!" *Ruth 1:16-17*

"Let me go to the field and glean among the ears of grain, behind someone in whose sight I may find favor." *Ruth 2:2*

"Why have I found favor in your sight, that you should take notice of me, when I am a foreigner?" *Ruth 2:10*

Then she said, "May I continue to find favor in your sight, my lord, for you have comforted me and spoken kindly to your servant, even though I am not one of your servants." *Ruth 2:13*

"The name of the man with whom I worked today is Boaz." *Ruth 2:19*

"He even said to me, 'Stay close by my servants, until they have finished all my harvest.'" *Ruth 2:21*

"All that you tell me I will do." *Ruth 3:5*

"I am Ruth, your servant; spread your cloak over your servant, for you are next-of-kin." *Ruth 3:9*

"He gave me these six measures of barley, for he said, 'Do not go back to your mother-in-law empty-handed.'" *Ruth 3:17*

Ruth's story

Ruth's story is delightful. Loyalty, risk, danger, poverty, hard work, sex, family...it's all here. And there is something else: her undeniably beautiful voice that carries through the ages. For background, read the previous two chapters. Better yet, read the story in the Bible. And as you do, think about Ruth being childless for ten years in Moab. Little did she know what adventures and rewards awaited her after the death of her first husband.

While Naomi may get the credit for scheming, Ruth is a hands-on kind of woman. Once she and her mother-in-law reach Bethlehem, she wastes no time. The first thing Ruth says is that she will go gleaning "behind someone who might notice her"—presumably, a well-to-do man.

And she does. Her hard work impresses a fellow worker and also draws the attention of wealthy Boaz, who discovers she has treated her mother-in-law exceedingly well.

Sacrifice, perseverance, and an open heart serve to free Ruth from the bonds of poverty and loneliness. And given her origin as a woman of Moab, she is worthy of even more respect—for the Moabites were despised among the Hebrew people. Descendants of Lot and his daughters through scandal (see page 40), the Moabites were considered both immoral and unclean (Numbers 25). Somehow Ruth transcends these challenges as the winds of the Spirit blow quietly behind the scenes.

Consider this

Small feet. Calloused hands. Huge heart. Flat stomach from hunger and lack of children. While such terms are not mentioned in the Bible, they seem to describe Ruth.

Once a woman married into a Jewish family, the custom was to join that family fully, leaving her original family behind. Even though it would have been acceptable to stay with her own people in Moab, Ruth's marriage vows prescribed a course of action from which she refused to depart.

In this story Ruth is as iron-willed as Naomi, yet within her exists a certain sacramental grace. Called *chesed* in Hebrew, it means sacred kindness: not just normal kindness, but extraordinary, grace-filled, looking-out-for-the-other, God-filled kindness.

What mother-in-law, especially one who is lonely and widowed, would not love to hear these words? *(Read aloud for full effect)*.

"Entreat me not to leave you or to return from following you;
for where you go I will go,
and where you lodge I will lodge;
your people shall be my people, and your God my God;
where you die I will die,
and there I will be buried.
May the Lord do so to me and more also
if even death parts me from you."
Ruth 1:16-17

"Don't force me to leave you; don't make me go home. Where you go, I go; and where you live, I'll live. Your people are my people, your God is my god; where you die, I'll die, and that's where I'll be buried, so help me God—not even death itself is going to come between us!" Ruth 1:16-18 (*The Message*, Eugene H. Peterson)

And then there is the not-so-slight matter of Boaz. No doubt, Ruth did not think of him as a potential husband, for she was only one of many hungry and potentially homeless women working his fields. She was astonished that Boaz even noticed her, since she wasn't an Israelite.

By taking Naomi's advice, Ruth put herself in danger; the whole plan could have backfired. Ruth could have been raped on the threshing room floor by one or more of the workers; she could have been scorned and despised by Boaz; she could have developed a scandalous reputation by lying next to Boaz and pulling his clothes back.

By the end of Ruth's story, however, Ruth's *chesed* and willingness to follow Naomi's direction has given the young woman a new start. She has endured poverty, widowhood, and suffering—and found redemption along the way.

A final note. Boaz just might have learned values from his mother: Rahab, the prostitute and hero. She would have known what it was like to be poor, not knowing the source of her next meal, and it appears she shared those values with her son.

What might we learn from Ruth?

▷ It can pay to listen to your elders or mother-in-law.

▷ Sacred kindness is a gift to others.

▷ Grief can be turned to joy when our focus turns to the survival of others.

▷ Faith, hard work, obedience, and kindness can bring good fortune.

For reflection

1. How did Ruth exemplify *chesed*—the art of sacred kindness? To what extent do you practice (or did you practice) *chesed* with parental figures in your family?

2. Think about the risks that Ruth took to accomplish her journey. Are there people in your life for whom you would take similar risks?

3. This is one of the most beloved stories in the Bible. Why is it such a favorite?

4. How do race issues in contemporary society compare to the ones faced by Ruth?

5. How does your family compare to the mixed cultural identities of the Naomi-Ruth-Boaz combined family unit? Any lessons to be learned here? Any similar joys?

RUTH

THE WOMEN OF BETHLEHEM

Three groups

PROFILE: LOW

▷ **READ THEIR STORY:** Ruth 1:19; 4:14-15,17

▷ **CLASSIC MOMENT:** Shouting, "A son has been born to Naomi!" (Translation: Old women like us are useful and have meaning)

▷ **LIKELY CHARACTERISTICS:**
Group #1: Catty, Demeaning, Snarky, Curious
Group #2: Wise, Celebratory, Affirming, Faithful, Bold
Group #3: Joyful

▷ **DATA:** 64 words[40]

Who were the women of Bethlehem?

Three groups that surround Naomi at different transition points upon her return to Bethlehem // Jewish women of faith // Friends and neighbors of Naomi, some current, some prior

What did the Women of Bethlehem say?

Group #1: **"Is this Naomi?"** *Ruth 1:19*

Group #2: **"Blessed be the LORD, who has not left you this day without next-of-kin; and may his name be renowned in Israel! He shall be to you a restorer of life and a nourisher of your old age; for your daughter-in-law who loves you, who is more to you than seven sons, has borne him."** *Ruth 4:14-15*

Group #3: **"A son has been born to Naomi."** *Ruth 4:17*

The women of Bethlehem's story

Group #1: **Ruth 1:19**

Imagine Naomi on her entry into Jerusalem: poor, bedraggled, and starving. When she left Bethlehem years earlier because of famine, her head was high, and three men walked beside her. Now there are murmurings...whispers... involuntary stares. The whole town is abuzz.

And then the women ask: "Is that Naomi?"

Translation: "Terrible, she looks just terrible! She could keel over any day! What happened to her? Where are her sons? Where is her husband? Who is that girl behind her?

She's not one of us."

Leave me alone, Naomi thinks. I am nothing now. I am just here to die.

One does not get the sense here that women step forth to help Naomi. Would Naomi have accepted their help? Doubtful.

Group #2: **Ruth 4:14-15**

Undeniably, this group of women is thrilled for Naomi. They also give her the greatest compliment of all, saying that Ruth loves her and is worth more than seven sons. In ancient Israel, love was not taken for granted. For spouses, it was an occasional by-product of a long marriage—or not. For parents and children, it was most often present—but to be loved by a daughter-in-law was a great honor.

To say that Ruth was worth more than seven sons was also extraordinary. Sons were the top prize, and the number "seven" meant rare good fortune.

God has restored Naomi to a life of love. God has redeemed her from hunger and poverty, granting her a future through her grandson.

Group #3: **Ruth 4:17**

Imagine the joy of Naomi's friends upon hearing that Naomi is a grandmother. In her they see a woman who has come back from the edge of despair. Her struggle to get home has resulted in new life, and the line of Naomi's sons is secure. Plus, there is a new baby to cuddle!

The women also give Obed his name, which in Hebrew means "servant." It is as if God's breath is moving through this group, helping them articulate that joy is one of the highest forms of love.

Consider this

Group #1. We don't know if any of the women who glanced at Naomi offered her food or shelter for the night. Given Naomi's penchant for isolation, she and Ruth may well have been homeless. Even if Naomi did not want a friendly greeting, we hope that someone from this group offered a warm meal.

Group #2. Praising Naomi and Ruth indicates that they have joined or rejoined a circle of women friends in Bethlehem. Especially since Ruth is a migrant worker, and Moabites were regarded as nothing more than crushed rock by the Israelites, such praise is a huge step.

Group #3. Not only are neighborhood women rejoicing here, but angels in heaven are rustling their wings as well. God's divine hand is showing here, with such joy in the foreign daughter-in-law who has produced a son for the ages.

What might we learn from the women of Bethlehem?

▷ Look for the good things in life; don't dwell on the bad.

▷ Be grateful for what you have.

▷ Choose your friends carefully, as attitude matters.

For reflection

1. Why did the women say, "Naomi has a son" instead of "Ruth has a son?"

2. How do the women transition in this story from being catty and curious to celebratory and affirming? What caused them to make the switch?

3. The women did not know that they were witnessing a substantial event in Judeo/Christian history, one that would deeply affect both faiths. How might we know if something of such magnitude stands before us?

4. Celebrating with others is an important part of the Christian life. How have you helped others celebrate recently? How might you plan to help others celebrate this week?

RUTH

CHAPTER 9

WOMEN WHO SPEAK IN 1 SAMUEL

Picture yourself climbing a beautiful mountain trail. On your right, steep cliffs threaten to swallow you like a whale eats krill, barely noticing. The terrain is uneven, and occasionally you stumble. There are no guardrails. Such terrain is like what the women in 1 Samuel faced. If they made the wrong decision, rejection, and even death might be the result. Particularly handy were skills in diplomacy, humility, negotiation, and prayer—and those traits glow brightly here.

1 Samuel has eight instances where women speak, for over a thousand words. Slightly less than half of them come from Hannah, a woman it would be hard not to like.

By the numbers

Words spoken by women in 1 Samuel: 1,055

Number of women who speak: Five individuals (Hannah, Phinehas's wife, Michal, Abigail, and the witch of Endor) and three groups (girls fetching water, women of Israel, women attending Phinehas's wife)

HANNAH

Tears and transformation

PROFILE:
MODERATELY
HIGH

▷ **READ HER STORY:** 1 Samuel 1-2

▷ **C LASSIC MOMENT:** Praying so hard for a son that an onlooker thought she was drunk

▷ **LIKELY CHARACTERISTICS:** Resourceful, Independent, Faithful, Decisive, Honorable

▷ **DATA:** 474 words

Who was Hannah?

The woman who spoke the most in 1 Samuel // A faith-filled woman who kept her promises // Samuel's mother, after years of infertility // A prophet who foretold history // The second wife of Elkanah (in a polygamous marriage)

What did Hannah say?

She was deeply distressed and prayed to the LORD, and wept bitterly. She made this vow: **"O LORD of hosts, if only you will look on the misery of your servant, and remember me, and not forget your servant, but will give to your servant a male child, then I will set him before you as a nazirite until the day of his death. He shall drink neither wine nor intoxicants, and no razor shall touch his head."** *1 Samuel 1:10-11*

But Hannah answered, **"No, my lord, I am a woman deeply troubled; I have drunk neither wine nor strong drink, but I have been pouring out my soul before the LORD. Do not regard your servant as a worthless woman, for I have been speaking out of my great anxiety and vexation all this time."** *1 Samuel 1:15-16*

"Let your servant find favor in your sight." Then the woman went to her quarters, ate and drank with her husband, and her countenance was sad no longer. *1 Samuel 1:18*

In due time Hannah conceived and bore a son. She named him Samuel, for she said, "**I have asked him of the** LORD." *1 Samuel 1:20*

The man Elkanah and all his household went up to offer to the LORD the yearly sacrifice, and to pay his vow. But Hannah did not go up, for she said to her husband, "**As soon as the child is weaned, I will bring him, that he may appear in the presence of the** LORD, **and remain there forever; I will offer him as a nazirite for all time.**" *1 Samuel 21-22*

And she said, "**Oh, my lord! As you live, my lord, I am the woman who was standing here in your presence, praying to the** LORD. **For this child I prayed; and the** LORD **has granted me the petition that I made to him. Therefore I have lent him to the** LORD; **as long as he lives, he is given to the** LORD." *1 Samuel 1:26-28*

Hannah prayed and said,

"My heart exults in the LORD;
my strength is exalted in my God.
My mouth derides my enemies,
  because I rejoice in my victory.

There is no Holy One like the LORD,
  no one besides you;
  there is no Rock like our God.
Talk no more so very proudly,
  let not arrogance come from your mouth;
for the LORD **is a God of knowledge,**
  and by him actions are weighed.
The bows of the mighty are broken,
  but the feeble gird on strength.

Those who were full have hired themselves out for bread,
  but those who were hungry are fat with spoil.
The barren has borne seven,
  but she who has many children is forlorn.
The LORD kills and brings to life;
  he brings down to Sheol and raises up.
The LORD makes poor and makes rich;
  he brings low, he also exalts.
He raises up the poor from the dust;
  he lifts the needy from the ash heap,
to make them sit with princes
  and inherit a seat of honor.
For the pillars of the earth are the LORD's,
  and on them he has set the world.

He will guard the feet of his faithful ones,
  but the wicked shall be cut off in darkness;
  for not by might does one prevail.
The LORD! His adversaries shall be shattered;
  the Most High will thunder in heaven.
The LORD will judge the ends of the earth;
  he will give strength to his king,
and exalt the power of his anointed." *1 Samuel 2:1-10*

Hannah's story

When her story opens, Hannah is heartsick and unable to eat because her greatest desire—bearing a son—continues to elude her. Child after child is born to her husband's first wife, Peninnah, who brazenly taunts Hannah. "Her rival used to provoke her severely, to irritate her, because the LORD had closed her womb" (1 Samuel 1:6).

Yet Hannah perseveres. Pouring out her heart at the temple in Shiloh, so much that the priest thinks she is drunk, she bargains with God: give her a son and she will turn him back over to the Lord's service when he has finished nursing. Hannah conceives, bears little Samuel, and as promised, brings him back to live and serve permanently in the temple when he is weaned.

Thankfully, she gives birth to other children, but mothers do not replace their firstborns like they do light bulbs. Each year, she brings Samuel a little blue coat she has made for him, weave by weave, stitch by stitch. Wearing it under his priestly tunic, the coat keeps both his body and soul warm.

Little Samuel grows to be the last judge and military leader of Israel at a time when the nation is particularly violent and morally corrupt. Like his mother, however, he is faithful and just, committed to serving God and country.

It's a straightforward, recurring story: another infertile woman conceives, finally, and gives birth to a high-achieving firstborn. But as one child is not a carbon copy of another, neither is the story of this mother and son. They sport the longest-running life story in the Bible, as we come to know Hannah. Read on, leaving old crusty commentaries behind.

Consider this

Hannah married a good man. And while men are not the central figures in this book, when one deserves a word of praise, we point it out. And here, Elkanah deserves mention, as he observes Hannah crying and senses great tribulation in her soul. "Why are you so sad?" he asks. "Am I not worth more to you than ten sons?"

Wow! A husband who cares how his wife is feeling and inquires about it. Except for Jesus, this is the only man in the Bible who asks why a woman is sad. Jesus' words to grief-stricken Mary Magdalene on the morning of the resurrection are virtually the same ones said by Elkanah when Hannah is in despair.

Elkanah to Hannah: "Why are you so sad?"

Jesus to Mary Magdalene: "Woman, why are you weeping?"

Empty womb transformed; empty tomb transformed.

Grace and promise abide in the midst of anguish. Perhaps through studying the scriptures as a boy, Jesus admired the way that Elkanah treated Hannah.

Hannah is the clearest example of a kind of prayer that many dismiss: bargaining with God. "Give me a son and I will set him free to serve you," she begs. Note that she goes right to the top. She does not need a mediator, although Eli the priest steps in as one—after he chastises her—and joins her in prayer.

Prayerful souls might think it is wrong or ineffective to bargain with God, yet here we see a stunning example of a Bible woman doing just that, successfully. She asked for what she wanted most—a son. To our knowledge, she did not say, "If it be your will," or "Whatever you want is fine with me, God." She drew from her own power, as she envisioned it: the potential to bear a child. And she promised to give back to God her most precious treasure.

Although it must have been extraordinarily difficult, she kept that promise to God. When Samuel was barely weaned, she returned to Eli and let Samuel go, trusting that God had better things in mind for him than she could even ask or imagine.

Such a move symbolizes Hannah's love: life-giving and freeing. As such, she is a rich resource from which to draw when learning how to let go as a parent. Think of mothers who release their children for adoption, knowing it is the best move for the child. Consider parents who die while their children are still young, or the grief of parents whose children die before they do. Letting go is never easy; those we love always die before we are ready, but Hannah provides a graceful example of letting her son step confidently into his future.

What might we learn from Hannah?

▷ Pray for sons and daughters who have left home.

▷ Do not be afraid to pray passionately, despite what others may think.

▷ Bargaining with God is a valid option.

▷ Sometimes children leave home when they are grown; sometimes they must leave much sooner.

▷ Take the high road when dealing with close relatives and clergy.

For reflection

1. Who caused Hannah so much grief? What was her response, and how did she avoid being bitter and full of revenge?

2. What might we learn from Hannah about hope and desire?

3. Have you ever bargained with God? What was the result?

4. How did Hannah stay in touch with Samuel? How might her actions help those who are unable to stay in touch with their children?

5. Compare the Song of Hannah in 1 Samuel 2:1-11 with the *Magnificat* in Luke 1:46-55. Name the similarities and the differences.

1 SAMUEL

▷ READ THEIR STORY: 1 Samuel 4: 19-22

▷ CLASSIC MOMENT: Announcing Ichabod's birth to comfort Phinehas's widow

▷ LIKELY CHARACTERISTICS: Calm, Encouraging, Nurturing

▷ DATA: 10 words

Who were the women attending the wife of Phinehas?

Servants who announced the birth of Ichabod // The second group of women to attend a dying mother // A bridge between life and death // Bringers of comfort and hope for the future of God's people

What did the women attending the wife of Phinehas say?

"Do not be afraid, for you have borne a son." *1 Samuel 4:20*

The women attending the wife of Phinehas's story

On our imagined "Scale for Happy Bible Stories," this chapter rates below zero, as there is much death and woe here.

Upon hearing the news earlier that day that her soldier-husband had been killed in battle, Phinehas's wife has gone into premature labor. Worse, she is dying—and laments from her deathbed that her family has failed God.

Urging her not to be afraid, her servants concentrate on the one bright light in the darkness: the birth of a son. Even though she is near death and her other sons are now deceased, a new son meant that her life's work and labor will carry on. The family will not be forgotten, and she has done all she could to bring new life to a dysfunctional and corrupt family.

Consider this

Question: Of whom do you think when you hear the name "Ichabod?"

Perhaps Ichabod Crane, the headless horseman, described so well by Washington Irving in "The Legend of Sleepy Hollow." Doom and gloom fill that story—and this one as well. (Learn more about the birth attendants' valiant efforts in the next section.)

Death waits just outside the door, yet the servants surround their charge, giving her emotional as well as physical support in her final moments. While it is not recorded in the Bible, we assume they prepared her for the grave as well.

These women symbolize the value of all those engaged in the healing arts, including chaplains, nurses, ministers, and doctors—for like the servants here, these people, too, provide comfort in the darkest of nights. By saying, "Do not be afraid," they remind us of workers who toil in the service of another. Kind acts by millions of caretakers have gone unrecognized over time; this narrative reminds us of how much simple deeds and words mean in times of stress and sorrow—and how important they are to God's unfolding story.

What might we learn from the women attending the wife of Phinehas?

▷   Be quick to encourage others and point out good news.

▷   Reach out to those who are suffering.

▷   Stay the course.

▷   Know that faith connections are more transparent in crisis situations.

For reflection

1. With Phinehas's wife dying following the deaths of her husband and sons, these servants must have been in shock—and most likely, they would soon be unemployed. Yet they carried on bravely. What does that say about them?

2. Who has been kind to you in a difficult moment? What was it about that gesture that you particularly remember?

3. What does it take to stay calm in difficult situations? Why does it help to be with other women in such times?

4. Ichabod was an innocent party to the suffering he would face as an orphan. What relevance does this story hold for those who are orphaned because of political or ecological upheavals?

▷ **READ HER STORY:** 1 Samuel 4: 19-22

▷ **CLASSIC MOMENT:** Naming her son while dying in childbirth

▷ **LIKELY CHARACTERISTICS:**
Rueful, Sorrowful, Despairing, Faithful

▷ **DATA:** 14 words

Who was the wife of Phinehas?

Eli's daughter-in-law // A new widow // A mother who died in labor // A member of a dysfunctional family // The wife of an unfaithful husband

What did the wife of Phinehas say?

"The glory has departed from Israel, for the ark of God has been captured."
1 Samuel 4:22

The wife of Phinehas's story

Bible scholars disagree on the character of Phinehas's wife: some say she was corrupt like her husband and sons (1 Samuel 2:12), while others say she was a woman of faith. What do the facts suggest?

While dying in childbirth, she names her son Ichabod, which means: "Where is the glory?" She elaborates, "The glory has departed from Israel, for the ark of

God has been captured." What she does not say, but weighs heavily on her soul, is that the ark has departed under her family's leadership. She has, however, at the cost of her own life, given Israel a gift that only a mother can—the birth of a son, the birth of renewed hope.

Consider this

Her statement does not strike us as a faithless comment. Remember that this poor woman has just received terrible news: her husband and sons have died in battle. She has also heard how her father-in-law, Eli, reacted to that news. He was so stunned that he fell over backward from his chair, breaking his neck.

Yet rather than dwell on those deaths, she grieves Israel's standing. For her, the tragedy is that the Philistines have captured the Ark of the Covenant[41] in battle. Grieving that loss, she cries out—for losing the ark means losing the actual presence of God. In ancient times, where the ark was, God was; where the ark was not, God was not.

Given this context, Phinehas's wife is not a bitter, despondent woman; rather, she is a woman of faith with a voice of power. In her last breath, she commemorates Israel by giving her son a name that will express the depth of her concern for her beloved nation and its relationship to God.

What might we learn from the wife of Phinehas?

- ▷ Slivers of hope can be found even when all seems lost.

- ▷ Names are often more than they seem.

- ▷ Bad choices in life may grieve us on our deathbeds.

For reflection

1. What must have life been like for Phinehas's wife? Do you think the birth of her new son gave her peace or turmoil?

2. Are the things you may have said in childbirth worth repeating? How might you have reacted had you been this woman?

3. The Bible calls Phinehas a "scoundrel" (1 Samuel 2:12). What are some things to know if you find yourself married to a scoundrel?

4. In periods of deep grief, sometimes beliefs that mean the most to us rise to the surface. What have you come to understand in times of mourning or anxiety?

5. Names are significant. If you are reading this book in a group, learn the full names of those who are studying this book with you and what those names mean.

▷ **READ THEIR STORY:** 1 Samuel 9: 11-13

▷ **CLASSIC MOMENT:** Directing Saul to Samuel and telling him to hurry

▷ **LIKELY CHARACTERISTICS:** Confident, Friendly, Articulate, Knowledgeable, Chatty

▷ **DATA:** 77 words

Who were the girls fetching water?

Town residents and friends // Maidens, most likely // The bringers of water for their families and animals

What did the girls fetching water say?

"Yes, there he is just ahead of you. Hurry; he has come just now to the town, because the people have a sacrifice today at the shrine. As soon as you enter the town, you will find him, before he goes up to the shrine to eat. For the people will not eat until he comes, since he must bless the sacrifice; afterward those eat who are invited. Now go up, for you will meet him immediately." *1 Samuel 9:12-13*

The girls fetching water's story

In this simple but beautiful story, a group of girls unknowingly connect the desires of heaven with the political, religious, and military voids in the emerging nation of Israel.

On a downhill slide for several hundred years, the Hebrew people are becoming increasingly alienated from each other. There is no unified authority, save God, and moral values seem to be at an all-time low. Many have demanded a king; the judges (rulers) have been opposed, because God is the only King. Yet as society seems to plummet toward a path of no return, God's hand is working.

The fateful day begins like most, with young people doing routine chores. Girls are on their way to the town well to draw water, and a young man named Saul is searching for donkeys that have wandered away from his father's land.

When Saul and his servant cannot locate the animals, they ask the girls how to find the holy man in town, "the seer," who might be able to help. The group points up the hill, urging Saul to hurry, for the seer has pressing obligations and is on the move.

The young men take the advice, and it's a good thing they do. The holy man is none other than Samuel, Hannah's son, the last judge of Israel. God has informed him that the first king of Israel will soon be in his sights—and there stands Saul, the chosen one.

As the sun dawns the next morning, Samuel anoints Saul and sends him on his way. Still shocked to be identified as the future king, Saul remains quiet. After about forty days and much drama, he is crowned king.[42]

And yes, the donkeys are safe. Samuel correctly judged that they found their way home. If the girls had not been alert and urged Saul to hurry, Israel's future may have turned out quite differently.

Consider this

Drawing water was a task assigned to marginalized groups: girls, women, and male servants. Certainly the job was physically taxing (picture children balancing large water jugs on their heads), but it also must have provided a chance to get out of the house and chat with others.

No doubt the girls noticed Saul and his servant approaching them; perhaps they slowed their steps to allow the young men to catch up. After all, the Bible says that he was the most handsome man in Israel, and stood head and shoulders above everyone else (1 Samuel 9:2). Or perhaps the young men took special notice of the girls. Either way, wells were a place of refuge, romance, and news. There, a girl might find a husband (like Rebekah and Zipporah did), talk with God (as Hagar did near a spring), or meet a handsome stranger and his servant (as the girls did here).

Saul seemed to be exceptionally polite; the girls were well informed and articulate. A chance meeting? Probably more of a God-moment.

Readers may question whether the girls spoke all the words together for which they are credited. Remember that, in this book, we are looking for the eternal truths found in stories. Stories don't tell us what is true, but rather, what must be true. These girls helped make possible God's plan. Without them, the future king might have missed his date with destiny.

What might we learn from the girls fetching water?

▷ Readily help others when they ask for your assistance.

▷ Strive to give others clear and thorough answers to their questions.

▷ Stay abreast of current events.

▷ Go out for fresh air.

For reflection

1. If the girls had lingered, or had given Saul and his servant bad directions, what might have happened?

2. How is the Holy Spirit present in this story?

3. Where in the Bible did other important events happen at a well, spring, or river? What does the gift of water have to do with contemporary Christians?

4. Is there something in your life that you should be doing quickly? Something that God would not have you avoid? How might the girls in this story inspire you to complete that task?

▷ READ THEIR STORY: 1 Samuel 18: 6-7

▷ CLASSIC MOMENT:
Cheering for David and taunting Saul

▷ LIKELY CHARACTERISTICS:
Joyful, Bold, Political, Flip

▷ DATA: 10 words

Who were the women of Israel?

Women and girls who came out to cheer for David after he killed Goliath // Women and girls from many towns along David's victory route home

What did the women of Israel say?

As they were coming home, when David returned from killing the Philistine, the women came out of all the towns of Israel, singing and dancing, to meet King Saul, with tambourines, with songs of joy, and with musical instruments. And the women sang to one another as they made merry, **"Saul has killed his thousands, and David his ten thousands."** *1 Samuel 18:6-7*

The women of Israel's story

Happiness. Joy. A brave Israelite warrior named David has killed the most ferocious Philistine warrior of all: Goliath. As the women across Israel line the streets on David's victory route home, they cheer and shake their tambourines, chanting: "Saul has killed his thousands, and David his ten thousands!"

Given there was no vote in ancient Israel, women had few ways to voice their collective opinion—and clearly find a way here. Political commentary directed at a healthy leader is one thing, but criticizing an unstable one is another. What the women do know is this: Saul has become an increasingly ineffective leader, David is a better warrior, and Saul is exhibiting strange and unsettling behavior. Wisely, Saul promotes David, making him a commander of a thousand soldiers. But still the demons linger within.

Consider this

The seemingly obscure chant voiced by the women of Israel is obscure only because most Bible commentators tend to skip it. Even in researching women of the Bible, this moment floats around like dust, easily brushed away. With forces of jealousy and sabotage afoot, however, it must have felt like stinging nettles to Saul.

By the time David emerges victorious over Goliath, Saul has been told by God (via Samuel, Hannah's son) that he is no longer in God's favor. At issue, ironically, is that Saul does not follow God's wishes to the letter in battle; he often shows more mercy than God would have wished. The Lord torments Saul with an evil spirit (1 Samuel 18:10), his beloved son Jonathan disobeys him without even knowing it and ends up cursed (1 Samuel 14:42-45), he becomes unstable, and Samuel tells him that God has abandoned him (1 Samuel 15:26).

Enter David. And enter hundreds, if not thousands, of women cheering for the handsome young warrior and comparing him to the impotent and tortured king.

Saul had shown signs of despair long before David came on the scene. The women of Israel's scorn intensified the situation but did not cause it; Saul had displeased God and God had responded by agitating Saul with evil spirits. Yet as the women shouted in unity, their voices were heard—and may it always be so!

What might we learn from the women of Israel?

▷ Women's communication systems are intense and powerful.

▷ There is safety in numbers.

▷ Our words may affect others more than we know.

For reflection

1. The women of Israel used the God-given gift of free speech to express their views. How does their ability to do so hearken back to the story of Eve? What other women in the Bible, either individually or collectively, did the same?

2. Where is God in this story? Did God hear their voices and send a spirit to trouble Saul—or is it an example of how all things work for good (as in the Joseph narratives) for those who believe?

3. What happens to a country or organization when a leader is disabled and even dangerous? What contemporary events resemble the women of Israel cheering David and taunting Saul? What role does faith play...and how does one know what side God is taking?

MICHAL

A pawn in a kingly chess game

PROFILE: LOW

▷ **READ HER STORY:** 1 Samuel 18-19, 25:44; 2 Samuel 3:13-14, 6:14-23; 1 Chronicles 15:29.

▷ **CLASSIC MOMENT:** Lambasting David as he returns the Ark of the Covenant to Jerusalem

▷ **LIKELY CHARACTERISTICS:** Bold, Lonely, Brave, Jealous, Sarcastic

▷ **DATA:** 54 words (28 in 1 Samuel, 26 in 2 Samuel)

Who was Michal?

A princess, the daughter of King Saul // A bride-prize // The first wife of King David // The common-law wife of Paltiel // Eventually, an angry and embittered woman

What did Michal say?

Saul sent messengers to David's house to keep watch over him, planning to kill him in the morning. David's wife Michal told him, "**If you do not save your life tonight, tomorrow you will be killed.**" *1 Samuel 19:11*

So Michal let David down through the window; he fled away and escaped. Michal took an idol and laid it in the bed; she put a net of goats' hair on its head, and covered it with the clothes. When Saul sent messengers to take David, she said, "**He is sick.**" *1 Samuel 19:12-14*

Saul said to Michal, "Why have you deceived me like this, and let my enemy go, so that he has escaped?" Michal answered Saul, **"He said to me, 'Let me go; why should I kill you?'"** *Samuel 1 19:17*

David returned to bless his household. But Michal the daughter of Saul came out to meet David, and said, **"How the king of Israel honored himself today, uncovering himself today before the eyes of his servants' maids, as any vulgar fellow might shamelessly uncover himself!"** *2 Samuel 6:20*

Michal's story

Michal's story is a sad one. Like a pale and spindly sapling forever caught under a canopy of larger trees, Michal is emotionally trapped by the men around her: her father, King Saul, and her husband, King David. Decisions are made for her as she is handed off from one man to another and trapped by power grabs. She is eventually cast aside, having no children to call her own.

By the time Michal is of marriageable age, mental instability has caused Saul to view David as an imminent threat. Given that David is a formidable warrior, skilled musician, and highly attractive man—and that Samuel has even told Saul that God was rejecting him as king—Saul's fear is not without reason.

Saul soon uses David for target practice. For example, the king promises his elder daughter, Merab, in marriage to David if the young warrior can bring back the foreskins of one hundred Philistines. Since foreskins are not obtained easily—the Philistines would have had much incentive to win that battle—it appears that Saul was hoping David would be killed.

Imagine the look on Saul's face when the brave warrior returns with double the required number of foreskins. As a reward, Michal, not the promised older sister, is given to him. Apparently Saul sees Michal as second best. Scripture says that she loved David (1 Samuel 18:20), but significantly, he never says he loves her…or any of his wives.

Michal is a valuable asset to David, at least initially. One evening, soon after their wedding, he is chased into his quarters by a spear-throwing Saul and his warriors. Quick thinking on Michal's part saves his life. After lowering him out of the window, she grabs a life-sized household idol, adds goat hair, and puts it under the covers, making it look as though her husband is sleeping. David escapes into the wilderness for several years, but Michal does not join him.

In David's absence, Saul sends Michal to another man, Paltiel, even though she is still married to David. Estimates vary, but she seems to have spent many years with Paltiel.

Eventually David demands her return for what seems to be the political goal of expanding his power base (he has gained several wives in the intervening years, for much the same reason). As David's soldiers hustle Michal away, Paltiel runs after the caravan, weeping. Clearly he loves Michal. Her feelings for him are not known, but he seems to have provided her a decent home life.

Back at the palace, Michal becomes cynical and embittered. When David returns the Ark of the Covenant to Jerusalem and struts through the city like a prize athlete, Michal snaps, publicly berating David for being almost nude in front of his servants' wives; the word "vulgar" jumps from her mouth. He never sleeps with her again, and she is not recorded in the official list of David's wives, probably because she never bore him children.

Consider this

In the history of Israel, David's reign symbolizes a high point: all twelve tribes come together (although substantial conflicts still exist); God is worshiped across the kingdom; military strength is advanced; the land is more secure; psalms (many by David) are composed; and Israel is more economically viable.

That would be the big picture. Conversely, Michal's brutal story tells of a woman torn between the old and the new. Like a pawn in a chess game between Saul and David, she seems never able to emerge as a mature, self-actualized adult. Would it have made a difference if she had accompanied David into the wilderness? Perhaps. What if she had refrained from humiliating David in public? Would it have mattered? Maybe, maybe not.

Old Testament times were heartless and cold-blooded for women and men both. But if a man can be judged by how he treats others, David's treatment of Michal was disheartening at best and cruel at worst.

Like a soldier who has died in battle and is honored posthumously, Michal is honored here. May she have found peace, at the last.

What might we learn from Michal?

▷ Even if our lives are constrained, there still may be options.

▷ Being married to a person in leadership is more complicated than it first appears.

▷ Comparing values before marriage is a wise thing to do.

For reflection

1. Was there more that Michal could have done to improve her situation? If so, what might that have been? If not, why not?

2. To what extent did mental illness and a dysfunctional family system affect Michal's life? Have you experienced similar dynamics in your family? What actions did you take to survive and to heal?

3. One biblical commentator says that the marriage between Michal and David was "the worst marriage in biblical history,"[43] and that she needed to be with her husband in his early wilderness travels, rather than staying back at the palace with Daddy. Is this a fair criticism, or is Michal being blamed for something that was out of her control? What are your thoughts?

4. What does Michal and David's marriage have in common with the unions of someone like King Henry VIII? Why has history tended to judge David in a brighter light than Henry?

ABIGAIL

A woman of diplomacy

▷ **READ HER STORY:** 1 Samuel 25; 2 Samuel 2:2, 3:3; 1 Chronicles 3:1

▷ **CLASSIC MOMENT:** Persuading David to relinquish his sword and not kill her household

▷ **LIKELY CHARACTERISTICS:** Responsible, Beautiful, Diplomatic, Independent, Discerning, Faithful, Brave, Persuasive

▷ **DATA:** 316 words

Who was Abigail?

Nabal's wife, then David's // A diplomat and negotiator // A prophet // A woman marked for death // The mother of Daniel/Chileab, son of David

What did Abigail say?

"Go on ahead of me; I am coming after you." *1 Samuel 25:19*

"Upon me alone, my lord, be the guilt; please let your servant speak in your ears, and hear the words of your servant. My lord, do not take seriously this ill-natured fellow, Nabal; for as his name is, so is he; Nabal is his name, and folly is with him; but I, your servant, did not see the young men of my lord, whom you sent." *1 Samuel 25:24-25*

"Now then, my lord, as the Lord lives, and as you yourself live, since the Lord has restrained you from blood-guilt and from taking vengeance with your own hand, now let your enemies and those who seek to do evil to my lord be like Nabal. And now let this present that your servant has brought to my lord be given to the young men who follow my lord." *1 Samuel 25:26-27*

"Please forgive the trespass of your servant; for the LORD will certainly make my lord a sure house, because my lord is fighting the battles of the LORD; and evil shall not be found in you as long as you live. If anyone should rise up to pursue you and to seek your life, the life of my lord shall be bound in the bundle of the living under the care of the LORD your God; but the lives of your enemies he shall sling out as from the hollow of a sling. When the LORD has done to my lord according to all the good that he has spoken concerning you, and has appointed you prince over Israel, my lord shall have no cause of grief, or pangs of conscience, for having shed blood without cause or for having saved himself. And when the LORD has dealt well with my lord, then remember your servant." *1 Samuel 25:28-31*

"Your servant is a slave to wash the feet of the servants of my lord." *1 Samuel 25:41*

Abigail's story

On the run from King Saul, David has returned to his old line of work in the wilderness: protecting sheep and keeping order. Having spent more time in the fields than in towns, he is comfortable and skilled in the wild. He and his men protect shepherds and their animals from marauding bands of thieves; they also protect landowners from thugs and bloodthirsty land-grabbers. Like a mafia lord, David expects something in return: loyalty, money, food, and a place to camp with his six hundred men.

Nabal, Abigail's husband and a wealthy area landowner, is preparing for sheep-shearing season, a time of celebration, food, and drink. Respecting Nabal's stature, David sends ten polite fellows to ask for food. Pointing out that no harm has come to the Nabal's shepherds or sheep, the request seems simple:

some food for David and his men, please, in return for their safeguarding property and livestock.

Nabal explodes. "Just who is this David? Who is his father? There are many inconsequential men wandering out there and he is one...why should I give him food?"

Enraged, David straps on his sword—and orders four hundred men to accompany him. Adrenaline and anger flowing, they set out to kill Nabal and his household.

Thankfully, one of Nabal's servants reaches Abigail first and tells her the news; immediately she understands her husband's folly and springs into action. Soon two hundred loaves of bread, two hundred cakes of figs, and other mouthwatering provisions are loaded onto donkeys for David and his men. The caravan sets out, with Abigail in the lead.

Picture her on the road, laden down with food, meeting David and hundreds of restless soldiers behind him.

"Forgive my husband," Abigail pleads. "He is spiteful and malicious. I did not know your men asked for food, or I would have filled their saddlebags. Have mercy on us. You are fighting God's battles, and evil shall not be found in you. You are the prince of Israel. Because God has treated you well, show the same concern for us."

Much as David's singing had once pacified King Saul, Abigail's words calm David. Taking the high road, he orders his troops to stand down.

When Abigail returns home from her successful negotiations, Nabal is "very drunk" (1 Samuel 25:36)—so drunk that she does not talk with him. Good move.

Sober the next morning, Nabal learns that his surliness with David almost cost them everything. Nabal goes white, suffering what appears to be the first official heart attack in the Bible: "his heart dies within him; he became like a stone" (1 Samuel 25:37). Yet he stays alive for another ten days, until God strikes him dead. Really dead, this time.

David soon sends his servants to collect Abigail for marriage. No doubt he could have had her through force, but her response indicates a choice. Graceful as always, she is thrilled—or sees it as her best option (which it is). "I will wash the feet of your servants," she says, and rides to join him with five of her maids.

Eventually, Abigail and David have a son, Chileab (Daniel), of whom nothing more is known. David widens his holdings by acquiring Nabal's land, and Abigail gains a sober spouse.

Consider this

Some women crumble under pressure; others rise to the top, showing extraordinary grace. Abigail was not a crumbler. Had she been one, her story might have faded into obscurity, for it's likely she and Nabal would have been bludgeoned to death.

Abigail could have approached Nabal and gotten his approval to talk with David. Or she could have panicked. She could have fled to the woods. She could have refused to listen to her husband's servant. She could have asked David to kill Nabal and leave her alive.

But with wisdom and clarity, she acted, saving the lives of all involved. She recognized David's sacred calling, articulated her husband's folly, and expressed her own desire to live. Such an action exhibits what AA (Alcoholics Anonymous) calls "detachment with love": the ability to preserve one's sanity and balance through practical, reasoned actions, rather than losing oneself in a whirlpool of constant anxiety.

Abigail was a class act. Through the gifts of food, discretion, and discernment, she resolved what could have been a bloody crisis. She did not describe herself as a victim or present herself as a body of nerves. Rather, she acted, and is forever remembered as a woman of grace and diplomacy.

What might we learn from Abigail?

▷ While anxiety may be an automatic response, it is not particularly productive in times of stress.

▷ We often need to act to protect ourselves and those we love.

▷ Clarity of vision, love, and honesty can be roads to both survival and deliverance.

▷ Abigail recognized God's hand at work in David's life and the ultimate role God had for him as ruler of Israel. Especially as we confront adversity, we need such spiritual discernment.

For reflection

1. Can you remember a time when you untangled someone else's problem? What happened?

2. Abigail rose above her husband's drinking, thought clearly, and protected her household. What coping mechanisms would she have developed over the years to survive with him? Has your life been affected by someone abusing drugs or alcohol? If so, how did you find sanity, balance, and God's presence?

3. Abigail seems humbled to marry David and offers to care for his servants (washing someone's feet was a sign of respect and hospitality). Perhaps she sees herself joining David on a holy mission: to care for and protect God's people. Or perhaps she is just relieved to be alive and in safe hands. What is your sense of Abigail's motivations?

▷ **READ HER STORY:** 1 Samuel 28

▷ **CLASSIC MOMENT:** Bringing back Samuel's spirit for Saul, who learns of his imminent death

▷ **LIKELY CHARACTERISTICS:** Skeptical, Countercultural, Wise, Clairvoyant, Intuitive, Hospitable, Compassionate

▷ **DATA:** 126 words

Who was the witch of Endor?

A woman from Endor who could summon the spirits of the dead // An independent contractor (paid by the session) // A woman living alone // An outcast

What did the witch of Endor say?

"Surely you know what Saul has done, how he has cut off the mediums and the wizards from the land. Why then are you laying a snare for my life to bring about my death?" *1 Samuel 28:9*

"Whom shall I bring up for you?" *1 Samuel 28:11*

"Why have you deceived me? You are Saul!" *1 Samuel 28:12*

"I see a divine being coming up out of the ground." *1 Samuel 28:13*

"An old man is coming up; he is wrapped in a robe." *1 Samuel 28:14*

"Your servant has listened to you; I have taken my life in my hand, and have listened to what you have said to me. Now therefore, you also listen to your servant; let me set a morsel of bread before you. Eat, that you may have strength when you go on your way." *1 Samuel 28:21-22*

The witch of Endor's story

Imagine an old woman, living alone in a hillside cave outside the small town of Endor. She is known by several names: fortune-teller, medium, witch. An outcast, she supports herself through her remarkable ability to predict the future. Most jobs are closed to females; she exercises one of the few vocations in biblical times through which a woman could earn a few cents.

On a night unlike all others, an old man stumbles to her door, asking her to rouse a friend from the afterlife. She refuses, telling him that King Saul has banned such activity. For all she knows, the man dressed in what appear to be old battle fatigues, or the two men with him, is employed by Saul to find and arrest lawbreakers like her.

"There will be no punishment," says Saul. "Trust me."

She takes a chance, inviting them inside. "Who is it you wish to speak with?"

"Samuel," he says. "Samuel."

She nods, locates Samuel in the netherworld, summons him—and then screams, finding herself standing between the two most powerful men in Israel, one alive and the other dead—or kind of dead. Grumpy-dead.

Angry that he has been roused, Samuel does not lighten the mood. Instead, he announces that death will take the king the very next day. Samuel disappears, and Saul falls to the ground. Condemned to die, he is also exhausted, for he has not eaten in over twenty-four hours.

With surprisingly deep compassion, the old woman begs the exhausted monarch to stay for a bite of bread so that he might have strength for the morrow. First he refuses, then accepts. Knowing that this will be Saul's last meal, she prepares a meal that is indeed fit for a king.

As was foretold that night because of her action, Saul dies the next day on the battlefield. Knowing that his life is to end and not wanting to die by the hands of the Philistines, he falls on his own sword, thus ending the tenure of the first king of Israel.

Consider this

Ostracized for most of her life, the witch of Endor has finally found a place where she can live in relative safety and practice her vocation. When the knock on her door comes, she is justifiably concerned, for the punishment for practicing witchcraft is death.

We can see why Saul sought her counsel: With the death of Samuel, Saul has lost the only person he could trust and the one who had advised him for years. Chased by David's troops and tortured by God's demons, Saul was a broken man.

No wonder the witch screams. Perhaps she had been enjoying a quiet moonlit night. Perhaps she had been drifting off to sleep…but now, in her rocky living room, stand Israel's past and present.

But she does not run. Her vocation is one of both intuition and hospitality.

Like Mary of Bethany washing and anointing Jesus' feet with priceless oil (John 12:1-8), she offers Saul her most valuable material resource: a fatted calf. Like Mary, who helped to give Jesus the strength to walk to the cross, the witch gives Saul physical and emotional support during his last hours. In the crazed last night of an old man's life, she gives him what he sorely needs: a moment of peace.

What might we learn from the witch of Endor?

▷ Be insistently generous.

▷ Consider all gifts to be from God and use them wisely.

▷ People who seek healing are often hungry, in more ways than one.

▷ Give what you can while you can.

For reflection

1. The witch of Endor had a range of God-given gifts. What were they?

2. Why did Saul seek out this woman? Was it a reasonable thing for him to do? Do you think it was bravery on her part to conjure up Samuel or was she afraid for her life? Did God inspire them to come together? If so, why? If not, why not?

3. The witch had two of the most powerful men in Israel standing with her, even though she had to practice her vocation on the edges of town, in the shadows. In some ways she is like a prostitute, visited by men under the cover of darkness. What does it mean that this witch and several prostitutes have such a strong presence in scripture?

4. Have you ever agreed to help someone and then been terrified at the result? If so, why?

CHAPTER 10

WOMEN WHO SPEAK IN 2 SAMUEL

It's all about David and the women who are affected by his actions in 2 Samuel; all the women who speak are caught up in various parts of his adult life. Halfway through the book though, we see an interesting turn. After hearing from three named women who deal directly with David (wife, daughter, wife), the remaining three are unnamed, but still caught in the web of dynamics surrounding his life and actions as king.

By the numbers

Words spoken by women in 2 Samuel: 642

Number of women who speak: Six (Michal, Bathsheba, young Tamar, the wise woman of Tekoa, the woman of Bahurim, the wise woman of Abel)

BATHSHEBA

*One bath
too many*

▷ **READ HER STORY:** 2 Samuel 11-12, 1 Kings 1:15-31, 1 Kings 1-2, 1 Chronicles 3:5

▷ **CLASSIC MOMENT:** When she is bathing on her roof and King David spots her

▷ **LIKELY CHARACTERISTICS:** Beautiful, Sensual, Loyal, Purposeful, Intelligent, Diplomatic

▷ **DATA:** 192 words (3 in 2 Samuel, 189 in 1 Kings)

Who was Bathsheba?

A wife of Uriah the Hittite, who dies in battle // A faithful wife to David, second king of Israel // A mother who mourns the death of her firstborn // The mother of Solomon, third king of Israel // The woman who speaks the most in 1 Kings

What did Bathsheba say?

The woman conceived; and she sent and told David, **"I am pregnant."** *2 Samuel 11:5*

Bathsheba bowed and did obeisance to the king, and the king said, "What do you wish?" She said to him, **"My lord, you swore to your servant by the Lord your God, saying: Your son Solomon shall succeed me as king, and he shall sit on my throne. But now suddenly Adonijah has become king, though you, my lord the king, do not know it. He has sacrificed oxen, fatted** cattle, and sheep in abundance, and has invited all the children of the king, the priest Abiathar, and Joab the commander of the army; but your servant Solomon he has not invited. But you, my lord the king—the eyes of all Israel are on you to tell them who shall sit on the throne of my lord the king after him. Otherwise it will come to pass, when my lord the king sleeps with his ancestors, that my son Solomon and I will be counted offenders." *1 Kings 1:17-21*

Then Bathsheba bowed with her face to the ground, and did obeisance to the king, and said, "**May my lord King David live forever!**" *1 Kings 1:31*

Then Adonijah son of Haggith came to Bathsheba, Solomon's mother. She asked, "**Do you come peaceably?**" He said, "Peaceably." Then he said, "May I have a word with you?" She said, "**Go on.**" *1 Kings 2:13-14*

"And now I have one request of you; do not refuse me." She said to him, "**Go on.**" *1 Kings 2:16*

"**Very well; I will speak to the king on your behalf.**" *1 Kings 2:18*

The king rose to meet her, and bowed down to her; then he sat on his throne, and had a throne brought for the king's mother, and she sat on his right. Then she said, "**I have one small request to make of you; do not refuse me.**" And the king said to her, 'Make your request, my mother; for I will not refuse you." She said, "**Let Abishag the Shunammite be given to your brother Adonijah as his wife.**" *1 Kings 2:19-21*

Bathsheba's story

Into the late afternoon sun steps Bathsheba, ready to purify herself after her monthly period. An age-old ritual for all Israelite women in their childbearing years, Bathsheba takes an extra minute, for there is no rush. Her husband Uriah, a general in David's army, is off fighting the Philistines, so she is alone. Or so it seems. Out for a stroll, King David stands transfixed on his palace roof, unable to turn away from the beautiful naked woman.

He must have her. He sends messengers to collect her, has sex with her, sends her home. Done. Finished, perhaps forgotten. Until she sends three powerful words back to him: "I am pregnant."

How easy it would have been for David had Bathsheba not conceived. Now, he must deal with an awkward reality: the fact that she is married—and not to him. He does not need another wife; he already has several. Even worse, he has committed adultery with the wife of a soldier under his command.

To solve his "problem," David summons Uriah from combat, hoping that he will sleep with Bathsheba soon enough to make it look like he is the father of her child. A good soldier, however, does not abandon his king, especially in times of war—and Uriah is fiercely committed to both country and king. To leave David would be to leave God, for David is God's anointed one. Uriah, ever the loyal subject, spends his precious night of furlough at the palace gate instead of with his wife.

David tries one more time to send Uriah home; again, the general refuses. "Enough," thinks David. "Enough!"

He orders Uriah back to the war zone, giving the soldier a missive for Joab, the battlefield commander. In that missive are David's tragic and harsh instructions, penned in his own hand: "Send Uriah into the worst part of battle. Make sure he gets killed."

Shortly thereafter, Uriah lies dead on the battlefield. After giving Bathsheba time to mourn, David sends for her and marries her—and finds that God does not approve of adultery or murder. We might also think that it would be hard for Bathsheba to sleep with the man who killed her husband, but neither her words nor her thoughts on that subject are recorded.

Through Nathan the prophet, David learns that the child Bathsheba carries will die, that there will be strife in his household, and that David's wives will be given to his neighbors (2 Samuel 12:11). No mention is made of Bathsheba's emotions about the death of her firstborn son, yet her grief must have run deep. Other sons are eventually born to her and David, including Solomon, but no more of her words are recorded until David is old and dying.

By that time, with many of David's sons viewing the throne like candy, power struggles abound. Bathsheba notes these spats, yet rarely mentions them to David, until Adonijah, David's oldest living son, names himself the next king even before David has died (1 Kings 1:5). Carefully, on the request of Nathan (prophet and advisor), Bathsheba tells David that his legacy and her life will be endangered should he not act to make their son Solomon king. David agrees and officially names Solomon as his successor.[44]

Envy between brothers continues to flare. Soon after Solomon establishes his power, Adonijah approaches Bathsheba. No wonder her first words to him are, "Do you come peaceably?"

Well, sort of, it turns out.

Adonijah wants her help in obtaining Abishag the Shunammite[45], one of David's other wives, for his own wife. Bathsheba dutifully visits Solomon, presenting the request without bias. Known for his wisdom, the king refuses. Sensing correctly that such a move would rob him of his power—one sign of power was to have sex with an adversary's concubines or wives—he has Adonijah beheaded. Perhaps that was Bathsheba's hope all along—but given her decades-long experience in surviving palace politics, she presented the rebel's request to her son without opinion. After all, had Adonijah survived, she would need to be on his good side.

Consider this

Stories that involve King David are difficult to interpret. They are, after all, about David and the dynamics of palace life some three thousand years ago. Whether he is being persecuted by Saul, lusting after Bathsheba, playing songs on his harp, killing Goliath, mourning the death of a child, leading the way in battle, or dancing before the Ark, scripture sets David as the central and golden figure at this time in Israel's history.

Given this David-lens, it is difficult to accurately judge the reactions and emotions of Bathsheba. It is reasonable to think that she might have been unhappy about being summoned to the palace. Did David rape her? Was she grief-stricken over the event? Sex with David was hardly consensual, as she had no right to refuse him; the power was all in his hands. David could take whomever he wanted, even the wife of his general.

Power dynamics are still at the heart of sexual violence. When populations of women are raped, often in war, the message is usually meant for the men of the land: we have invaded and conquered both your land and your women. This was true in biblical times, and especially during David's and Solomon's tenures.

It is not known if Bathsheba loved Uriah or David, for there is no mention of how she feels. She could have seen David on the palace roof and wanted to be with him. Or she could have loved Uriah dearly and been horrified upon losing him to such treachery. How she could have managed to sleep with the one who arranged for her husband to be killed is hard to imagine.

We do know that God was not pleased with David's crime of adultery and punished him by causing the death of Bathsheba's firstborn. Again, the trauma for Bathsheba must have been overwhelming.

After the initial turmoil and sorrow, Bathsheba became a favored wife, court presence, advisor, diplomat, and queen mother. And like so many other women of the Bible, she was, indeed, a survivor.

What might we learn from Bathsheba?

▷   One's life events may be determined by others.

▷   Power dynamics are almost always present in relationships.

▷   Love is not a given.

▷   While time may not heal all wounds, it heals many.

▷   Being a survivor is better than being dead.

For reflection

1.   Bathsheba had no choice but to obey King David's summons and eventually become his wife. Where do you see her heart during the different stages of her life?

2.   Bathsheba suffered the loss of a child conceived through adultery but went on to have four sons and a daughter. Have you experienced the loss of a child? Did faith help you through the grief process? Do you still mourn?

3.   What part did politics play in Bathsheba's story? Are there places in the world today that experience the same kind of dynamics described here? If so, where?

4.   Do dysfunctional family patterns run from one generation to the next? If so, how might God work to heal them?

2 SAMUEL

YOUNG TAMAR

Tragedy upon tragedy

PROFILE: LOW

▷ **READ HER STORY:** 2 Samuel 13:1-22

▷ **CLASSIC MOMENT:** Being raped by her half-brother

▷ **LIKELY CHARACTERISTICS:** Beautiful, Obedient, Kind, Abused, Abandoned, Ostracized

▷ **DATA:** 82 words

Who was young Tamar?

The only daughter of King David listed in the Bible // A girl not yet married, probably between ten and fourteen years of age // The half-sister of Amnon, David's eldest son, who raped her // The full sister of Absalom // An obedient daughter and a clear thinker // A societal outcast after being raped and then rejected by Amnon

What did young Tamar say?

"No, my brother, do not force me; for such a thing is not done in Israel; do not do anything so vile! As for me, where could I carry my shame? And as for you, you would be as one of the scoundrels in Israel. Now therefore, I beg you, speak to the king; for he will not withhold me from you." *2 Samuel 13:12-13*

"No, my brother; for this wrong in sending me away is greater than the other that you did to me." *2 Samuel 13:16*

Young Tamar's story

The story of young Tamar is heart-wrenching. Tamar's half-brother Amnon desires her sexually, but he knows that it is immoral and criminal to sleep with his half-sister. And there seems to be no way to get near her, as she is watched around the clock by palace guards. On a day that would forever define the life of young Tamar, Amnon, and Jonadab (cousin of both Amnon and Tamar) hatch a plan.

"Pretend you're sick," advises Jonadab. "Have your father send Tamar to make those nice little cakes for you. Remember, look sick. Look hungry."

The plan works. King David orders Tamar to do what Amnon asks.

Once she is within reach, Amnon orders his servants to leave, forces Tamar into his inner chamber, and encourages her to sleep with him. As a young woman who knows that virginity is both prized and expected of her, she adamantly refuses. "Speak to my father," she says. "If you want me, then arrange our marriage."

Instead, Amnon rapes her. The assault marks her as a wanton woman; robbing the young Tamar of her innocence and her future.

Yet even after the worst moment of her life, Tamar is rational enough to propose a face-saving option: that Amnon marry her, thus allowing her some exemption from humiliation. She would have been considered unfit for marriage to any other man after the rape, as it would have been viewed as her fault. Being married to her attacker would have at least given her the opportunity to bear children and erase her shame. It's an unthinkable solution in some (but not all) cultures today, but in Tamar's society this was a logical option. Coldly, Amnon rejects her, condemning her to a life of solitude and grief.

After she tells her brother Absalom of the assault, he encourages her to remain silent, but he also reports the rape to King David. David is enraged but does nothing. Three years later, Absalom invites Amnon to a family gathering, gets him drunk, and has him killed to avenge Tamar.

Consider this

This text is one of several terribly dark stories[46] about women in the Old Testament. Not only is Tamar raped by a half-brother (who was aided by a cousin), but there is no redemption for her, no light at the end of her nightmare. Her life has been destroyed; she experiences dysfunctional family systems at their worst.

Her half-brother rapes her and her cousin helps plan the crime. Her father does nothing. Her brother Absalom tells her to be quiet, and then kills Amnon, thus giving new life to family strife and hatred. Because of the murder, Absalom is also forced to flee to the wilderness for three years; it is assumed that Tamar followed, for she took refuge with Absalom's family.

Is there redemption for Tamar? Is there some goodness in life for her? The one small sliver of recognition after the rape may have been when Absalom named his daughter Tamar (2 Samuel 14:27). But that is small compensation for the loss of her innocence, identity, and future.

The object of lust and the victim of sexual assault, Tamar is handed a life sentence of despair woven by her father, brothers, and male cousin. Like a butterfly trussed in a spider's web, there is no escape. She is pierced and wounded and disappears down the maw of brutal cultural norms, sexual violence, and powerful political ambitions.

Unfortunately, this is not just a times-gone-past story. Life is still not easy for many women, especially those who suffer physical and emotional abuse. And sometimes, tragically, girls and women are still lost to the forces of evil: killed, starved, beaten to death. Our hope for them is not only that we will be God's instruments to change such evil in this world, but also that in the Resurrection, these women will pass into God's loving embrace. That they will hear the words: "Welcome, my daughter. I love you. You are safe here. You are created in my image and I cherish you. Welcome, my beautiful daughter. You are home."

What might we learn from young Tamar?

▷ Some tragedies defy human understanding.

▷ Options are not always possible.

▷ Some of the greatest evils can be committed by family members.

▷ It is our responsibility to stand up for those who have been victimized.

For reflection

1. Because of the assault, young Tamar's future implodes. Name the ways she is hurt by family members. How could an action by any one of them have changed her situation for the better?

2. In what ways is her story about power rather than sex?

3. Tamar's story is often compared to that of Jephthah's daughter (Judges 11:29-40), or the concubine who was cut into twelve pieces and delivered to the twelve tribes of Israel (Judges 19:22-39). What are the similarities? What are the differences?

4. How do we reconcile the terrible actions in these stories—or equally difficult events in our own lives—with our understanding of a loving God?

5. Have you experienced any of these dynamics in your family? Has healing been possible, and to what extent?

THE WISE WOMAN OF TEKOA

A storyteller fit for a king

▷ READ HER STORY: 2 Samuel 14:1-21

▷ CLASSIC MOMENT: Telling King David a story that would encourage him to forgive Absalom

▷ LIKELY CHARACTERISTICS: Wise, Brave, Articulate, Fearless, Persuasive

▷ DATA: 437 words

Who was the wise woman of Tekoa?

The woman who spoke the most in 2 Samuel // A respected and outspoken local leader // The mother of two sons // An eloquent storyteller // An envoy sent by Joab

What did the wise woman of Tekoa say?

When the woman of Tekoa came to the king, she fell on her face to the ground and did obeisance, and said, "**Help, O king!**" The king asked, "What is your trouble?" She answered, "**Alas, I am a widow; my husband is dead. Your servant had two sons, and they fought with one another in the field; there was no one to part them, and one struck the other and killed him. Now the whole family has risen against your servant. They say, 'Give up the man who struck his brother, so that we may kill him for the life of his brother whom he murdered, even if we destroy the heir as well.' Thus they would quench my** one remaining ember, and leave to my husband neither name nor remnant on the face of the earth." *2 Samuel 14:4-7*

Then the king said to the woman, "Go to your house, and I will give orders concerning you." The woman of Tekoa said to the king, "**On me be the guilt, my lord the king, and on my father's house; let the king and his throne be guiltless.**" *2 Samuel 14:8-9*

"Please, may the king keep the Lord your God in mind, so that the avenger of blood may kill no more, and my son not be destroyed." *2 Samuel 14:11*

"Please let your servant speak a word to my lord the king." He said, "Speak." *2 Samuel 14:12*

The woman said, "Why then have you planned such a thing against the people of God? For in giving this decision the king convicts himself, inasmuch as the king does not bring his banished one home again. We must all die; we are like water spilled on the ground, which cannot be gathered up. But God will not take away a life; he will devise plans so as not to keep an outcast banished forever from his presence. Now I have come to say this to my lord the king because the people have made me afraid; your servant thought, 'I will speak to the king; it may be that the king will perform the request of his servant. For the king will hear, and deliver his servant from the hand of the man who would cut both me and my son off from the heritage of God.' Your servant thought, 'The word of my lord the king will set me at rest'; for my lord the king is like the angel of God, discerning good and evil. The Lord your God be with you!" *2 Samuel 14:13-17*

Then the king answered the woman, "Do not withhold from me anything I ask you." The woman said, "**Let my lord the king speak.**" The king said, "Is the hand of Joab with you in all this?" The woman answered and said, "**As surely as you live, my lord the king, one cannot turn right or left from anything that my lord the king has said. For it was your servant Joab who commanded me; it was he who put all these words into the mouth of your servant. In order to change the course of affairs your servant Joab did this. But my lord has wisdom like the wisdom of the angel of God to know all things that are on the earth.**" *2 Samuel 14:18-20*

The wise woman of Tekoa's story

Ah, the power of storytelling to influence young tots and old kings alike. Like many rulers, King David is difficult to approach or to criticize, for the power is all his. Yet the woman of Tekoa, with a well-told story, persuades him to restore his broken relationship with his son Absalom.[47]

She is well-rehearsed and convincing, due in no small part to Joab, David's chief military officer, whose ambition is to be near the seat of power. Joab believes it is time for David and Absalom to reconcile. Three years have passed since Absalom killed Amnon for the rape of Tamar; Absalom is still in line for the throne, and Joab is covering his bets.

In Tekoa, he has heard of a sage old woman. He instructs her to wear mourning clothes and tell David that one of her two sons has killed the other, and that conflict has riddled the family ever since. (She apparently did have two sons, so her motherly instinct was easy to call up.) David listens. Then he perceives the meaning of the story and asks the old woman if Joab's hand was involved. She admits this but convinces David from her heart that reconciling with Absalom would be good for all of Israel.

The wise old woman is allowed to return home and resume a normal life, probably enjoying some prestige for having conversed with King David—and causing a major policy shift.

Consider this

The woman of Tekoa would make an excellent intelligence officer—and did. The stakes were high. The good news is that she was not asked to undertake an evil assignment. Unity for royal father and son would theoretically be a good thing for Israel.

What might we learn from the wise woman of Tekoa?

▷ Wisdom comes in many forms, including being able to protect ourselves.

▷ Truth is sometimes found in fiction.

▷ A non-anxious presence is an indispensable asset.

For reflection

1. Tekoa was a region of olive growing, and olive oil was thought to give wisdom, thus the "wise woman from Tekoa." She also must have had some status, or Joab would not have sought her out to help him reason with King David. Describe someone like her that you might know or see in the news.

2. What synonyms would you use to describe the word "wise?" Why must a person (usually) be advanced in years to possess the quality of wisdom?

3. Spiritual and emotional dysfunction seems to play a large role in the Davidic dynasty. What aspects of this dysfunction, if any, have you witnessed in your own family? Where might God's hand be found in the healing process?

THE WOMAN OF BAHURIM

A human life jacket

▷ **READ HER STORY:** 2 Samuel 17:17-21

▷ **CLASSIC MOMENT:** When she protected two of King David's men, who were hiding in an empty cistern on her land

▷ **LIKELY CHARACTERISTICS:** Brave, Intelligent, Faithful, Clever

▷ **DATA:** 8 words

Who was the woman of Bahurim?

A homemaker // A loyal subject of King David // A lifesaver // A convincing person // A quick thinker

What did the woman of Bahurim say?

"They have crossed over the brook of water." *2 Samuel 17:20*

The woman of Bahurim's story

Political unrest never seems to stay in one place, and it is clearly encircling both Jerusalem and its countryside when Absalom revolts, challenging David openly for the crown. Perhaps because youth is on his side and he seems the best bet for the future, Absalom's army is larger than David's. When it appears that Absalom might indeed purge his father from Jerusalem, David and his household flee, leaving behind ten concubines to watch the palace. And then one of the most unseemly crimes in the Old Testament takes place: Absalom marches the concubines up to the roof and rapes them, "in the sight of all Israel," trying to solidify his takeover (2 Samuel 16:22).

Contrast that scene with this one, happening at roughly the same time. In the countryside surrounding Jerusalem, where David is on the run, he is a beloved figure. He is also one of the people—a country boy and shepherd. One of his supporters is a woman who lives in Bahurim, just miles from the Mount of Olives. She knows that great debates are taking place in Jerusalem on how best to kill the king—and thousands of soldiers are preparing to ride out on Absalom's command.

She is not surprised, then, when two men race onto her property, apparently being chased. Recognizing them as David's people, she sees the pair slip down her cistern. Quickly she spreads a cloth over the top as if to dry grain in the sun.

Absalom's soldiers arrive within minutes.

"We heard David's men went this way!" they say. "Where are they? Tell us!"

The woman nods, then turns and points past a creek, saying, "They went that way; they crossed over that water." In full pursuit, the men run the way she has directed.

Shaking out the cloth, she signals David's men to climb out of the well. Later she will learn that they were carrying vital information for the king—telling him his location had been discovered and that Absalom was planning on killing him that very night. Like almost all the locals, the woman knows David's hiding place. Because of her clear thinking, he will be safe.

Consider this

This is the second of three stories about unnamed, everyday women doing what they can to bring peace to Israel and to save their families and towns. The woman of Bahurim used the tools she had within reach—a cloth, grain, and wits—to act, and she successfully turned away what could have been a deadly confrontation.

Without her support, the men hiding in the well could have been killed. The woman and her family could have been slain too. King David could have been murdered, along with his troops. And the king of Israel might have been Absalom: a murderer, disloyal son, and rapist.

What might we learn from the woman of Bahurim?

▷   Work with the tools at hand to create change.

▷   Maintain a non-anxious presence; it helps others trust you.

▷   Keep your ear to the ground to be aware of community developments.

▷   Take risks for what you believe.

For reflection

1. What do you think went through the woman's mind when she watched first David's men, then Absalom's soldiers race into her yard?

2. When is deceit justified? Was this woman deceitful, or was she serving her God and king? Or was it both?

3. What other stories about women does this remind you of? (Hint: Check the Book of Joshua, chapters two and six.)

4. Do women in the Bible generally conduct business with a more non-violent approach than men? If so, to what extent? Name women on both sides.

2 SAMUEL

THE WISE
WOMAN
OF ABEL

*A golden
diplomat*

PROFILE:
LOW, LIKE A CLAM
WASHED UP ON
THE BEACH

▷ **READ HER STORY:** 2 Samuel 20: 14-22

▷ **CLASSIC MOMENT:** Convincing the people of Abel to behead a local ringleader so her townspeople will be spared destruction

▷ **LIKELY CHARACTERISTICS:** Steely, Courageous, Influential, Diplomatic, Ruthless

▷ **DATA:** 86 words

Who was the wise woman of Abel?

A brave, intelligent woman who saved her people // A woman of influence and initiative // A diplomat // A pragmatist

What did the wise woman of Abel say?

Joab's forces were battering the wall to break it down. Then a wise woman called from the city, **"Listen! Listen! Tell Joab, 'Come here, I want to speak to you.'"** He came near her; and the woman said, **"Are you Joab?"** He answered, "I am." Then she said to him, **"Listen to the words of your servant."** He answered, "I am listening." Then she said, **"They used to say in the old days, 'Let them inquire at Abel'; and so they would settle a matter. I am one of those who are peaceable and faithful in Israel; you seek to destroy a city that is a mother in Israel; why will you swallow up the heritage of the LORD?"** *2 Samuel 20:15-19*

"His head shall be thrown over the wall to you." Then the woman went to all the people with her wise plan. And they cut off the head of Sheba son of Bichri, and threw it out to Joab. *2 Samuel 20:21-22*

The wise woman of Abel's story

Bam! Bam! Bam! Fast and hard, David's army batters the wall protecting the town of Abel. Within minutes, it will be breached and the population annihilated—all because a fugitive is hiding out behind the gates. (The criminal, Sheba, has supported Absalom's quest to gain the throne and encouraged Israel's ten northern tribes to break away from David.)[48]

From the growing panic inside emerges a confident voice: the wise woman of Abel. Shoulders thrown back, she asks to see the army's commander, Joab. The battering pauses.

A warrior steps forward. And with her words, "Are you Joab?" comes the first of several clues why she was known as a woman of wisdom. The man standing before her could have been anyone, ready to plunge a dagger into her abdomen.

"I am," he says. Negotiation is the first step of diplomacy, and she has opened the conversation, calling him by name.

Then the second clue: "Listen to the words of your servant." She establishes by the word servant that she is on his side. Knowing full well that he is a man who would kill first and ask questions later, the right words are essential.

"I am listening," he says. Major accomplishment.

In remarks worthy of a seasoned diplomat, she indicates that people have traditionally sought out Abel as a place of peace and conflict resolution. The third and fourth clues to her wisdom are that she establishes her age and authority by saying, "in the old days" and asks him why he would destroy such a place that is "a mother in Israel." Note the double meaning here: mothers are good. Why would you want to destroy your mother, whether that mother is a peace-seeking town or a wise woman like me?

The fifth clue is that she appeals to Joab's faith. Don't destroy the Lord's heritage, she tells him. This is bigger than we are. This is God's part of town. We have, together, a legacy.

The final clue to her wisdom is that she offers Joab a ready-made solution. "You want Sheba's head? We'll give it to you. We'll work this out together. We don't like him, either." Joab agrees. She goes back behind the walls and explains the situation, and minutes later, Sheba's head comes flying over the wall.

Consider this

This story is a powerful one, and follows two other positive accounts about women taking action in a time of political strife. Imagine the old woman standing at the town's gate—using skills of diplomacy, negotiation, shared history—and then appealing to her townspeople, saying, "Where's the traitor? We need his head!" Formidable. In charge. Quick to act when needed.

Note as well the contrast in Joab's two interactions with wise women. He summons the wise woman from Tekoa and uses her as his mouthpiece. In contrast, the wise woman of Abel asks Joab to come to her—and suggests a scenario that would benefit all. (Except for Sheba, who was a goner either way.)

The wise woman of Abel knew she had power, and she used it. God bless her.

What might we learn from the wise woman of Abel?

▷ Harsh decisions may have to be made for the greater good of many.

▷ Quick thinking and a sense of reason at a time of crisis may bring peace.

▷ Identify your opponent before you start negotiating.

▷ In a time of stress, it helps if all warring parties receive something, rather than nothing.

For reflection

1. Joab stopped the siege of Abel in order to listen to the wise woman. How did she reason with him? What about her argument persuaded him to settle for the life of one man rather than many?

2. The citizens of Abel did not owe Sheba anything; he used their city to hide from David's army. He was a common enemy. Can the sacrifice of one for the good of many be justified?

3. The woman claimed her town as God's town, thus demonstrating her values. How might the stating of one's values help in negotiations?

CHAPTER 11

WOMEN WHO SPEAK IN 1 KINGS

From poverty-stricken prostitutes to an inordinately wealthy queen, distinctive and memorable characters take the stage in 1 Kings. Their narratives are some of the most compelling in the Bible. At least two of them— the queen of Sheba and Jezebel—also have crossed over into contemporary secular media—screenplays, movies, and books.

Learn, mark, and inwardly digest. You won't be the only one digesting material in this chapter, for those hungry palace dogs had a good meal as well.

By the numbers

Words spoken by women in the 1 Kings: 685

Number of women who speak: Six (Bathsheba, the real mother, the false mother, the queen of Sheba, the widow of Zarephath, Jezebel)

1 KINGS

PROFILE:
MODERATE

▷ **READ HER STORY:** 1 Kings 3:16-27

▷ **CLASSIC MOMENT:** Telling Solomon to give her son to a hateful companion rather than kill him

▷ **LIKELY CHARACTERISTICS:**
Self-sacrificing, Outspoken, Maternal, Loving

▷ **DATA:** 165 words

Who was the real mother?

A woman who loved her new baby // A woman seeking justice // A prostitute // A survivor of hard times

What did the real mother say?

"Please, my lord, this woman and I live in the same house; and I gave birth while she was in the house. Then on the third day after I gave birth, this woman also gave birth. We were together; there was no one else with us in the house, only the two of us were in the house. Then this woman's son died in the night, because she lay on him. She got up in the middle of the night and took my son from beside me while your servant slept. She laid him at her breast, and laid her dead son at my breast. When I rose in the morning to nurse my son, I saw that he was dead; but when I looked at him closely in the morning, clearly it was not the son I had borne." *1 Kings 3:17-21*

"No, the dead son is yours, and the living son is mine." *1 Kings 3:22*

"Please, my lord, give her the living boy; certainly do not kill him!" *1 Kings 3:26*

The real mother's story

One of the most haunting stories in the Old Testament, this case symbolizes the best of a mother's love and the surprising solution offered by King Solomon. Two women, living with each other and surviving from their earnings as prostitutes, give birth to sons within three days of each other. One woman accidentally crushes her newborn while sleeping; the other embraces her son carefully, falling asleep with him at her breast. When the baby crusher discovers her son has died, she steals the other woman's infant for her own.

In heated conflict, they appear before the king, asking for judgment on the case. When no immediate resolution is found, Solomon gives the terrible order: slice the child in half, so that each may have a part of him. Hearing that nightmare scenario, the real mother emerges—for she is indeed the one who loves the boy enough to let him go.

Consider this

Study the real mother's words as she describes her life. Men come and go, life is hard, joys are few. Most likely she owns nothing of value. If this is her first child, which it seems to be, the woman is probably a teenager. Yet she is willing to give up her greatest treasure of all, her newborn son, so that he might live.

In the spirit of full disclosure, we don't really know which mother is the biological mother—and that was Solomon's point. It doesn't take matching DNA to make a real mother.

What might we learn from the real mother?

▷ Sometimes love mandates that we give our children up much earlier than we would like.

▷ Love is sacrificial and puts the other first.

For reflection

1. Traditionally, this story has been taught to reflect the wisdom of Solomon— but just as important is the teaching of what makes a real mother. What traits did this woman have that made her a real mother?

2. How does she compare to other real mothers in the Bible? Name several and how they compare to this woman.

3. Some women have no biological children and yet make wonderful mothers. How is it possible to be a real mother without giving birth?

▷ **READ HER STORY:** 1 Kings 3:16-27

▷ **CLASSIC MOMENT:** Telling King Solomon to slash the child in half

▷ **LIKELY CHARACTERISTICS:** Selfish, Cold-hearted, Careless, Deceitful, Bitter

**PROFILE:
MODERATE**

▷ **DATA:** 21 words

Who was the false mother?

A careless, irresponsible mother // A prostitute // A liar // A survivor of hard times

What did the false mother say?

"No, the living son is mine, and the dead son is yours." *1 Kings 3:22*

"It shall be neither mine nor yours; divide it." *1 Kings 3:26*

The false mother's story

The bitterness in this mother's heart is so dark that she calls for the murder of her neighbor's newborn baby. Somehow she has rolled over in the night and smothered her own son, and then stolen the other baby from his mother's arms. Given a choice of whether the boy should live (and be given to someone else) or die, she says to kill him, thus revealing that she is not the boy's real mother.

Consider this

Why are women prostitutes? Often for financial reasons. Perhaps the false mother had been raped and thus was no longer "fit for marriage." Perhaps she had been widowed or her husband had divorced her with a wave of his hand.

Prostitution, then as now, found women on the bottom of society's ladder. Even concubines had a more secure life than did prostitutes: a home, the companionship of other women, a lineage for their children, food on their plates.

Yet despite the probable severity of her life, this woman demonstrated hatred when she could have chosen love. She acted to deny her companion a child because she had been denied hers. Caught in poverty, depression, and rejection, she screamed out for justice in the only way she knew: revenge and pain for another.

End of discussion...or not? When God talks of redemption and raising up the outcast, we often think of those who are crippled, imprisoned, hungry, or blind. But this woman, morally corrupt as she may be, is still in God's sights. No one is beyond the reach of God's love.

What might we learn from the false mother?

> ▷ Sometimes grief or envy causes us to harm others.

> ▷ Homicidal instincts may be only a step away, especially in times of fatigue and stress.

> ▷ Even in the worst of circumstances, there are choices.

For reflection

1. What extenuating circumstances might have driven the false mother to steal another's child? Do her circumstances matter?

2. How might this woman find redemption? How do people find redemption after life if they cannot find it in this life?

3. Have you ever wanted to destroy another's happiness out of your own brokenness?

4. Name a situation in which you forgave someone—or name a situation in which you found it impossible to forgive. How was God involved, or not?

THE QUEEN OF SHEBA

Solomon's match

PROFILE:
MODERATELY
HIGH

▷ **READ HER STORY:** 1 Kings 10:1-13, 2 Chronicles 9:1-12

▷ **CLASSIC MOMENT:**
Traveling to Solomon's kingdom by caravan loaded with riches and spices

▷ **LIKELY CHARACTERISTICS:**
Adventuresome, Questioning, Diplomatic, Intelligent, Powerful, Sensual, Wealthy

▷ **DATA:** 228 words (106 in I Kings, 122 in 2 Chronicles)

Who was the queen of Sheba?

An ambassador and wealthy woman // A ruler, probably of a land in southwestern Arabia // An intelligent, sensual, and diplomatic woman // A journeyer

What did the queen of Sheba say?

"The report was true that I heard in my own land of your accomplishments and of your wisdom, but I did not believe the reports until I came and my own eyes had seen it. Not even half had been told me; your wisdom and prosperity far surpass the report that I had heard. Happy are your wives! Happy are these your servants, who continually attend you and hear your wisdom! Blessed be the LORD your God, who has delighted in you and set you on the throne of Israel! Because the LORD loved Israel forever, he has made you king to execute justice and righteousness." *1 Kings 10:6-9*

"The report was true that I heard in my own land of your accomplishments and of your wisdom, but I did not believe the reports until I came and my own eyes saw it. Not even half of the greatness of your wisdom had been told to me; you far surpass the report that I had heard. Happy are your people! Happy are these your servants, who continually attend you and hear your wisdom! Blessed be the LORD your God, who has delighted in you and set you on his throne as king for the LORD your God. Because your God loved Israel and would establish them forever, he has made you king over them, that you may execute justice and righteousness." *2 Chronicles 9:5-8*

The queen of Sheba's story

The queen of Sheba: eloquent of speech, shrouded in mystery, and bathed from childhood in precious oils. Sparking the imagination as few others have, she is memorialized not only in the Bible, but the Qur'an as well. Her likeness has also appeared in books, plays, classical music, movies, and poems. Even Jesus refers to her twice, calling her the queen of the South (Matthew 12:42, Luke 11:31).

Where exactly is she from? Where is "Sheba?" Most likely this refers to southwestern Arabia, possibly the area of modern-day Yemen. Another tradition says she ruled Ethiopia, north of current-day Somalia and east of South Sudan.

Why did she travel to meet Solomon? She may have been trying to align herself with Solomon's strong kingdom, to secure current and future trade possibilities, to sate her curiosity, and to come home with new resources. According to the two short chapters describing her, she met those goals. (And according to various non-biblical legends, there was one substantial added benefit that some say emerged about nine months later…kicking and screaming.)

The Bible identifies her as the ruling queen of a wealthy land south of Jerusalem.[49] We know that her country is affluent because she brought with her "120 talents of gold," or in today's market, the equivalent of roughly $165 million.[50] Her caravan is loaded down with exotic spices and never again "did spices come in such quantity" to Israel, sandalwood, and an extraordinarily flamboyant caravan of camels and servants (1 Kings 10:10).

She arrives prepared, bringing both gifts and questions. Not until her questions are answered sufficiently does she give Solomon the gifts (one assumes she brought with her a strong military presence to guard those materials while she pursued her answers).

She is a keen observer and diplomat. She assesses his wealth and infers that he would be helpful to her, and then compliments him on both his wisdom—the one quality that Solomon had requested from God—and his prosperity (in biblical times, a sure sign of God's favor). She meets Solomon as an intellectual equal by asking him hard questions.

She establishes her authority through her intellect and position, then points to the values they share: intelligence, security, and peace. She links Solomon to a higher power, invoking God's name, even though she may have been a polytheist: God "has made you king over them that you may execute justice and righteousness" (2 Chronicles 9:8).

Consider this

The Bible does not report that Solomon and the queen of Sheba had a relationship outside their business dealings. The queen of Sheba was a powerful and exotic woman, diplomat, ruler, and trader, and stood comfortably on her own two feet. Having said that, there exist legends from multiple sources stretching over some three thousand years that their relationship was more than just a business friendship. Because of their consistency in wide-ranging cultures, it would be irresponsible not to mention them here. There are also these lines from the Bible that seem just a bit more suggestive than average biblical prose: the queen of Sheba discussed with him "all that was on her mind" (2 Chronicles 9:1), and was granted "every desire that she expressed" (2 Chronicles 9:12).

Clearly Solomon was attracted to women. 1 Kings 11 says among his wives were seven hundred princesses and three hundred concubines. (If every woman averaged two children, that would be two thousand children.) Foreign women in particular seemed to be an irresistible draw to him (which eventually angered God). King Solomon "loved many foreign women" along with the daughter of Pharaoh, including Moabite, Ammonite, Edomite, Sidonian, and Hittite women. The Bible says, "Solomon clung to these in love" (1 Kings 11:1-2).

While we do not know all the dynamics of the relationship between the queen of Sheba and Solomon, what is important is this: she was bright, diplomatic, beautiful, and a bit exotic. She lit up the imaginations of those around her—and the fires still burn.

What might we learn from the queen of Sheba?

▷ Taking the initiative to build relationships in times of peace is a strong diplomatic move.

▷ Preparation and affirmation are key to successful business relationships.

▷ Risk and danger are part of leadership.

▷ Mixing business and a more personal relationship might have worked for the queen of Sheba; chances are it won't work for you.

For reflection

1. What comes to your mind as you visualize the queen of Sheba? From where does her power come?

2. Although the queen must have traveled with a military presence, she would have been a target for theft, murder, and rape—as well as possible heat stroke in the desert. Describe what drove her to set out on what could have been a fatal journey.

3. The queen of Sheba appears to have been an extraordinary ruler, wise enough to seek lessons from a gifted colleague. Have you been in a situation where you found valuable help by seeking the wisdom of others? Describe.

4. As with many of the great biblical events (Sarah and Abraham's desert sojourn, Ruth and Naomi's return to Bethlehem, Mary's flight to visit Elizabeth), this story takes place within the context of a long journey. Given that travel is no longer done on foot or on camels (thus giving travelers less time to reflect and grow), what might that mean for us?

▷ **READ HER STORY:** 1 Kings 17

▷ **CLASSIC MOMENT:** Seeing her beloved son brought back to life by Elijah

▷ **LIKELY CHARACTERISTICS:** Despondent, Humble, Self-giving, Faithful, Protective, Tenacious

▷ **DATA:** 104 words

Who was the widow of Zarephath?

A poverty-stricken mother who was preparing for death // A woman whom God instructed the prophet Elijah to seek out // A straightforward, assertive woman // A witness to two of God's miracles // A foreigner to Israel, living in the heart of Baal territory

What did the widow of Zarephath say?

"As the LORD your God lives, I have nothing baked, only a handful of meal in a jar, and a little oil in a jug; I am now gathering a couple of sticks, so that I may go home and prepare it for myself and my son, that we may eat it, and die." *1 Kings 17:12*

"What have you against me, O man of God? You have come to me to bring my sin to remembrance, and to cause the death of my son!" *1 Kings 17:18*

So the woman said to Elijah, "Now I know that you are a man of God, and that the word of the LORD in your mouth is truth." *1 Kings 17:24*

The widow of Zarephath's story

See this story first for what it is: a faith statement by a seemingly ordinary woman as she looks into starvation's gaping maw.

Because of God's anger toward Jezebel and others who have been worshiping Baal, the countryside has suffered a famine for almost three years. Only a few can afford to buy precious grains for bread, some have died, and others are so close to death that they almost don't feel the flies scurrying on their faces. One of those is the widow of Zarephath. Month after month, day after day, she has put away whatever grains she could find, whatever drops of oil she could save. Now, with her son near death, she expects to bury him—then waste away herself, ignored by all but birds of prey.

It hurts to move. It hurts to breathe. It hurts to walk away from her boy, knowing he may not be alive when she returns. Nonetheless, she must find firewood to prepare their last meal together, so she forages outside the city gate, searching for a few sticks.

Mirage-like, a man appears in her path. She recognizes him as a man of God because of the mantle that is wrapped around his shoulders. He, too, is emaciated, but God has cared for him, commanding ravens to share their food with him twice a day. Rotting flesh is better than no food at all. At least it has kept him alive.

If the woman had come earlier or later to the town's gates, she would not have seen the prophet. If she had searched for wood in another part of town, she would not have seen him. Intuition? Coincidence? More likely a "God-moment" (1 Kings 17:8-9), even though she is not an Israelite.

Elijah is there because his own water supply has dried up, and because God has directed him to the heart of this Baal-worshiping country, where God has told him that a widow will provide food.

"Give me some water," he says. As she leaves to get it, he tells her to bring some bread back as well.

"I have no food, sir! What bits I have left I will give to my son so that he may live another day!"

"Do not be afraid," he answers. "Cook a biscuit for me first and then you will both eat—for God says your grains and oil will not fail you."

Somehow, she summons the courage to do as Elijah asks—and remarkably her containers stay full, brimming over with grains and oil. But the crisis has not ended, for instead of recovering, her son deteriorates to the point of no return.

She snaps. "What have you against me, O man of God? You have come to cause the death of my son!"

Elijah gathers the lifeless boy into his arms, takes him upstairs (where the woman has provided lodging), pleads with God, then stretches his body on top of the boy's, begging God to fill his lungs with air.

And God does. The woman is overjoyed.

Consider this

This is a tough story. A starving woman is asked to feed a wandering prophet before she feeds her dying son, before she feeds herself—and she does. Even though her failing strength would barely allow her to search for sticks, she recognized God's presence in the prophet, and responded unconditionally.

Did she respond because she thought Elijah would save her? That correlation does not jump from the Bible's pages. Did she respond because in the excitement of seeing a prophet, she forgot her son? No.

She gave food to Elijah first because she trusted him, instinctively knowing that he was a man of God. Her jug of oil kept flowing; her container of grain stayed full. Her cup truly overflowed—until her boy stopped breathing. Then she unloaded her anger on Elijah, blaming herself for her boy's condition (as many mothers would, whether logical or not). Through the prophet, God restores the boy to health.

This woman is the first individual cited by Jesus in the Gospel of Luke after he returns from his forty-day trial in the wilderness. Reading the scriptures in his hometown synagogue, he tells them, "The Spirit of the Lord is upon me, because he has anointed me to bring good news to the poor...to let the oppressed go free." He announces that "today this scripture has been fulfilled in your hearing" (Luke 4:20).

The crowd responds, "Is this not Joseph's son? Who does he think he is? Why, we've known him since he was a boy!"

Jesus says, "Truly I tell you, no prophet is accepted in the prophet's hometown" (Luke 4:24).

And then he shares the story of the widow in Zarephath, and how God sent Elijah only to her, not to the many widows and lepers in Israel who were also starving. Hidden here is the uncomfortable truth that while God continues to love the people of the covenant, others are included in God's expansive grasp. The people get so angry with Jesus that they try to kill him, but he passes through their clutches and moves on to the next town.

What might we learn from the widow of Zarephath?

▷ God is present in moments of despair.

▷ God's true representatives bring messages of faith and healing.

▷ Taking risks is part of being in relationship with God.

▷ The church is catholic (with a small "c") because it proclaims the whole faith to all people, to the end of time;[51] and this is a good example of such outreach.

For reflection

1. Why did the widow of Zarephath trust Elijah? What did it mean that she fed the prophet even though her preference was to be with her son?

2. In 1 Kings 17:18, Elijah restored her son to life. When her son was dying, Zarephath blamed herself, although the nature of the sin she mentions is never explained. It is common for women to blame themselves. To what extent have you blamed yourself for circumstances out of your control?

3. Elijah's restoration of the widow's son might remind you of another story. What stories in the Bible are similar?

4. How might this story be a good text for interfaith study?

JEZEBEL

Treachery personified

PROFILE: HIGH

▷ **READ HER STORY:** 1 Kings 16:31, 18:4, 13, 19; 19:1-2, 1 Kings 21, 2 Kings 9

▷ **CLASSIC MOMENT:** Being thrown out a palace window and eaten by dogs for her treachery

▷ **LIKELY CHARACTERISTICS:** Vain, Bloodthirsty, Arrogant, Ruthless, Cruel, Powerful, Murderous, Tasty

▷ **DATA:** 108 words (100 in 1 Kings, 8 in 2 Kings)

Who was Jezebel?

A Phoenician princess married to King Ahab of Israel // A mother and grandmother of kings // A devotee to the pagan god Baal // A bloodthirsty persecutor of Elijah and other Hebrew prophets // The epitome of wickedness and treachery // A woman with a "painted" face

What did Jezebel say?

Then Jezebel sent a messenger to Elijah, saying, **"So may the gods do to me, and more also, if I do not make your life like the life of one of them by this time tomorrow."** *1 Kings 19:2*

His wife Jezebel came to him and said, **"Why are you so depressed that you will not eat?"** *1 Kings 21:5*

His wife Jezebel said to him, "**Do you now govern Israel? Get up, eat some food, and be cheerful; I will give you the vineyard of Naboth the Jezreelite.**" *1 Kings 21:7*

She wrote in the letters, "**Proclaim a fast, and seat Naboth at the head of the assembly; seat two scoundrels opposite him, and have them bring a charge against him, saying, 'You have cursed God and the king.' Then take him out, and stone him to death.**" *1 Kings 21:9-10*

As soon as Jezebel heard that Naboth had been stoned and was dead, Jezebel said to Ahab, "**Go, take possession of the vineyard of Naboth the Jezreelite, which he refused to give you for money; for Naboth is not alive, but dead.**" *1 Kings 21:15*

When Jehu came to Jezreel, Jezebel heard of it; she painted her eyes, and adorned her head, and looked out of the window. As Jehu entered the gate, she said, "**Is it peace, Zimri, murderer of your master?**" *2 Kings 9:30-31*

Jezebel's story

As we deconstruct rumors and allegations, we often find women to be smarter, healthier and more faithful than they have been portrayed, both in scripture and in history. That is not the case here—for Jezebel is one of the most destructive women in the entire Bible.

Originally from Phoenicia, Jezebel married King Ahab of Israel (their marriage improved trade routes for both countries). Like her people, she worshiped Baal, the pagan god of fertility and agriculture. By this time, Israel was divided into two countries: the northern ten tribes (Israel) and the southern two tribes (Judah). Ahab ruled over the north, and it was there that Jezebel actively sought to replace Yahweh with Baal. Some four hundred and fifty priests of Baal and four hundred priests of Asherah, Baal's consort, were guests at Jezebel's table.

Long ago, however, God had insisted that Israel be a monotheistic nation, dedicated completely to him and he to them ("You shall have no other gods before me...for I the LORD your God am a jealous God" Exodus 20:3-5). In the name of Baal, however, sexual rituals and temple prostitution increasingly raged across the land, destroying both the moral and the theological fiber of Israel. This intentional seduction of Israel from its faithfulness to God is Jezebel's great treachery. Among her other crimes are murder and conspiracy to commit murder—and right in the middle of it is the prophet Elijah, a substantial thorn in the side for both Ahab and Jezebel.

Elijah and Jezebel are at odds before they even meet. When God sends Elijah to tell King Ahab that he will soon send rain to famine-starved Israel, they argue about whose gods are strongest. Elijah puts Ahab to the test: "Send all your prophets to Mount Carmel and have them prove they can do the simplest task—creating rain from dry skies!"

The prophets of Baal and Asherah fail miserably, while Yahweh prevails. After defeating the pagan prophets, Elijah rounds them up, marches them to the Kidron Valley (the same place where Deborah had led the troops), and slaughters them.

Jezebel is not pleased and sends word to Elijah that she will have him killed. He flees. She pulls back her claws. Temporarily.

But Jezebel is not finished with her treachery. From the palace walls in Samaria, King Ahab admires his great land holdings, unbroken and beautiful...except for a postage stamp-sized vineyard next door. He covets the patch and tries to convince its owner, Naboth the Jezreelite, to sell it. But it is not for sale; the plot had been handed down to Naboth by his father. Under Mosaic law, Naboth was forbidden to sell his piece of the promised land—and didn't want to, anyway.

Ahab is so depressed that he throws himself on his bed and refuses to eat. Jezebel taunts him, telling him that he is the king. He should get up and be cheerful; she will obtain the land for him. She arranges a mock trial for Naboth, which (no surprise) ends in his death by stoning...and Ahab takes the land.

Bad deeds do not go unnoticed. God sends Elijah to tell Ahab that he and Jezebel will die a particularly gruesome death, and that dogs will lick up their blood just as they had Naboth's. King Ahab dies in battle, and that part of the prophecy is fulfilled.

Jezebel continues to swat down God's prophets, but in the end, the tide turns. After Ahab is killed, Jehu rides to the palace in Jezreel to defeat Ahab's successor Joram, avenge the slaying of Naboth, punish Jezebel for her treachery, and restore the sacred city to the service of God. When Jezebel hears of his arrival, she puts on lavish makeup and looks out from an upstairs window (2 Kings 9:30). Ornery to the end, she leans out and taunts Jehu, reminding him of Zimri, a commander who had tried to steal the throne forty years ago and failed.

Jehu eyes her, then demands: "Who is with me?"

Several eunuchs, who are behind Jezebel, see their chance and push the queen out of the window, giving the hungry palace dogs a fresh snack.

Consider this

The name "Jezebel" has always carried negative connotations, beyond race and community of origin. You probably wouldn't name your daughter Jezebel any more than you'd name your son Judas. Jezebel is known throughout history for her murderous ways, and it is hard not to celebrate her downfall (a word that takes on new meaning with this story).

Jezebel's attempt to seduce the Israelites away from their faith was a violation at the deepest level. Destruction of the human spirit, rejection of God, and turning away from the faith were crimes that could not be ignored.

What might we learn from Jezebel?

▷ Arrogance and ruthlessness can lead to a terrible end.

▷ God will win the battle in the end; evil will not go unpunished.

▷ Listen to God's prophets.

For reflection

1. What was Jezebel's greatest fault? What damage did she do to Israel?

2. Jezebel has been criticized throughout history for dominating King Ahab. Would the same be said for a powerful man behind a woman?

3. In the same vein, the issue of Jezebel painting her face seems to jump off the pages of the Bible, for it is as if the writer is saying that only evil women wear makeup. Would the issue of vanity have been a problem if a man had been in charge? Why the focus on cosmetics?

CHAPTER 12

WOMEN WHO SPEAK IN 2 KINGS

The order for the women who speak here is exactly the opposite of that in 1 Kings: unnamed women speak first, followed by an equal number of named ones. Yet whether named or unnamed, all these individuals tell compelling stories. Here, for example, we see one of the saddest events of all time: a war-ravaged mother who eats her son.

At the end of 2 Kings, look for one of the surprise jewels in the Old Testament: a beautifully eloquent woman, once a housewife, now a prophet as well. Skills developed at home—prayer, study, and listening—had served her family well, and eventually blessed both the monarchy and the faith community of Israel.

By the numbers

Words spoken by women in 2 Kings: 486

Number of women who speak: Seven (the wife of a member of the company of prophets, the Shunammite woman, the servant girl of Naaman's wife, the woman who ate her son, Jezebel, Athaliah, and Huldah)

▷ **READ HER STORY:** 2 Kings 4:1-7

▷ **CLASSIC MOMENT:** Telling Elisha her children would be sold into slavery

▷ **LIKELY CHARACTERISTICS:** Faithful, Trusting, Proactive, Scared

▷ **DATA:** 43 words

Who was this wife (with the inescapably long title)?

The widow of a man who had served in a prophetic order guided by Elisha // An impoverished woman // A mother who followed Elisha's instructions // The recipient of a miracle

What did the wife say?

Now the wife of a member of the company of prophets cried to Elisha, **"Your servant my husband is dead; and you know that your servant feared the LORD, but a creditor has come to take my two children as slaves."** Elisha said to her, "What shall I do for you? Tell me, what do you have in the house?" She answered, **"Your servant has nothing in the house, except a jar of oil."**
2 Kings 4:1-2

When the vessels were full, she said to her son, **"Bring me another vessel."** But he said to her, "There are no more." Then the oil stopped flowing. *2 Kings 4:6*

The wife's story

Her husband, the family breadwinner, has died. The bills are piling up, and she stands to lose her children.

Some three thousand years later, we can still hear the agony and suffering in her voice. Yet she, like so many other Bible women, is a survivor. She acts, reaching out to Elisha, Elijah's successor, because her husband had worked in Elisha's company of prophets.

Her husband would have received some compensation for his work—low, but enough to keep the wolf from the door. Now that is no longer the case. She stands to lose everything and faces the horror of seeing her children sold into slavery.

"What shall I do for you?" Elisha asks. "What do you have in the house?"

"Nothing but a jar of oil," replies the widow.

Elisha commands, "Go borrow other jugs and jars and vases and containers— and bring back as many as you can!"

She gathers all the vessels she can find, takes her children inside, shuts the door, and begins pouring oil. Jug after jug becomes full; they pour until there are no more containers.

Elisha tells her to sell the oil, pay her debts, and then use the rest for living expenses.

2 KINGS

Consider this

Note that Elisha does not procure the oil, nor does he produce it; clearly a gentle and powerful miracle occurs by God's hand. But miracles do not happen out of the blue—the heart must be receptive, even if only known to God. Consider the ways in which the widow had tilled the soil to prepare for a miracle:

- She expressed her concerns to the prophet

- She advocated for her children rather than giving up

- She used the materials she had

- She worked in community with her neighbors

- She did what God's agent said to do

Perhaps most importantly, though, she had never let her supply of oil completely exhaust itself—there was something for God to work with, to transform.[52] She would not give up the fight for her children until there was no more breath within her.

What might we learn from this woman?

▷ Let nothing stop you from protecting your family.

▷ Involve others in solving a crisis.

▷ Believe in God's agents.

▷ Be open to miracles.

▷ Do your part to give God something to work with.

For reflection

1. This woman was willing to do all she could to keep her children from slavery. What were her options?

2. Throughout the Bible, there are instances of God caring for widows and orphans. How does this story manifest that value?

3. Symbolizing God's love, the oil flowed until there were no more containers to hold it. Have you known a troublesome time in your life when God's love felt abundant? Is it easier or harder to recognize abundance in prosperous times?

4. This woman appealed to Elisha almost as one would approach a corporation to pay life insurance. Perhaps without knowing it, this was her business plan. Are you prepared in case something happens to your income?

5. Jesus said, "Blessed be the poor in spirit, for theirs is the kingdom of heaven" (Matthew 5:3). How might this story illustrate that theme?

2 KINGS

THE SHUNAMMITE WOMAN

"It will be all right!"

▷ **READ HER STORY:**
2 Kings 4:8-37; 8:1-6

▷ **CLASSIC MOMENT:** Appealing to Elisha directly to save her son

▷ **LIKELY CHARACTERISTICS:**
Forthright, Purposeful, Hospitable, Generous, Intelligent, Tenacious

▷ **DATA:** 150 words

Who was the Shunammite woman?

A wealthy woman from the town of Shunem who bears a son as foretold by Elisha // A woman who creates a holy space in her home // A woman who won't take no for an answer

What did the Shunammite woman say?

"Look, I am sure that this man who regularly passes our way is a holy man of God. Let us make a small roof chamber with walls, and put there for him a bed, a table, a chair, and a lamp, so that he can stay there whenever he comes to us." *2 Kings 4:9-10*

"I live among my own people." *2 Kings 4:13*

"No, my lord, O man of God; do not deceive your servant." *2 Kings 4:16*

"Send me one of the servants and one of the donkeys, so that I may quickly go to the man of God and come back again." *2 Kings 4:22*

"It will be all right." *2 Kings 4:23*

Then she saddled the donkey and said to her servant, "Urge the animal on; do not hold back for me unless I tell you." *2 Kings 4:24*

"It is all right." *2 Kings 4:26*

"Did I ask my lord for a son? Did I not say, Do not mislead me?" *2 Kings 4:28*

"As the LORD lives, and as you yourself live, I will not leave without you." *2 Kings 4:30*

The Shunammite woman's story

Awesome. Underrated. No holds barred. A role model. A woman who created a holy space in her home as well as in her heart. A mother who would take no prisoners in the quest to heal her son. You can place your bets on her, and this is why:

The Shunammite (pronounced shoo-na-mite) woman is observant. She observes Elisha and becomes certain that he is "a holy man of God." Perhaps she has seen him do a miracle. Perhaps she has seen him pray. Perhaps she has seen him guide his company of prophets.

So she makes room for God's presence in her house. Elisha is God's agent; therefore, as she constructs a space for him, she is making room for God in both her home and her heart. She nurtures Elisha. She provides for God's servant by giving him a place to rest, complete with a bed, chair, table, and lamp. Her ministry of hospitality runs strong.

When Elisha tells the barren woman that she will bear a child, she is skeptical, like Sarah. Her answer was something like, "Don't mess with me if you're not serious." A son arrives; Elisha isn't messin' with her.

She embraces her son in death as in life. While working with his father in the fields, the boy complains of a headache. His father sends him home to his mother. By noon that day, while sitting in her lap, he dies.

She does not crumble. She takes charge. Rather than arranging for burial, she takes the boy up to Elisha's bed, lays him there, and tells her husband to get a servant and a donkey ready because she is going to find the prophet. When his questions become a bit, well, irritating ("Why are you doing this now?"), she utters her classic line: "It will be all right." Saddling the donkey herself—because time is of the essence—she rides about fifteen miles to Mount Carmel, where Elisha lives.

She speaks truth to power, saying, "Didn't I tell you not to mislead me?" In other words, "My son has died. You messed with me." Picture her response when Elisha tells her he will send Gehazi to lay his staff on her son's face. Gehazi goes ahead, but the staff does not heal the boy, which is no surprise to the woman. She will not settle for anything less than the prophet himself, so Elisha accompanies her home.

She sees her hope fulfilled after Elisha personally tends to the boy. Performing what appears to be CPR, the prophet feels the boy grow warm, watches him sneeze seven times (seven is always a fortuitous number in the Bible), then calls his mother. She falls to her knees in gratitude, then picks up her son and takes him downstairs.

Consider this

The Shunammite woman had an extraordinarily deep and strong spiritual core. She knew who she was and what needed to be done to save her son, and she did it. A wonderful example of how to be a mother, she is indeed a role model—especially for those who may feel their options and power are limited.

What might we learn from the Shunammite woman?

▷ Keep a light burning for God.

▷ Saddle up that donkey and get going.

▷ Take your complaint right to the top when necessary.

For reflection

1. The woman had made a space for the presence of God in her home. What did that say about her?

2. Think about your home. Is there a place set apart for God's presence? If so, how do you use it?

3. She was very blunt with Elisha, at one point saying, "Did I not say, Do not mislead me?" Is there a loved one in your life who needs you to be an advocate? Who should you approach to solve the problem? Pray for God's wisdom and strength and set out.

5. Does the Shunammite woman remind you of other women in history? If so, who and why?

2 KINGS

THE SERVANT GIRL OF NAAMAN'S WIFE

God's voice through a child

▷ **READ HER STORY:** 2 Kings 5:2-4

▷ **CLASSIC MOMENT:** Directing the leprous Naaman toward Elisha

▷ **LIKELY CHARACTERISTICS:** Compassionate, Well-intentioned, Resilient, Forgiving, Sincere

▷ **DATA:** 19 words

Who was the servant girl of Naaman's wife?

An Israelite girl taken captive by the Aramean army // A kind and trusting person

What did the servant girl say?

"If only my lord were with the prophet who is in Samaria! He would cure him of his leprosy." *2 Kings 5:3*

The servant girl's story

There are young saints in the Bible, and this girl is one of them. Captured in war and brought back to enemy lands, she becomes bound to the wife of Naaman, the commander-in-chief of the Aram-Damascus army. She will never see her original family again.

Yet she does not show anger or distress. She sees that Naaman is suffering from leprosy and knows that Elisha, were he present, would cure him. Naaman's wife passes this news on to her husband; he travels to Samaria to see the prophet and is healed—although through his skepticism, Naaman makes the healing process harder for himself than he should.

Consider this

Normally in this book we stick to the stories of the girls and women who speak. Naaman's actions, though, serve to bring home the message expressed by the girl: God heals—and sometimes speaks in soft ways from unexpected sources. Things do not have to be as complicated as we make them. The unnamed servant girl has no power, yet here she works as a mighty evangelist by pointing the path to Elisha, who heals on behalf of God. Because she is taking an active role in caring for the enemy and keeping her faith, God is able to use her in reaching the hardened hearts of others.

What might we learn from the servant girl?

▷ Readily forgive others for treating us sinfully.

▷ Don't hold back helpful information out of spite.

▷ Separate our opinions of others from our compassion for them.

▷ Keep the faith in all circumstances.

2 KINGS

For reflection

1. The servant girl was a stranger in a strange land, kidnapped from her home and living among those who had killed her people. Yet she willingly shared knowledge so that her captor might be healed. To what extent might Jesus have been thinking of her, and other such forgiving children, when he said, "Let the little children come to me, and do not stop them; for it is to such as these that the kingdom of heaven belongs" (Matthew 19:14)?

2. By offering hope to Naaman, how did she communicate God's love?

3. Which is more difficult for you: forgiving the deep sins of others or living with anger? What might we learn from this girl?

THE WOMAN WHO ATE HER SON

Unfathomable grief, horrifying actions

▷ **READ HER STORY:** 2 Kings 6:24-32

▷ **CLASSIC MOMENT:** Eating her son

▷ **LIKELY CHARACTERISTICS:**
Gullible, Desperate, Selfish, Impulsive, Not too bright

▷ **DATA:** 55 words

Who was the woman who ate her son?

A Samaritan mother // A starving woman who had lost hope // A woman who was incapacitated due to trauma, grief, and hunger // An easy prey

What did she say?

"Help, my lord king!" *2 Kings 6:26*

He said, "No! Let the Lord help you. How can I help you? From the threshing floor or from the wine press?" But then the king asked her, "What is your complaint?" She answered, **"This woman said to me, 'Give up your son; we will eat him today, and we will eat my son tomorrow.' So we cooked my son and ate him. The next day I said to her, 'Give up your son and we will eat him.' But she has hidden her son."** *2 Kings 6:27-29*

2 KINGS

The woman's story

No way around it, this is a complex and terrible story. Even in the worst of times, the thought of a mother eating her child is horrifying—and here, a mother kills, cooks, and consumes her son.

The context is that the city of Samaria—the capital of the northern kingdom of Israel—has been besieged by the armies of Aram, its neighbor to the north. And with such devastation come the ravages of war: starvation, disease, grief, chaos, and torture. It is that picture that confronts the king as he walks along the top of the city's remaining walls. Suddenly a woman cries out to him from below for help.

He hears her horrific story. She and another woman agreed to eat their children, starting with her son, followed by the other woman's son. She kept her end of the deal, killing her son so the two mothers could cook and eat him. But when it was time to consume the second son, the boy had disappeared, hidden by his mother. Now the first woman's despair is overwhelming.

The king tears his clothes in grief over the actions of the woman, and the events that have caused them. Then he blames Elisha, the prophet, vowing that he will kill him.

Consider this

Right minds do not always prevail in horrible circumstances like war; morals often disintegrate like shattered windows. Still, this story rightfully jolts the reader into a state of disbelief, even nausea. Most likely, the mother had lost her mind due to the extenuating circumstances. If she was of sound mind, God is the only one who understands her actions. Even with famine, despair, and death on all sides in times of war, the vast majority of mothers would not eat their children or allow them to be consumed.

Recognize, however, that desperate circumstances tempt men and women to engage in desperate acts—acts that would not even be considered when stomachs are full, minds and hearts engaged.

Stories in the Bible are usually about more than the event described, and that is true here. The message here is that because Israel has fallen away from God, the moral fiber of society has broken apart.

What might we learn from the woman who ate her son?

- ▷ Do not eat our children.
- ▷ Starvation kills both spirit and body.
- ▷ Make bargains carefully.
- ▷ Fight to hold onto our values during times of physical and emotional affliction.

For reflection

1. What might have caused this woman to make the decision she did? Are there other similar, terrible decisions that people have made in times of war or famine?

2. Whose sin is greater: the woman who ate her own son, or the second woman who apparently encouraged the murder?

3. Where is God in this story? How might Saint Paul's words from Romans 8:38-39 help here?

2 KINGS

ATHALIAH

"Treason, treason!"

PROFILE: LOW

▷ **READ HER STORY:** 2 Kings 8:26, 2 Kings 11, 2 Chronicles 22-23, 2 Chronicles 24:7

▷ **CLASSIC MOMENT:**
Killing her grandchildren

▷ **LIKELY CHARACTERISTICS:**
Ruthless, Bloodthirsty, Evil, Arrogant, Power-obsessed

▷ **DATA:** 4 words (2 in 2 Kings, 2 in 2 Chronicles)

Who was Athaliah?

Daughter of King Ahab of Israel (some say sister) // Possibly the daughter of Jezebel // Wife of Jehoram, King of Judah // Mother of Ahaziah, King of Judah // A ruler of Judah for seven years // A murderess and supporter of Baal

What did Athaliah say?

When Athaliah heard the noise of the guard and of the people, she went into the house of the LORD to the people; when she looked, there was the king standing by the pillar, according to custom, with the captains and the trumpeters beside the king, and all the people of the land rejoicing and blowing trumpets. Athaliah tore her clothes and cried, **"Treason! Treason!"** *2 Kings 11:13-14*

Athaliah tore her clothes, and cried, **"Treason! Treason!"** *2 Chronicles 23:13*

Athaliah's story

A thaliah is the only woman to have ruled Judah, which sounds noteworthy until you know that she arranged to have her grandchildren murdered. Her story is an interesting one.

Although she was an Israelite (many commentators miscast her as a foreigner)[53], she was the daughter of King Ahab, and thus a descendant of David and an Israelite by blood.

In 867 BCE, a peace treaty calms the waters between Judah (the two southern tribes) and Israel (the ten northern tribes). To seal the deal, Ahab gives his daughter Athaliah to Jehoram, the prince of Judah. Athaliah moves from Samaria, the capital of the north, to Jerusalem, the capital of the south. Jehoram dies some fifteen years later, and Ahaziah, Jehoram's son with Athaliah, is crowned king.

Some time later, Ahaziah goes to visit his uncle, the king in Samaria. This is an unlucky time to visit, for it's the day of the bloodiest royal coup in the history of the northern kingdom. As Jezebel's body lies in the courtyard, soldiers also kill Ahaziah, the king of Judah; Joram, the king of Israel; and sadly, all seventy of Athaliah's half-brothers.

Back in Jerusalem, Athaliah goes on a rampage. She oversees the killing of all those with royal blood, including her own grandchildren, except one who remains in hiding. That one, Joash, is spirited out of the palace into the temple by the wife of the high priest. During the next seven years, while the boy's existence is kept secret, Athaliah rules her people with a cruel and bloody hand.

When the boy reaches the age of reason, the high priest has him brought back to the palace, along with the spears and shields that had been David's. Armed guards surround the palace as trumpets blast the good news. The high priest crowns the boy and all the people of the land rejoice—except for Athaliah.

Tearing her clothes in an age-honored sign of grief, she shouts the only words credited to her in scripture: "Treason! Treason!"

Minutes later, she is put to death. No one mourns her.

Consider this

One could consider this another evil-woman story, for it surely is, yet with a new twist: a grandmother who has her grandchildren murdered. On our cringe-worthy scale, this action comes in only a bit lower than the mother who ate her son, for it is a particularly demonic action.

Over the years, scholars have searched for a logical reason for her action (if there ever could be one). One would think that she would want to keep her grandchildren safe so they could grow to reign in her stead. Perhaps she killed them because she suspected her rule would come to ruin and didn't want them to see it, but that is not obvious in scripture. Scholar Mayer I. Gruber, among others, suggests that Athaliah tried to centralize power after her son King Ahaziah was murdered (2 Kings 9:27) by Jehu (the same king who had caused Jezebel's death).[54] No warm and comforting grandmother was she, as she oversaw the annihilation of nearly all the potential heirs to the throne. Clearly, no good reason exists for her actions. She joins the legion of those in this world who are simply evil, who have neither heart nor conscience.

One bit of good news is that she was punished for her crimes. Justice was done. Good won over evil. Her little grandson grew to reign over Judah for forty years, and for most of that time, Joash was a strong and faithful leader.

Yet it is hard to shake off her haunting deeds.

What might we learn from Athaliah?

This space is intentionally left blank.

For reflection

1. Although a person may grow up in a negative environment (and it is likely that Athaliah did, with Jezebel and Ahab as parents), being a responsible adult means sorting out good from evil. Why do you think Athaliah was unable or unwilling to do that? How can you?

2. What could have been Athaliah's motivation for destroying all of her remaining heirs?

3. Where is God in this story, especially for the deceased grandchildren?

4. God allowed Jerusalem to be destroyed because its people had sinned, greatly. Could this kind of behavior have caused God's anger?

HULDAH

First responder

▷ **READ HER STORY:** 2 Kings 22:14-20, 2 Chronicles 34:22-28

▷ **CLASSIC MOMENT:** Being consulted by leaders sent by the king so that he might better understand God's word

▷ **LIKELY CHARACTERISTICS:** Prophetic, Devout, Intellectual, Trusted, Direct

▷ **DATA:** 416 words (209 in 2 Kings, 207 in 2 Chronicles)

Who was Huldah?

A prophet[55] from Jerusalem // The woman who spoke the most in 2 Kings and 2 Chronicles // A messenger of God's word // A respected woman // The wife of the "keeper of the wardrobe"[56]

What did Huldah say?

She declared to them, "Thus says the LORD, the God of Israel: Tell the man who sent you to me, 'Thus says the LORD, I will indeed bring disaster on this place and on its inhabitants—all the words of the book that the king of Judah has read. Because they have abandoned me and have made offerings to other gods, so that they have provoked me to anger with all the work of their hands, therefore my wrath will be kindled against this place, and it will not be quenched.' But as to the king of Judah, who sent you to inquire of the Lord, thus shall you say to him, 'Thus says the Lord, the God of Israel: Regarding the words that you have heard, because your heart was penitent, and you humbled yourself before the Lord, when you heard how I spoke against this place, and against its inhabitants, that they should become a desolation and a curse, and because you have torn your clothes and wept before me, I also have heard you, says the Lord. Therefore, I will gather you to your ancestors, and you shall be gathered to your grave in peace; your eyes shall not see all the disaster that I will bring on this place.'" *2 Kings 22:15-20*

She declared to them, "Thus says the Lord, the God of Israel: Tell the man who sent you to me, 'Thus says the Lord: I will indeed bring disaster upon this place and upon its inhabitants, all the curses that are written in the book that was read before the king of Judah. Because they have forsaken me and have made offerings to other gods, so that they have provoked me to anger with all the works of their hands, my wrath will be poured out on this place and will not be quenched.' But as to the king of Judah, who sent you to inquire of the Lord, thus shall you say to him: 'Thus says the Lord, the God of Israel: Regarding the words that you have heard, because your heart was penitent and you humbled yourself before God when you heard his words against this place and its inhabitants, and you have humbled yourself before me, and have torn your clothes and wept before me, I also have heard you, says the Lord. I will gather you to your ancestors and you shall be gathered to your grave in peace; your eyes shall not see all the disaster that I will bring on this place and its inhabitants.'" *2 Chronicles 34:23-28*

Huldah's story

By the time that Huldah speaks (around 630 BCE), the northern part of the once-united Davidic kingdom has been destroyed for almost a hundred years, having fallen to the Assyrians in 722 BCE. Josiah, who has been king of the southern kingdom of Judah since he was eight years old, is seen as a noble king—unlike his father (Amon) and grandfather (Manasseh).

Despite the destruction of Israel and the dysfunctional, idol-worshiping leadership of his family members, Josiah restores the temple in Jerusalem, smashes altars and idols of pagan gods, insists that his people follow the law of Moses, and recognizes the word of God when an ancient scroll is found in the temple.

And that is where the prophet Huldah comes into the picture. After reading the scroll, also called the Book of the Law,[57] King Josiah falls into deep grief (2 Kings 22:11). Realizing that Judah has fallen far short of God's desires and instructions, he immediately dispatches the priest Hilkiah and others to the temple to ask the Lord for more clarity.

They do not go directly to the temple but to Huldah's house in the Second Quarter of Jerusalem.[58] They consult with her there.

Hold it! The king sends them to talk with the Lord at the temple and instead, they seek out and engage Huldah? Big move here.

Clearly, they know Huldah to be a voice of the Lord, or in other words, a prophet. They trust her to give them an accurate reading. She could downplay the whole thing, telling them not to worry. Huldah, however, affirms the worst of what has scared Josiah: the people have not followed God's law and will be destroyed. Moreover, God will do the destroying. But Josiah won't live to see it. Because he has humbled himself, he will be gathered to his grave in peace before the devastation comes (2 Kings: 22:20).

Did her words, or rather the Lord's words, come true? For the most part. Judah was invaded and conquered in 587 BCE. But Josiah had died fighting the Egyptians around 609 BCE. A small blessing: he did not witness firsthand the destruction of Jerusalem.

Consider this

Following horrific stories of women whose demise parallels the disintegration of the monarchy, Huldah's comments come as a welcome relief. Stark as her message may be, she is a truth teller, relaying God's message clearly and without regret.

By speaking God's word, Huldah helped renew the spiritual life of Judah, for Josiah instituted immediate reforms.

Saint Paul once said, "If I proclaim the gospel, this gives me no ground for boasting, for an obligation is laid on me, and woe to me if I do not proclaim the gospel!" (1 Corinthians 9:16). We get the sense that Huldah would have understood words such as these. Woe to us if we do not share what God has told us, for it is both an obligation and an honor.

What might we learn from Huldah?

▷ Do not hold back what you know in your heart.

▷ Discernment is best done with others.

▷ Huldah's vocation as a prophet was key to Israel's understanding of itself.

▷ Sometimes the best advice is given freely, without regard for payment.

For reflection

1. The high priest and others went straight to Huldah's home after King Josiah had asked them to go to the temple and consult the Lord. What qualities must Huldah have possessed to be as well-regarded as she was?

2. Obviously Huldah was an honest person. What would it have been like for her to give the news she did?

3. How did Huldah's words strike you? To what extent are they relevant today?

4. The theme of God punishing those who strayed away from the Law is a common reference in the Old Testament. Compare that theme to Jesus' actions and words in the New Testament.

CHAPTER 13

WOMEN WHO SPEAK IN 1 CHRONICLES

This is a bit of a strange book, and was originally joined with 2 Chronicles, Ezra, and Nehemiah.[59] The chronicler presents the days of the kings, not as a reporter would, but as an op-ed writer might: clearly on the side of King David, as God's chosen leader, leading God's chosen people. And that is, of course, what good storytellers do. They draw us in, strengthen our resolve, and help us know who we are—and why.

By the numbers

Words spoken by women in 1 Chronicles: 6

Number of women who speak: One (the mother of Jabez)

(Note: in 2 Chronicles, 331 words are also spoken by a total of three women. However, since all of them—the queen of Sheba, Athaliah, and Huldah—are profiled in other chapters, there is no separate chapter on 2 Chronicles.)

THE MOTHER OF JABEZ

Post-partum blues

PROFILE: VERY LOW

▷ **READ HER STORY:** 1 Chronicles 4:9

▷ **CLASSIC MOMENT:** Naming her son for her pain in childbirth

▷ **LIKELY CHARACTERISTICS:** Dramatic, Fertile

▷ **DATA:** 6 words

Who was the mother of Jabez?

A mother of several children // A woman who endured a particularly painful childbirth

---

What did the mother of Jabez say?

Jabez was honored more than his brothers; and his mother named him Jabez, saying, **"Because I bore him in pain."** *1 Chronicles 4:9*

The mother of Jabez's story

This woman's story seems a bit odd. She is quoted, all of six words, because she is saying why she named her son Jabez (which in Hebrew means "painful"). Giving birth to Jabez was terribly painful, she says, more so than her other deliveries. Jabez grows to be the most honored of his brethren, thus elevating his mother a bit in Israel's eyes.

However odd it appears, the inclusion of this woman and her difficult delivery helps to make this genealogical list real. After all, the author of Chronicles is writing for Jews who are returning from exile in Babylon. The chronicler is reminding them (and teaching the ones who are learning for the first time) of their identity as children of God. In 1 Chronicles 4, Judah's descendants are being recounted. As one Bible translation points out,[60] this is not a linear compilation of descendants, but rather a broad network of different groups of Judah's descendants.

Consider this

Learning family history is more than learning lists of names, for such history often invokes the odd story or the rare ancestor, such as the mother of Jabez. Many women have pain in childbirth, but they don't normally name their children, "Pain." Despite the strange naming of her son, it seems the mother of Jabez was a good soul and taught her son the ways of the Lord. When he later called out to God for his blessing and protection, God apparently granted his prayer.

Like his mother, Jabez disappears from view after his short utterance. In the last century, Jabez has been rediscovered by the evangelical faith community, but his mother has never emerged from obscurity. We can only wish them both well and hope that Jabez's mother has somehow come to terms with the pain involved in giving birth to this thoughtful child.

What might we learn from the mother of Jabez?

- ▷ Teach your children well.
- ▷ Giving birth can be extraordinarily painful and should not be underestimated.

For reflection

1. We have more questions than answers regarding this mother. We do not know, for example, why Jabez was more honored or honorable than his brothers. We do not know why the birth of Jabez was so painful or why she would choose to name her son using the Hebrew word for pain. What does your intuition tell you about the mother of Jabez?

2. His mother's teachings helped Jabez form a strong faith foundation. How can a mother or grandmother or aunt help young children draw close to God?

3. To what extent, or not, does the mother of Jabez remind you of other mothers in the Bible? What do they have in common? What is different?

CHAPTER 14

WOMEN WHO SPEAK IN ESTHER

One of the most beloved figures in Judeo/Christian history, Esther would be an excellent poker player. Dealt a lovely body and high emotional intelligence, she, over a period of weeks, lays down her other high cards: patience, bravery, and grace. A straight royal flush for an authentic royal—one who fully earns the respect of her people.

By the numbers

Words spoken by women in Esther: 416

Number of women who speak: One (Esther)

ESTHER

An ambassador for her people

▷ **READ ESTHER'S STORY:**
The Book of Esther

▷ **CLASSIC MOMENT:** Asking the king to spare her people and denouncing Haman as their persecutor

▷ **LIKELY CHARACTERISTICS:**
Beautiful, Courageous, Deliberate, Patient, Intelligent, Obedient

▷ **DATA:** 416 words

Who was Esther?

An orphan of the tribe of Benjamin; raised by her cousin Mordecai in Persia (where they were exiled) // A "draftee" into King Ahasuerus's (Xerxes's) harem // A queen // A protector of the Jewish people, saving them from annihilation in Persia //A woman whose actions inspired the Jewish feast of Purim

What did Esther say?

Then Esther spoke to Hathach and gave him a message for Mordecai, saying, **"All the king's servants and the people of the king's provinces know that if any man or woman goes to the king inside the inner court without being called, there is but one law—all alike are to be put to death. Only if the king holds out the golden scepter to someone, may that person live. I myself have not been called to come in to the king for thirty days."** *Esther 4:10-11*

Then Esther said in reply to Mordecai, "Go, gather all the Jews to be found in Susa, and hold a fast on my behalf, and neither eat nor drink for three days, night or day. I and my maids will also fast as you do. After that I will go to the king, though it is against the law; and if I perish, I perish." *Esther 4:15-16*

Then Esther said, "If it pleases the king, let the king and Haman come today to a banquet that I have prepared for the king." *Esther 5:4*

"This is my petition and request: If I have won the king's favor, and if it pleases the king to grant my petition and fulfill my request, let the king and Haman come tomorrow to the banquet that I will prepare for them, and then I will do as the king has said." *Esther 5:7-8*

"If I have won your favor, O king, and if it pleases the king, let my life be given me—that is my petition—and the lives of my people—that is my request. For we have been sold, I and my people, to be destroyed, to be killed, and to be annihilated. If we had been sold merely as slaves, men and women, I would have held my peace; but no enemy can compensate for this damage to the king." *Esther 7:3-4*

Then King Ahasuerus said to Queen Esther, "Who is he, and where is he, who has presumed to do this?" Esther said, "A foe and enemy, this wicked Haman!" *Esther 7:5-6*

"If it pleases the king, and if I have won his favor, and if the thing seems right before the king, and I have his approval, let an order be written to revoke the letters devised by Haman son of Hammedatha the Agagite, which he wrote giving orders to destroy the Jews who are in all the provinces of the king. For how can I bear to see the calamity that is coming on my people? Or how can I bear to see the destruction of my kindred?" *Esther 8:5-6*

"If it pleases the king, let the Jews who are in Susa be allowed tomorrow also to do according to this day's edict, and let the ten sons of Haman be hanged on the gallows." *Esther 9:13*

Esther's story

Esther's wisdom and courage have won her a place in the hearts of many Jewish and non-Jewish women (and men) alike. These comments are but a summary of Esther's story; do not miss reading the book itself.

As the book begins, Esther is living in Persia, where she is being raised by her cousin Mordecai. News comes from the palace that King Ahasuerus is searching for a new queen.

Vashti, the current queen, has been ousted for not obeying the king's orders to "show the peoples and the officials her beauty" during a celebration to commemorate "the great wealth of his kingdom" (Esther 1). Reasons that Vashti might not have appeared: 1) she was tired of entertaining, as the party was at the end of 187 days of feasting; 2) the king's eunuchs arrived to "collect" her, probably somewhat undiplomatically; 3) the king was drunk (the Bible says "merry with wine") and 4) Ahasuerus's order for her to wear her crown might have made her wonder if that was all she would be wearing.

Her refusal embarrasses the king in front of other men, causing him to send word throughout the country that such behavior will not be tolerated and that, "every man should be master in his own house" (Esther 1:22). Vashti disappears. Eventually a net is cast to gather all the beautiful young virgins into the king's harem, and Esther is caught up in the sweep. When her night with Ahasuerus arrives, she apparently pleases him and is named queen.

Soon her cousin Mordecai, sitting on a bench outside the palace gate, overhears two of the king's eunuchs discuss their plans to assassinate Ahasuerus. He tells Esther, who tells the king. The men are hanged, and the event is recorded in the palace books.

Soon after, the king promotes his favorite advisor, Haman, to be his top official and requires that all bow and do obeisance to Haman. But when Haman passes Mordecai on his way home one day, the old Jew refuses, knowing that he is to bow only to God. The Bible says that although Haman is infuriated, he thinks it beneath him to censure Mordecai directly. Rather, he swears to eliminate all Jews throughout the kingdom, and the king actually agrees.

With Jews in deep mourning throughout the country, Mordecai puts on sackcloth and ashes and goes wailing through the city "with a loud and bitter cry" (Esther 4:1). Esther hears of his distress and learns that she and her people are facing genocide. Mordecai then urges her to intervene with the king—but there is a problem. No one, including Esther, is allowed to talk with the king without first being summoned by him. The penalty for violating this protocol is death.

The king still does not know that Esther is Jewish. And in a move that resonates through the ages, she asks for three days of fasting from her fellow Jews. Saying she will fast as well, she agrees to go to the king, "though it is against the law; and if I perish, I perish" (Esther 4:16). Dressed in her royal robes, she stands in the king's hallway, waiting permission to enter. He sees her, summons her, and she invites him and Haman to a party that she will throw in the king's honor.

Puffed up with pride that he will attend, Haman walks home to share the good news with his wife and friends, also telling them about the irritating Mordecai who still refuses to bow when he passes by. They respond: Build a gallows fifty cubits high[61] and hang him!

Meanwhile, King Ahasuerus is haunted by the image of the newly built gallows and cannot sleep. He fights his insomnia by having the palace ledger read to him, hoping that the minutiae will leave him snoring—but jerks to attention when he hears the detailed notation about Mordecai saving him from the earlier assassination attempt.

Realizing that he has never rewarded Mordecai, he asks his servants, "What shall be done for the man whom the king wishes to honor?" (Esther 6:6). Haman, overhearing this, assumes that Ahasuerus wants to honor him and suggests a royal parade through the city.

"Great," replies the king. "Go get Mordecai." And so the tide turns.

The promised party occurs. The king asks Esther again to make her request, and she does, pleading for her own life and that of her fellow Jews. The truth comes out. Ahasuerus is incensed at Haman, and when the king walks away to the palace garden for a minute, Haman throws himself on Esther, begging her forgiveness. Bad goes to worse for Haman, for the king thinks he is sexually assaulting his wife.

A body swings from the gallows that very day—and it is not Mordecai's. Haman has met his match in God's servant Esther.

Consider this

One of only two books in the Bible named after women, this story has caught the imagination and hearts of generations of Jews and Christians. Esther is beautiful, brave, kind, patient, and smart—and uses those gifts to save her people from annihilation. From this event has come the celebration of Purim, a yearly remembrance.

Esther's name (which is *Hadassah* in Hebrew) appears fifty-five times in ten chapters of the book.[62] Surprisingly, God's name is never mentioned. When Esther calls for a time of fasting, one may assume she was praying to God. God must have been guiding her actions so she could save the Jewish population in Persia.

Postscript: The last two chapters of the Book of Esther reveal that Mordecai was promoted within the royal ranks and used that position to solidify his people's gains. Upward of 75,000 enemies of the Jewish people died by the sword. In a sign of respect (may it count for something), no plunder was taken.

It's all about "point of view." Such killings could be seen as good news for the Jewish people who had been carried away in captivity from their sacred land. Some say the Book of Esther should not have been included in the Bible—and indeed, there are additions and deletions made to the Greek version (see the Apocrypha comments on p. 338) to make the story more palatable. Some say it is based on historical events; others say it is fiction, written to help believers keep their faith and culture intact.

Remember that stories do not tell us what is true; they tell us what must be true. Eternal truths dominate Esther's story. Take a minute to reflect on what those truths are.

What might we learn from Esther?

▷ Timing is all-important.

▷ Sometimes we must take personal risks to make a difference.

▷ Our lives are linked to larger communities for which we must care.

▷ There comes a time to stand up and be counted.

For reflection

1. Esther, an orphan raised by her cousin Mordecai, shows remarkable strength of character prior to her selection as queen. What about her was different from the other women in the harem? Why were those traits appealing?

2. The name Esther means "star," and true to form, she played an important role in saving the Jewish people. What other people throughout history compare to Esther?

3. Esther could have lost her life by taking the action she did. Why did she risk it all? Would you risk so much for a cause or people?

4. When have you stood up for your faith and faith community? What pressures did you face and what was your response?

CHAPTER 15

WOMEN WHO SPEAK IN JOB

There is something about Job's wife that is so refreshingly real, especially in the midst of profound epic narratives. Everything is going well for her...until the day it doesn't. She loses everyone and everything important to her, and finds her husband sitting on a garbage heap, being very philosophical about his suffering. In the eleven words that she says, she takes a very different approach.

By the numbers

Words spoken by women in Job: 11

Number of women who speak: One (Job's wife)

JOB'S WIFE

NOT long suffering

PROFILE: LOW

▷ **READ HER STORY:**
Job 2, Job 19:17, Job 31:10

▷ **CLASSIC MOMENT:** Yelling at her husband to curse God and die

▷ **LIKELY CHARACTERISTICS:**
Frustrated, Grief-stricken, Bold, Angry, Cynical

▷ **DATA:** 11 words

Who was Job's wife?

A woman who lived in the land of Uz with her husband Job // A woman who endured the loss of seven sons and three daughters // A witness to unbearable suffering // A spouse in an embroiled and flashy divine dispute

What did Job's wife say?

"Do you still persist in your integrity? Curse God, and die." *Job 2:9*

Job's wife's story

One of the most overlooked women in the Bible, the unnamed wife of Job suffers horrific losses, along with her husband. All of their children (seven sons and three daughters) die in a windstorm; Job becomes leprous and covered with boils; the family's oxen are carried off into captivity; a fire kills thousands of their sheep; some servants are kidnapped; and other servants die by enemy swords.

What Job and his wife do not know is this: all of these losses have been the direct work of the Adversary (*ha satan* in Hebrew—God's prosecuting attorney) with God's knowledge. As the Book of Job notes, "One day the heavenly beings came to present themselves before the LORD, and Satan also came among them" (Job 1:6). God and Satan have a conversation:

> God: What have you been up to, Satan?
>
> Satan: Going to and fro on the earth, and walking up and down on it.
>
> God: Have you considered my servant Job? There is no one like him. He is blameless and upright. He fears me and turns away from evil at every opportunity.
>
> Satan: What do you expect? You've given him everything he has. Take away all that he owns and he will curse you!
>
> God: Very well! Everything in his power belongs to you. Destroy it, but do not hurt Job.

And so calamity falls around Job and his wife, causing them to lose their children, wealth, servants, livestock, and social standing. As God had predicted, though, Job does not curse the Lord; he remains silent—at least initially.

Not so with his wife. In the one instance where she speaks, early on in the story, she confronts her husband as he sits on an ash heap outside the town walls, scraping off his leprous boils with a stray pottery shard. Lashing out, she says, "Do you still persist in your integrity? Curse God, and die."

Hissing back, he says, "You speak as any foolish woman would speak. Shall we receive the good at the hand of God, and not receive the bad?" (Job 2:10).

Ah, marital bliss. And stress. And heartbreak. The Book of Job explores the meaning of life and suffering, questions Job discusses with three male friends. Debated, amongst others, are these possibilities:

- Job has somehow caused his own suffering.

- God has caused it to punish him for some wrong.

- The events are meant to test him.

- There is no benefit in being righteous.

- Suffering is an opportunity to learn.

- His destiny is beyond his control.

In a final fiery blast between God and Job, the latter is silenced when God asks how he—and any human being—can possibly understand the depth and breadth of God's actions. Job understands that he is not being punished nor is God testing him. He sees that his suffering does not have to do with his character but with events beyond his control.

Job repents for trying to box God into human parameters and prays for his friends. He is rewarded with ten new children and double the amount of material goods (fourteen thousand sheep, six thousand camels, a thousand oxen, and a thousand donkeys). Given the birth of ten additional children, and no mention of a new wife, the narrative implies that she is still married to Job and is the mother of the new children.

Consider this

In this classic theological treatise, known across secular and religious spectrums, Job's wife is presented as a fairly minor, snarly, and unfaithful character. What do we really know about her? We know she suffered terribly. Her children had been struck dead; her husband was being punished by God (or so it appeared); her material possessions were gone; and there was no understanding the multiple disasters occurring around her.

Her recorded words to Job indicate spontaneous anger after losing everything. Whether commendable or not, the words are at least understandable and very human.

Job's wife has been criticized by many for appearing punitive and caustic. That may be true, but take a deeper look. Like several other women in scripture, she plays the role of a skeptic. That attitude is not without value, for biblically, it most often belongs to a woman or an "outsider" male, and it often precedes a deeper knowledge[63] of the heart or a major theological shift.

Think of Eve and her action of eating the fruit. While she separates herself from God, she also enables the human race to walk into the wider world. Think of Sarah. Skeptical that God would endow her with a child at age ninety, she laughs—yet that laughter is followed by the birth of a son and the emergence of a nation. Consider the woman at the well, bantering with Jesus. Skeptical at the start of their conversation, she grasps within minutes the real truth that Jesus is the Messiah. Then she runs to share the news with those outside the traditional boundaries of the Jewish faith.

Although Job's wife does not have the enthusiasm that these other women demonstrated, her comments do precede a theological change in the biblical meaning of suffering. Until then, misfortune was considered to be a divine response to immoral deeds. By the end of the Book of Job, it is evident that God is bigger than human understanding, that tragedy can strike anyone, and that God will not abandon us.

What might we learn from Job's wife?

- ▷ Misfortune and illness cause stress for family members.
- ▷ Tempers may explode without warning in the midst of grief.
- ▷ There is a larger picture that we may not understand.
- ▷ The suffering of others is often out of our hands.

For reflection

1. What is your sense of Job's wife? What did she mean by, "Curse God, and die?" How might her despair have directed her comments?

2. Do you think that Job would have heard her if she said something resembling the comments made by his male friends? What purpose did her words serve?

3. Job said his wife spoke "as any foolish woman would." What are your thoughts about his comment? What would have been a better response?

4. Have you, after experiencing great loss, ever said something that you regretted? Have you snapped at a spouse or friend?

CHAPTER 16

WOMEN WHO SPEAK IN THE SONG OF SOLOMON

This is one hot book. Don't miss reading it. Try not to make judgments before you finish.

Here, a woman speaks more than in any other book of the Old and New Testaments, yet the book is credited to Solomon because some say he wrote it.[64] As is pointed out in the next few pages, however, most will be able to see that these statements are clearly composed by a woman, not a man. More importantly, remember the adage on which this book is based: Stories don't tell us what is true. They tell us what must be true.

By the numbers

Words spoken by women in the Song of Solomon: 1,425

Number of women who speak: One (the Shulammite woman)

THE SHULAMMITE WOMAN

PROFILE: LOW

▷ **READ HER STORY:**
The Song of Solomon

▷ **CLASSIC MOMENT:** The deep sensuality expressed throughout makes this epic journey poem a classic in itself

▷ **LIKELY CHARACTERISTICS:**
Passionate, Beautiful, Sensual, Provocative, Eloquent, Loyal

▷ **DATA:** 1,425 words

Who was the Shulammite woman?

The woman who had more words recorded than any other in the Old or New Testaments // A beautiful young woman in love with a shepherd from her homeland // Brought to King Solomon's court by his emissaries to be a part of his harem // A woman who resists the temptations of the royal court and the king to remain loyal to her first love, the shepherd

What did the Shulammite woman say?

Let him kiss me with the kisses of his mouth! For your love is better than wine, your anointing oils are fragrant, your name is perfume poured out; therefore the maidens love you. Draw me after you, let us make haste. The king has brought me into his chambers. We will exult and rejoice in you; we will extol your love more than wine; rightly do they love you. I am black and beautiful, O daughters of Jerusalem, like the tents of Kedar, like the curtains of Solomon. Do not gaze at me because I am dark, because the sun has gazed on me. My mother's sons were angry with me; they made me keeper of the vineyards, but my own vineyard I have not kept! Tell me, you whom my soul loves, where you pasture your flock, where you make it lie down at noon; for why should I be like one who is veiled beside the flocks of your companions? *Song of Solomon 1:2-7*

While the king was on his couch, my nard gave forth its fragrance. My beloved is to me a bag of myrrh that lies between my breasts. My beloved is to me a cluster of henna blossoms in the vineyards of En-gedi. *Song of Solomon 1:12-14*

Ah, you are beautiful, my beloved, truly lovely. Our couch is green; the beams of our house are cedar, our rafters are pine. *Song of Solomon 1:16-17*

I am a rose of Sharon, a lily of the valleys. *Song of Solomon 2:1*

As an apple tree among the trees of the wood, so is my beloved among young men. With great delight I sat in his shadow, and his fruit was sweet to my taste. He brought me to the banqueting house, and his intention toward me was love. Sustain me with raisins, refresh me with apples; for I am faint with love. O that his left hand were under my head, and that his right hand embraced me! I adjure you, O daughters of Jerusalem, by the gazelles or the wild does: do not stir up or awaken love until it is ready! The voice of my beloved! Look, he comes, leaping upon the mountains, bounding over the hills. My beloved is like a gazelle or a young stag. Look, there he stands behind our wall, gazing in at the windows, looking through the lattice. *Song of Solomon 2:3-9*

My beloved speaks and says to me: "Arise, my love, my fair one, and come away; for now the winter is past, the rain is over and gone. The flowers appear on the earth; the time of singing has come, and the voice of the turtledove is heard in our land. The fig tree puts forth its figs, and the vines are in blossom; they give forth fragrance." *Song of Solomon 2:10-13*

My beloved is mine and I am his; he pastures his flock among the lilies. Until the day breathes and the shadows flee, turn, my beloved, be like a gazelle or a young stag on the cleft mountains. *Song of Solomon 2:16-17*

Upon my bed at night I sought him whom my soul loves; I sought him, but found him not; I called him, but he gave no answer. "I will rise now and go about the city, in the streets and in the squares; I will seek him whom my soul loves." I sought him, but found him not. The sentinels found me, as they went about in the city. "Have you seen him whom my soul loves?" Scarcely had I passed them, when I found him whom my soul loves. I held him, and would not let him go until I brought him into my mother's house, and into the chamber of her that conceived me. *Song of Solomon 3:1-4*

I adjure you, O daughters of Jerusalem, by the gazelles or the wild does: do not stir up or awaken love until it is ready! What is that coming up from the wilderness, like a column of smoke, perfumed with myrrh and frankincense, with all the fragrant powders of the merchant? Look, it is the litter of Solomon! Around it are sixty mighty men of the mighty men of Israel, all equipped with swords and expert in war, each with his sword at his thigh because of alarms by night. King Solomon made himself a palanquin from the wood of Lebanon. He made its posts of silver, its back of gold, its seat of purple; its interior was inlaid with love. Daughters of Jerusalem, come out. Look, O daughters of Zion, at King Solomon, at the crown with which his mother crowned him on the day of his wedding, on the day of the gladness of his heart. *Song of Solomon 3:5-11*

Awake, O north wind, and come, O south wind! Blow upon my garden that its fragrance may be wafted abroad. Let my beloved come to his garden, and eat its choicest fruits. *Song of Solomon 4:16*

I slept, but my heart was awake. Listen! my beloved is knocking. *Song of Solomon 5:2*

I had put off my garment; how could I put it on again? I had bathed my feet; how could I soil them? *Song of Solomon 5:3*

My beloved thrust his hand into the opening, and my inmost being yearned for him. I arose to open to my beloved, and my hands dripped with myrrh, my fingers with liquid myrrh, upon the handles of the bolt. I opened to my beloved, but my beloved had turned and was gone. My soul failed me when he spoke. I sought him, but did not find him; I called him, but he gave no answer. Making their rounds in the city the sentinels found me; they beat me, they wounded me, they took away my mantle, those sentinels of the walls. I adjure you, O daughters of Jerusalem, if you find my beloved, tell him this: I am faint with love. *Song of Solomon 5:4-8*

My beloved is all radiant and ruddy, distinguished among ten thousand. His head is the finest gold; his locks are wavy, black as a raven. His eyes are like doves beside springs of water, bathed in milk, fitly set. His cheeks are like beds of spices, yielding fragrance. His lips are lilies, distilling liquid myrrh. His arms are rounded gold, set with jewels. His body is ivory work, encrusted with sapphires. His legs are alabaster columns, set upon bases of gold. His appearance is like Lebanon, choice as the cedars. His speech is most sweet, and he is altogether desirable. This is my beloved and this is my friend, O daughters of Jerusalem. *Song of Solomon 5:10-16*

My beloved has gone down to his garden, to the beds of spices, to pasture his flock in the gardens, and to gather lilies. I am my beloved's and my beloved is mine; he pastures his flock among the lilies. *Song of Solomon 6:2-3*

I am my beloved's, and his desire is for me. Come, my beloved, let us go forth into the fields, and lodge in the villages; let us go out early to the vineyards, and see whether the vines have budded, whether the grape blossoms have opened and the pomegranates are in bloom. There I will give you my love. The mandrakes give forth fragrance, and over our doors are all choice fruits, new as well as old, which I have laid up for you, O my beloved. *Song of Solomon 7:10-13*

O that you were like a brother to me, who nursed at my mother's breast! If I met you outside, I would kiss you, and no one would despise me. I would lead you and bring you into the house of my mother, and into the chamber of the one who bore me. I would give you spiced wine to drink, the juice of my pomegranates. O that his left hand were under my head, and that his right hand embraced me! I adjure you, O daughters of Jerusalem, do not stir up or awaken love until it is ready! *Song of Solomon 8:1-4*

Set me as a seal upon your heart, as a seal upon your arm; for love is strong as death, passion fierce as the grave. Its flashes are flashes of fire, a raging flame. Many waters cannot quench love, neither can floods drown it. If one offered for love all the wealth of one's house, it would be utterly scorned. *Song of Solomon 8:6-7*

I was a wall, and my breasts were like towers; then I was in his eyes as one who brings peace. *Song of Solomon 8:10*

Make haste, my beloved, and be like a gazelle or a young stag upon the mountains of spices! *Song of Solomon 8:14*

The Shulammite woman's story

This book reads a bit like a Shakespeare play. If you sit back in the theater and fight the sometimes-antiquated and bawdy words, you'll miss what the author is trying to portray.

In the Song of Solomon, also known as the Song of Songs, we find themes of passion, romance, love, lust, and loyalty. The young Shulammite woman (pronounced shoo-la-mite) yearns deeply for her lover, freely using erotic and sensual language. Brimming over with desire for him, she describes in great depth her image of them uniting. At one point she goes out looking for him in the night and is beaten by the palace guards. She recovers, then continues to describe her longing.

But the words in this book do not just belong to the woman. The man speaks frequently, telling her how desirable she is, and how much he loves her. Brothers speak as well, as does a mysterious small group, appearing almost like a Greek chorus.

Consider this

Here's the thing: when credit is due, give the credit. The woman in these pages speaks more than any other woman in the Old and New Testaments. Hot, sensual, and evocative language holds sway here—and it is the top word count for a woman in the Bible, excluding the Apocrypha. (Once the Apocrypha is added, a murderer tops the list. Really.)

As one might guess, because of its evocative and sexual words spoken mostly by a woman, the authorship of the Song has been the subject of endless debates. One of two books in the Bible where God is not mentioned, the Song may be the product of a range of poets, writers, and oral storytellers. Others say it came from the pen of Solomon, describing one of his seven hundred marriages.

The longest-held belief regarding authorship is that the writings symbolized the love between God and Israel.[65] Christians likewise saw it as an allegory for the love between Christ and his church. Many Christians also saw the book, and continue to see it, as God's affirmation of the sacrament of marriage and a celebration of the physical expression of love between a man and a woman.

All of those theories may hold truth, yet there is a common thread missing.[66] Many of the thoughts recorded in the poem are not male thoughts. Through common sense and intuition, it becomes obvious that there must have been the hand and heart of a woman involved in expressing at least some of the words.

Upon careful reading and comparing of different threads, this seems the most plausible scenario: the Shulammite woman has been called to Solomon's harem, but desires to be with her true love, a shepherd. She has been away from him and misses him; she searches for him; she pictures him coming for her. She loves him deeply, expressing the most profound levels of personal intimacy and desire.

Raised to an intensity not seen anywhere else in the Bible, a woman's sexual and emotional desires are on full display. Remind yourself that this is sacred literature and consider what new light, if any, that might throw on your understanding of the Bible.

What might we learn from the Shulammite woman?

▷ Listen to your inmost hopes.

▷ Trust in God that the right developments will unfold.

▷ Sexuality is a God-given gift.

▷ Deep love has physical, spiritual, and emotional components.

▷ Love enhances the senses.

For reflection

1. The Shulammite woman's story is a mix of wonderful sensual images. What were your initial impressions as you read her thoughts? Did your first impression remain the same once you had time to consider her story?

2. Does her story—and the number of words recorded—expand or change the meaning of the Bible for you? If so, why and to what extent? If not, why not?

3. How might this story help you see love and passion as gifts from God?

CHAPTER 17

WOMEN WHO SPEAK IN JEREMIAH

Imagine yourself volunteering to work in a soup kitchen, dishing up soup to those who have little. You know it's good soup; you've spent all morning helping to make it. It upsets you, then, to hear a hungry woman say, "This food tastes like garbage!"

Maybe the soup is bad. Maybe it is not what she would have chosen. But her options are limited, and she is angry to be on the receiving end of the soup line, having to eat whatever is given her or go hungry.

The women of Pathros are a bit like that, with almost everything out of their control. When Jeremiah tells them they should return to Jerusalem and that God will care for them, they've had it. They are grief-stricken, feeling as though God has let them down. They've found a goddess that just might do a better job. So they are terribly insulting to the prophet Jeremiah, linking him to the God they connect with their hunger and grief. Off with your head, Jeremiah![67]

By the numbers

Words spoken by women in Jeremiah: 42

Number of women who speak: One group (the wives and women of Pathros)

THE WIVES AND WOMEN OF PATHROS

▷ **READ THEIR STORY:** Jeremiah 44

▷ **CLASSIC MOMENT:** Defying God by worshiping the "Queen of Heaven"

▷ **LIKELY CHARACTERISTICS:** Defiant, Tenacious, Proud, Independent, Polytheistic

PROFILE: VERY LOW, FELIX THE CAT IS BETTER KNOWN

▷ **DATA:** 42 words

Who were the wives and women of Pathros?

Women who fled from Judah to Pathros in Egypt // Women who took up the worship of an alternate goddess

What did the wives and women of Pathros say?

Then all the men who were aware that their wives had been making offerings to other gods, and all the women who stood by, a great assembly, all the people who lived in Pathros in the land of Egypt, answered Jeremiah: "As for the word that you have spoken to us in the name of the LORD, we are not going to listen to you. Instead, we will do everything that we have vowed, make offerings to the queen of heaven and pour out libations to her, just as we and our ancestors, our kings and our officials, used to do in the towns of Judah and in the streets of Jerusalem. We used to have plenty of food, and prospered, and saw no misfortune. But from the time we stopped making offerings to the queen of heaven and pouring out libations to her, we have lacked everything and have perished by the sword and by famine." And the women said, **"Indeed we will go on making offerings to the queen of heaven and pouring out libations to her; do you think that we made cakes for her, marked with her image, and poured out libations to her without our husbands' being involved?"** *Jeremiah 44:15-19*

Alternate reading: And then the women chimed in: **"Yes! Absolutely! We're going to keep at it, offering sacrifices to the Queen of Heaven and pouring out offerings to her. Aren't our husbands behind us? They like it that we make goddess cookies and pour out our offerings to her."** *Jeremiah 44:19* (Eugene H. Peterson, *The Message*)

The story of the wives and women of Pathros

Reading the alternate lesson above can't help but make one laugh, with its descriptor of "goddess cookies." Laughing, however, is far from what the women of Pathros are doing when they confront the prophet Jeremiah. In Jeremiah 44, the prophet (an important but never-popular-in-his-time religious leader), upbraids the Hebrew population which has fled Jerusalem after its destruction in 587–586 BCE despite God's admonition to stay. (Interestingly, Jeremiah's people kidnapped him and forced him to accompany them to Egypt, where they, apparently, still did not like him.)

Now, living as refugees in Egypt, they still worship God—but also the "Queen of Heaven." This goddess is named as Asherah in the New Revised Standard Version, but identified as Ashtoreth in other credible sources.[68] Jeremiah is incensed, noting (again) that fidelity to God is the foundation on which the human/divine relationship is based. The women circle around him as he tells them that God will bring even the remnants of Judah (them) to an end because of their idolatry.

Shouting back, the people say it doesn't matter—that their lives were better before King Josiah's efforts stopped the worship of Baal and Ashtoreth

(2 Kings 23:1-30). Putting an exclamation point on those words are the women of Pathros: "Do you think we did it on our own? We were all together in praying to the Queen of Heaven, for she is on our side! And we will keep doing it!"

Consider this

Fleeing one's home in time of war is a heartbreaking last resort. Victims don't leave for trivial reasons—because the price of food is too high. They run for their lives, in poverty, often alone, always in the shadows of death and destruction.

And in those great shadows, the women of Pathros still believed in God (most likely), but other gods and goddesses must have seemed like extra protection—especially the Queen of Heaven, who was said to increase fertility.

But looks can be deceiving. Alternate gods, or "comforters," can seem like an improvement, initially appearing to better our quality of life in a difficult time. In our own day we substitute contemporary "gods" such as alcohol, drugs, over-consumption, or the love of money. Long term, these are dead-end temptations that often make things worse.

Jeremiah knows that. Even in times of stress—especially in times of stress—he says, "Don't abandon God, or God will abandon you."

Even with all the wagons circled around Jeremiah, there may be an upside here that has been historically overlooked. As noted earlier, the women believed they had experienced more blessings when they were still praying to other gods, specifically the Queen of Heaven. Scholar Kathleen M. O'Connor, in *The Women's Bible Commentary*,[69] suggests they may have seen the Queen as connected to the God of Israel and that the women's intent was not ill-conceived. As "resourceful, independent women with their own subculture," O'Connor says the women opened the door to conversation as "religious agents, taking worship into their own hands, as are many women today." Some contemporary researchers suggest that Asherah was Yahweh's companion, and that ancient Israel prayed to both.[70] While that theory is unorthodox, it sheds light on feminine aspects of the divine.

In contemporary society, the phrase "Queen of Heaven" is one often attributed to Mary, the mother of Jesus—who for many is not an alternative to God but an approachable part of the faith story.

The open question here is whether this step of the wives and women of Pathros is a step forward—laying the groundwork, albeit unintentionally, for a later Christian devotional approach to the divine—or a misstep away from the one true living Lord. Either way, the last group of women to speak in the Old Testament exhibits some of the same qualities as did the first woman, Eve. Like the paradox of Eve's choice to leave the garden, these women aren't going back.

What might we learn from the wives and women of Pathros?

▷ Carefully examine other people's suggestions about what to believe.

▷ Keep and protect your faith.

▷ Surround yourself with people who share the same values.

▷ Respect the sacred ground of your ancestors.

▷ Use tradition, scripture, and reason when examining moral choices.

▷ Do not make anything called "goddess cookies." Stick with communion bread if you must bake.

For reflection

1. Why were the women of Pathros singled out by Jeremiah? What power did they have?

2. What motivated the women of Pathros to turn to the "Queen of Heaven?" What spiritual and emotional needs were being met? How do you understand their actions? Were they wrong?

3. Would you have done the same in their circumstance?

4. Have you ever held onto a belief for too long and regretted it? What did you learn? Where is God in the process of letting go of actions or beliefs that may be harmful in the long run? Conversely, how does God help expand our thinking?

5. How do you understand feminine aspects of the divine, knowing that God is too infinite for the human mind to fully grasp?

CHAPTER 18

WOMEN WHO SPEAK IN DANIEL

In the book of Daniel are several tales: Three men thrown into a blazing furnace and coming out unharmed, Daniel getting thrown to the lions and emerging without a scratch, and the jaw-dropping narrative of words mysteriously emerging on palace walls.

Behind the scenes, however, is a woman who speaks on only one evening—the night on which she tries desperately to save her son. In the midst of corruption, she seeks the truth. Sadly, the truth speaks volumes.[71]

DANIEL

By the numbers

Words spoken by women in Daniel: 104

Number of women who speak: One (King Belshazzar's mother)

KING BELSHAZZAR'S MOTHER

The Sherlock Holmes of the Bible

PROFILE: VERY LOW

▷ **READ HER STORY:** Daniel 5

▷ **CLASSIC MOMENT:**
Recommending Daniel to her son

▷ **LIKELY CHARACTERISTICS:**
Knowledgeable, Calm, Forthright,
Wise, Assertive

▷ **DATA:** 104 words

Who was King Belshazzar's mother?

Once the Queen of Babylon, married to King Nebuchadnezzar // The current queen-mother, mother of King Belshazzar // An influential woman of the court who remembered Daniel's reputation // The last woman to have her words recorded in the Old Testament

What did King Belshazzar's mother say?

The queen, when she heard the discussion of the king and his lords, came into the banqueting hall. The queen said, **"O king, live forever! Do not let your thoughts terrify you or your face grow pale. There is a man in your kingdom who is endowed with a spirit of the holy gods. In the days of your father he was found to have enlightenment, understanding, and wisdom like the wisdom of the gods. Your father, King Nebuchadnezzar, made him chief of the magicians, enchanters, Chaldeans, and diviners, because an excellent spirit, knowledge, and understanding to interpret dreams, explain riddles, and solve problems were found in this Daniel, whom the king named Belshazzar. Now let Daniel be called, and he will give the interpretation."**
Daniel 5:10-12

Belshazzar's mother's story

Be prepared for a few chills down your back, as this event is one of the spookier occurrences in the Bible, and delightfully so. As the curtain opens, Belshazzar (pronounced Bell-sha-zer, with the accent on the middle syllable), king of Babylon and son of Nebuchadnezzar, is in the midst of a bawdy and raucous party, surrounded by a thousand of his lords, wives, and concubines. Since the king was "drinking wine in the presence of the thousand," it is safe to assume that wine flowed freely for all the guests (Daniel 5:1).

Under the influence, great feats of Babylon were no doubt toasted, including what many considered one of its finest moments: laying siege to Judah by destroying the temple and stealing its treasures.

"Bring in the chalices," orders Belshazzar. "Let us drink from the cups of our enemies!"

Praising the gods of gold and silver, bronze and iron, wood and stone, the partygoers lift the sacred vessels to their lips. And immediately, a hand seems to emerge from a dark corner of the room, writing on the wall with long and elegant strokes. With his knees knocking together and his face growing pale, Belshazzar is terrified, unable to understand the mysterious writing.

"Bring in the magicians," he cries. "Bring in the wise men! Get anyone who can read this writing and tell me what it means!"

"Ahem! Ahem!" Ponder, grunt, mumble. The seers are unable to tell the king the meaning of the foreign words.

And then the door to the banquet hall opens, allowing the king's mother to sweep in, as only queen mothers do. She begs her son to call on Daniel, the faithful Jewish visionary who guided her husband through many trials, including hallucinations, dreams, and insanity.

Daniel, now an old man, is found. Grimacing, he reads the words on the wall, "MENE, MENE, TEKEL, PARSIN." (Read it for yourself: Many, many, tek-el, parson.)

"God has numbered the days of your kingdom," he translates. "You have been weighed on the scales and found wanting, and your kingdom will be divided between the Medes and the Persians."

That very night, Belshazzar is killed, and half the kingdom is given to Darius the Mede.

Consider this

Mothers are often the keepers of history. Belshazzar's mother remembers that Daniel had given the king a sense of order and God's presence through his difficult trials. She had seen Daniel and his friends walk through flames and not be singed; she had seen hungry lions lie down before him when he was thrown to them for food. She knows he is a holy man, one of God's people. And like most mothers, she wants the best for her son.

She discovers what so many parents sadly find out: the actions of their grown children are no longer under their control. Most mothers raise their children with the best of intentions, devoting their heart and soul to their offspring. Yet sometimes, children take another path. Some make wrong decisions and break the law. Others engage in bad habits. And still others are killed or harmed through no fault of their own.

Only parents who have lost a child can rightfully know the depth of pain that a mother or father feels in such an instance. Unfortunately, Belshazzar's mother is witness to a triple nightmare: the handwriting on the wall, Daniel's ensuing prophecy, and the death of her son.

What might we learn from King Belshazzar's mother?

▷ While the upbringing of a child does matter, the decisions made by grown children are theirs and theirs alone.

▷ Stay in contact with those people you know who have special gifts.

▷ Although a friend's message may be unwelcome, it is good to seek advice, especially when things are out of control.

For reflection

1. What kind of woman do you think Belshazzar's mother was? Wise, loving, protective or self-driven and thinking only of what was best for her family?

2. Have you, or someone you have known, lost a child? How do people come to grips with that kind of tragedy? Where is God in that process?

3. What power did Belshazzar's mother have? Did she use it well or badly?

DANIEL

THE WOMEN WHO SPEAK IN THE APOCRYPHA

"Give me strength today, O Lord God!" —Judith

In the Apocrypha exist some of the most fascinating, honest, and upright women in the Bible. Do not miss reading their stories, or you will miss some spectacular women—alternately solving problems, risking their lives, committing murder, and being brilliant anchors of faith for their children.

Here we find Judith, the woman who speaks the most in the Bible. Given that women in the Bible say about 14,000 words total—out of approximately 1.1 million words in the Bible, including the Apocrypha—Judith's approximately 2,700 words account for almost twenty percent of total words spoken by women.

In some ways, the women of the Apocrypha are easier to understand than other biblical women, because their stories are longer and more detail is given. The last story is especially heartbreaking. Be forewarned.

CHAPTER 19

WOMEN WHO SPEAK IN TOBIT

This is a book not to miss. Ordinary people deal with extraordinary suffering, turn to God, find redemption, and know both grief and joy as their children mature. Four women speak in Tobit—a good number, particularly because the book is relatively short.

TOBIT

By the numbers

Words spoken by women in Tobit: 531

Number of women who speak: Four (Anna, maid of Raguel, Sarah, Edna)

ANNA

"My child has perished!"

PROFILE: SNAKE-BELLY LOW, UNFORTUNATELY

▷ **READ ANNA'S STORY:**
The Book of Tobit, Apocrypha

▷ **CLASSIC MOMENT:**
When her son returns home after she assumed he was dead

▷ **LIKELY CHARACTERISTICS:**
Hardworking, Feisty, Pessimistic, Cranky, Anxious

▷ **DATA:** 151 words

Who was Anna?

The mother of one son, Tobias // The wife of Tobit // A weaver who supported her family after Tobit went blind // A grandmother to seven grandsons // A refugee from Galilee, living in Nineveh

What did Anna say?

"...it was given to me as a gift in addition to my wages." But I did not believe her, and told her to return it to the owners. I became flushed with anger against her over this. Then she replied, **"Where are your acts of charity? Where are your righteous deeds? These things are known about you!"** *Tobit 2:14*

"Why is it that you have sent my child away? Is he not the staff of our hand as he goes in and out before us? Do not heap money upon money, but let it be a ransom for our child. For the life that is given to us by the Lord is enough for us." *Tobit 5:18-20*

"My child has perished and is no longer among the living....Woe to me, my child, the light of my eyes, that I let you make the journey." *Tobit 10:4, 5*

She answered him, "Be quiet yourself! Stop trying to deceive me! My child has perished." *Tobit 10:7*

When she caught sight of him coming, she said to his father, "Look, your son is coming, and the man who went with him!" *Tobit 11:6*

Then Anna ran up to her son and threw her arms around him, saying, "Now that I have seen you, my child, I am ready to die." And she wept. *Tobit 11:9*

Anna's story

A nna comes to life within the larger book of Tobit, which is told by her husband (Tobit) in first-person narrative. The main characters: a magical fish (not identified gender-wise, thankfully, so not fish-profiled here), a demon named Asmodeus (male), an angel named Raphael (male), and a widow named Sarah. The latter has married seven times, only to have all seven husbands die after they have taken their wedding vows but before diving into the marriage bed. Entering the bridal chamber seems to have spelled their doom.

Anna and her family are refugees in Nineveh, exiled from Israel after its conquest by the Assyrians. They are short of money, because while burying a fellow Jew (as a good deed), Tobit was blinded when bird droppings fell into his eyes.

In this time of need, Tobit sends their son Tobias to a distant village to reclaim some money he has put in safekeeping there, while Anna earns money as a weaver. Yet after four years of Tobit's blindness, stress has so crippled this family that almost any event causes pain and recrimination. When Anna is given the gift of a goat for her good work as a weaver and brings it home—no doubt feeling affirmed and useful—Tobit accuses her of stealing the goat, and he becomes despondent.

TOBIT

311

When son Tobias leaves, upon the direction of Tobit, Anna breaks down as well. Her son is the one part of her life that is unharmed and whole, and she is filled with much anticipatory grief. She expects him back in a matter of days; he is gone for two weeks. Sick with worry and sure that Tobias is dead, she lashes out at Tobit, accusing him of killing her son.

Meanwhile Tobias has met and married "take-your-chances" Sarah. He survived his wedding night with the intervention of the angel Raphael, whom God sent in answer to Tobit and Sarah's separate prayers for help. Note that Raphael enlisted some assistants from both the animal and the fish kingdoms. A dog accompanies Tobias and Raphael on their journey, and the remains of a magic fish both repel the demon and heal Tobit's eyes, restoring his vision.

Imagine Anna's joy when her beloved Tobias walks up the road. Her joy is compounded over the years with the birth of seven grandsons, known in that time to be an extraordinarily strong sign of divine blessing.

Consider this

How many of us walk into situations we haven't bargained for? One spouse loses a job and the other becomes the sole supporter, one partner becomes ill and needs more physical assistance than the other can give, or one partner becomes depressed and the other worries and worries.

Anna and Tobit meet many of these challenges successfully, albeit painfully, and their marriage takes on added joy once their son returns home and Tobit's sight is restored. Family harmony and good fortune are symbolized, in the end, by Tobias being able to bury both his parents and Sarah's. The parents die normally of old age and are not preceded in death by their children. Everything is peaceful, and the young couple has time to spend with each set of parents before they die. The family unit, and their future, is secure. Strong faith carries the day.

What might we learn from Anna?

▷ Life can be extraordinarily difficult at times, but God's angels have us in their charge.

▷ Patience and optimism are hard to maintain when illness and stress undermine the family unit.

▷ Sometimes it is easier to be pessimistic than to be optimistic.

▷ Trust God that you will be able to survive should the worst occur.

▷ Prayer is a pathway forward.

▷ Put magic fish to work whenever you find them.

For reflection

1. Anna supports the family and does it well, yet Tobit accuses her of stealing when she comes home with a bonus. What do you make of Anna's reaction (Tobit 2:14)? Why does Tobit accuse her? Might it have to do with his unease at the change in roles?

2. Anna argues that the family has enough money on which to survive. Tobit disagrees, telling Tobias how to recover money that was set aside many years ago. Tobias does what Tobit wants. Have you experienced any loved ones going into danger, against your better judgment? Where was God in that experience? What helped you get through it?

3. Understandably, Anna is pessimistic and afraid to trust, for she has lost a great deal. When her son is missing, she fears he is dead. Why is it easier for her to see the worst than to hope for the best?

4. The steady hand behind the angel Raphael, of course, is God. Where do you see the Holy Spirit working in this story?

▷ **READ HER STORY:** Tobit 3:7-9

▷ **CLASSIC MOMENT:**
Viciously accusing Sarah of murder

▷ **LIKELY CHARACTERISTICS:**
Vengeful, Opinionated, Bold, Terrified

▷ **DATA:** 52 words

Who was the maid of Raguel?

A house servant // A woman under stress // A woman working in a difficult situation

What did the maid of Raguel say?

"You are the one who kills your husbands! See, you have already been married to seven husbands and have not borne the name of a single one of them. Why do you beat us? Because your husbands are dead? Go with them! May we never see a son or daughter of yours!" *Tobit 3:8-9*

The maid of Raguel's story

Most people prefer a quiet and safe workplace. That is not the case for this poor maid, for she works for a man in whose home seven husbands have been killed. All of the men die as they approach the daughter, Sarah, on their wedding night.

This outspoken maid has, most likely, helped to prepare the household for seven wedding celebrations. Perhaps a new dress had to be made each time. On every wedding night, the groom died and had to be carried out. The bride needed comfort, seven times. Perhaps the wedding chamber needed a freshening after each deathly struggle. And given that murder is rarely a silent crime, this servant may have overheard terribly brutal noises.

Clearly, the maid is close to the edge (with good reason). And perhaps it is not just the husbands who are at risk of death or injury, for she says, "Why do you beat us? Because your husbands are dead?" (Tobit 3:9).

Consider this

No wonder this maid spoke such harsh words about Sarah. Comments like hers were not normally tolerated by those in charge, but even the most skeptical of readers will admit that, here in the House of Seven Deceased Grooms, life is not normal.

Sarah becomes miserable after the maid's remarks. She goes upstairs to hang herself but then realizes such a move would only add to her father's burdens, for he loves her dearly. See the next story for her comments.

What might we learn from the maid of Raguel?

▷ On-the-job stress takes more of a toll than we realize.

▷ Fear often casts its voice in anger.

▷ Those we serve may be carrying heavy burdens, as may be those who serve us.

▷ We may hurt those around us more than we know.

For reflection

1. The maid of Raguel blamed Sarah for the murders, indicating that she didn't make a distinction between a demon committing the crimes and Sarah committing them; she just wanted Sarah gone. From her position, what would it have been like to work in that situation?

2. Does it make a difference if it was a demon responsible for the fate of the seven men? The Book of Tobit does not say if the demon was outside of Sarah's body or not; perhaps it was through her hands—inadvertent poison?!—that the demon worked.[72] What do you think about the possibility of demon possession?

3. Have you ever been in a work situation that seemed intolerable? What were your actions? What were the maid's options in this unbearable situation? Where is God's hand for this woman?

4. Sarah went to hang herself, based on the maid's withering criticism. Have you ever underestimated the power that your words had?

SARAH

"No rope for me"

PROFILE: LOW

▷ **READ HER STORY:**
Tobit 3:7-17; 6-8; 10-12; 14:3

▷ **CLASSIC MOMENT:** Experiencing a demon kill seven of her husbands

▷ **LIKELY CHARACTERISTICS:**
Sensible, Brave, Beautiful, Temporarily suicidal, Innocent, Sincere, Faithful

▷ **DATA:** 208 words

Who was Sarah?

The only child of Raguel and Edna // Wife to seven husbands, all killed by the demon Asmodeus // A woman who marries her kinsman Tobias // Daughter-in-law to Tobit and Anna // Eventually the mother of seven sons

What did Sarah say?

"Never shall they reproach my father, saying to him, 'You had only one beloved daughter but she hanged herself because of her distress.' And I shall bring my father in his old age down in sorrow to Hades. It is better for me not to hang myself, but to pray the Lord that I may die and not listen to these reproaches anymore." *Tobit 3:10*

"Blessed are you, merciful God! Blessed is your name forever; let all your works praise you forever. And now, Lord, I turn my face to you, and raise my eyes toward you. Command that I be released from the earth and not listen to such reproaches any more. You know, O Master, that I am innocent of any defilement with a man, and that I have not disgraced my name or the name of my father in the land of my exile. I am my father's only child; he has no other child to be his heir; and he has no close relative or other kindred for whom I should keep myself as wife. Already seven husbands of mine have died. Why should I still live? But if it is not pleasing to you, O Lord, to take my life, hear me in my disgrace." *Tobit 3:11-15*

And they both said, "Amen, Amen." *Tobit 8:8*

Sarah's story

What a nightmare for Sarah...and even worse for her seven grooms. According to the Book of Tobit, Asmodeus, a powerful demon, loves Sarah and will not allow any man to approach her in marriage. Seven times she has married, and seven times her betrothed has died within her chamber.

After Sarah hears the maid's terrible words of accusation about their deaths, she vows to kill herself. Yet because of the love she has for her father Raguel, she, thankfully, rejects suicide. In a heartbreaking prayer, she asks God to take her if it be pleasing to him. She asserts her innocence and speaks of her shame, asking God to at least hear her pain.

At the same moment, Tobit is praying as well. He does not blame God for his circumstances but rather asks for redemption. God hears both Sarah and Tobit—sending Raphael, one of seven archangels, to the rescue of both through a successful marriage between Sarah and Tobit's son, Tobias.

In a bizarre juxtaposition (Tobit 8:9), Sarah's father Raguel digs a grave for what he thinks will be the next groom to die (Tobias) at the same time that Sarah is giving thanks to God for new hope.

The angel Raphael saves the couple by leading Tobias to a magic fish whose inner organs not only fend off the demon, thus saving Tobias, but also eventually are used to cure his father, Tobit, of blindness!

Asmodeus, the demon, is sent fleeing to Egypt, where he is chased down by Raphael and bound powerless, no longer able to kill. And Sarah and Tobias? They live, as the story goes, happily ever after, producing seven sons, a propitious number.

Consider this

Sarah finds redemption. Living with a situation completely out of her control, God provides her with a husband—and an angel to ensure his survival—as well as their eventual peace, health, and offspring.

And Tobit finds redemption, living with a situation out of his control: blindness. God provides healing, restoration, and a renewed life for him.

The prayers of Sarah and Tobit—uttered separately and without knowledge of the other—are blended into one story of promise through the angelic messenger of God. Divine economy, indeed.

What might we learn from Sarah?

- ▷ Keep the faith, even in desperate circumstances.
- ▷ Faithfulness to God is always rewarded (sometimes in this life, sometimes in the next).
- ▷ Continue to pray, even when all seems hopeless.
- ▷ Be ready to move when the time is right.
- ▷ It can be inconvenient when a demon falls in love with you.

For reflection

1. Sarah experienced much terror and anguish in her life. How did she keep her sanity?

2. Raguel had his servants dig Tobias's grave at the same time that Sarah was giving thanks to God. How does one maintain a sense of hope and expectation like Sarah did, without giving into negative thoughts as did Raguel? Or was he justified in thinking the grave would be needed?

3. With the demon under control, Sarah was free to love her spouse and move on with life. Have you ever experienced such a demon in your life? What shape did it take? Were/are you successful in managing it?

TOBIT

EDNA

"Take courage, my daughter"

PROFILE: LOW

▷ **READ HER STORY:** Tobit 7; 8:19-21; 10:7-13; 14:13

▷ **CLASSIC MOMENT:** Comforting her daughter Sarah on her wedding night

▷ **LIKELY CHARACTERISTICS:** Gentle, Courteous, Sensitive, Compassionate, Selfless, Brave

▷ **DATA:** 120 words

Who was Edna?

The wife of Raguel and mother of Sarah // Eventually mother-in-law to Tobias // A courageous woman

What did Edna Say?

"Where are you from, brothers?" *Tobit 7:3*

"Do you know our kinsman Tobit?" *Tobit 7:4*

"Is he in good health?" *Tobit 7:4*

"Take courage, my daughter; the Lord of heaven grant you joy in place of your sorrow. Take courage, my daughter." *Tobit 7:16*

"My child and dear brother, the Lord of heaven bring you back safely, and may I live long enough to see children of you and of my daughter Sarah before I die. In the sight of the Lord I entrust my daughter to you; do nothing to grieve her all the days of your life. Go in peace, my child. From now on I am your mother and Sarah is your beloved wife. May we all prosper together all the days of our lives." *Tobit 10:12*

Edna's story

This woman has been to hell and back, yet she finds the inner strength to comfort and guide her daughter on two occasions: when Sarah is facing her eighth wedding night and when it is time for her beloved daughter to leave home. Note the verbal versus physical contrast here, as she takes her daughter to the bridal chamber: "She wept for her daughter. Then, wiping away the tears, she said, 'Take courage, my daughter'" (Tobit 7:16).

Wiping away tears. Being brave. Letting her go and hoping for the best, praying that her heart would not be broken again. No doubt Sarah had cried in her mother's arms with each loss, yet Edna still finds the strength to encourage her, to believe in life over death, in sanity over chaos.

Edna repeats that strength two weeks later, for Tobias insists on returning to Nineveh with Sarah. "In the sight of God, I entrust my daughter to you," she says. "Do not grieve her in any way, and I hope to see her and my grandchildren before I die."

Consider this

Edna has been her daughter's anchor—practical, articulate, and most of all, loving. Because she loves so deeply, she is able to both comfort her daughter in sorrow and celebrate with her in joy, supporting Sarah as she moves away with her new husband.

And here is some extra good news: back in Nineveh, Tobit realizes that the city will soon fall and urges his son to move back to Media to keep his family safe. When Tobit and Anna die, Tobias buries them next to each other and then moves to Media, as his father advised, no doubt making Edna ecstatic. (By this time, Edna probably was rested, for burying seven son-in-laws must have been exhausting.)

Later, Tobias is able to bury Raguel and Edna as well, in a passing of the generations. Everything works out better than anyone, save God, could have guessed.

What might we learn from Edna?

 ▷ Even when we are surrounded by chaos, it is possible to find strength to keep going.

 ▷ Edna stayed strong for her daughter through both suffering and joy; such consistency is difficult, but is the way of love.

 ▷ It is better to encourage those we love than to dig their graves.

 ▷ God will reward patience.

 ▷ Know when it is the right time to let your children go.

TOBIT

For reflection

1. Edna showed great compassion to both her daughter and future son-in-law. She welcomed Tobias and knew he might well be killed, but all she could do was shut the bedroom door and pray. Have you ever been in a situation where danger appeared imminent to loved ones and there seemed to be little you could do?

2. The loss of Sarah's seven husbands must have been almost as distressing for Edna as it was for Sarah. How does one find the strength to pray and give courage to another in such a mutual time of distress?

3. It is easy to underestimate the power of prayer. Where do you see the power of prayer in the Book of Tobit?

4. Being a good mother means knowing when to let go. How and when did Edna let go appropriately? What other women in the Bible were able to also let go at the right time? How might you do the same?

CHAPTER 20

WOMEN WHO SPEAK IN JUDITH

Shakespeare cannot top this drama—and no fully educated person should miss it, for it is one of intrigue, faith, and action. A widow who might have stayed at home and dressed in black for the rest of her days, Judith instead risks both her neck and reputation to save her people—and comes home with a special treat.

JUDITH

By the numbers

Words spoken by women in Judith: 2,689

Number of women who speak: One (Judith)

JUDITH

Head and shoulders above

PROFILE: MODERATE

▷ **READ HER STORY:**
The Book of Judith in the Apocrypha

▷ **CLASSIC MOMENT:**
Beheading King Holofernes

▷ **LIKELY CHARACTERISTICS:**
Brave, Beautiful, Profound, Outspoken, Decisive, Intelligent, Lethal

▷ **DATA:** 2,689 words

Who was Judith?

The woman who speaks more than any other woman in the Bible // A wealthy land-owning widow of the city of Bethulia // A faithful follower of God, determined to save her people // A person of great prayer and spiritual insight // The only woman in the Bible who pleads with God to bless her lies

What did Judith say?

"Listen to me, rulers of the people of Bethulia! What you have said to the people today is not right; you have even sworn and pronounced this oath between God and you, promising to surrender the town to our enemies unless the Lord turns and helps us within so many days. Who are you to put God to the test today, and to set yourselves up in the place of God in human affairs? You are putting the Lord Almighty to the test, but you will never learn anything! You cannot plumb the depths of the human heart or understand the workings of the human mind; how do you expect to search out God, who made all these things, and find out his mind or comprehend his thought? No, my brothers, do not anger the Lord our God. For if he does not choose to help us within these five days, he has power to protect us within any time he pleases, or even to destroy us in the presence of our enemies. Do not try to bind the purposes of the Lord our God; for God is not like a human being, to be threatened, or like a mere mortal, to be won over by pleading. Therefore, while we wait for his deliverance, let us call upon him to help us, and he will hear our voice if it pleases him. For never in our generation, nor in these present days, has there been any tribe or family or people or town of ours that worships gods made with hands, as was done in days gone by. That was why our ancestors were handed over to the sword and to pillage, and so they suffered a great catastrophe before our enemies. But we know no other god but him, and so we hope that he will not disdain us or any of our nation. For if we are captured, all Judea will be captured and our sanctuary will be plundered; and he will make us pay for its desecration with our blood. The slaughter of our kindred and the captivity of the land and the desolation of our inheritance—all this he will bring on our heads among the Gentiles, wherever we serve as slaves; and we shall be an offense and a disgrace in the eyes of those who acquire us. For our slavery will not bring us into favor, but the Lord our God will turn it to dishonor. Therefore, my brothers, let us set an example to our kindred, for their lives depend upon us, and the sanctuary—both the temple and the altar—rests upon us. In spite of everything let us give thanks to the Lord our God, who is putting us to the test as he did our ancestors. Remember what he did with Abraham, and how he tested Isaac, and what happened to Jacob in Syrian Mesopotamia, while he was tending the sheep of Laban, his mother's brother. For he has not tried us with fire, as he did them, to search their hearts, nor has he taken vengeance on us; but the Lord scourges those who are close to him in order to admonish them." *Judith 8:11-27*

"Listen to me. I am about to do something that will go down through all generations of our descendants. Stand at the town gate tonight so that I may go out with my maid; and within the days after which you have promised to surrender the town to our enemies, the Lord will deliver Israel by my hand. Only, do not try to find out what I am doing; for I will not tell you until I have finished what I am about to do." *Judith 8:32-34*

"O Lord God of my ancestor Simeon, to whom you gave a sword to take revenge on those strangers who had torn off a virgin's clothing to defile her, and exposed her thighs to put her to shame, and polluted her womb to disgrace her; for you said, 'It shall not be done'—yet they did it; so you gave up their rulers to be killed, and their bed, which was ashamed of the deceit they had practiced, was stained with blood, and you struck down slaves along with princes, and princes on their thrones. You gave up their wives for booty and their daughters to captivity, and all their booty to be divided among your beloved children who burned with zeal for you and abhorred the pollution of their blood and called on you for help. O God, my God, hear me also, a widow. For you have done these things and those that went before and those that followed. You have designed the things that are now, and those that are to come. What you had in mind has happened; the things you decided on presented themselves and said, 'Here we are!' For all your ways are prepared in advance, and your judgment is with foreknowledge.

"Here now are the Assyrians, a greatly increased force, priding themselves in their horses and riders, boasting in the strength of their foot soldiers, and trusting in shield and spear, in bow and sling. They do not know that you are the Lord who crushes wars; the Lord is your name. Break their strength by your might, and bring down their power in your anger; for they intend to defile your sanctuary, and to pollute the tabernacle where your glorious name resides, and to break off the horns of your altar with the sword. Look at their pride, and send your wrath upon their heads. Give to me, a widow, the strong hand to do what I plan. By the deceit of my lips strike down the slave with the prince and the prince with his servant; crush their arrogance by the hand of a woman.

"For your strength does not depend on numbers, nor your might on the powerful. But you are the God of the lowly, helper of the oppressed, upholder of the weak, protector of the forsaken, savior of those without hope. Please, please, God of my father, God of the heritage of Israel, Lord of heaven and earth, Creator of the waters, King of all your creation, hear my prayer! Make my deceitful words bring wound and bruise on those who have planned cruel things against your covenant, and against your sacred house, and against

Mount Zion, and against the house your children possess. Let your whole nation and every tribe know and understand that you are God, the God of all power and might, and that there is no other who protects the people of Israel but you alone!" *Judith 9:2-14*

"Order the gate of the town to be opened for me so that I may go out and accomplish the things you have just said to me." *Judith 10:9*

"I am a daughter of the Hebrews, but I am fleeing from them, for they are about to be handed over to you to be devoured. I am on my way to see Holofernes the commander of your army, to give him a true report; I will show him a way by which he can go and capture all the hill country without losing one of his men, captured or slain." *Judith 10:12-13*

"Accept the words of your slave, and let your servant speak in your presence. I will say nothing false to my lord this night. If you follow out the words of your servant, God will accomplish something through you, and my lord will not fail to achieve his purposes. By the life of Nebuchadnezzar, king of the whole earth, and by the power of him who has sent you to direct every living being! Not only do human beings serve him because of you, but also the animals of the field and the cattle and the birds of the air will live, because of your power, under Nebuchadnezzar and all his house. For we have heard of your wisdom and skill, and it is reported throughout the whole world that you alone are the best in the whole kingdom, the most informed and the most astounding in military strategy.

"Now as for Achior's speech in your council, we have heard his words, for the people of Bethulia spared him and he told them all he had said to you. Therefore, lord and master, do not disregard what he said, but keep it in your mind, for it is true. Indeed our nation cannot be punished, nor can the sword prevail against them, unless they sin against their God.

"But now, in order that my lord may not be defeated and his purpose frustrated, death will fall upon them, for a sin has overtaken them by which they are about to provoke their God to anger when they do what is wrong. Since their food supply is exhausted and their water has almost given out, they have planned to kill their livestock and have determined to use all that God by his laws has forbidden them to eat. They have decided to consume the first fruits of the grain and the tithes of the wine and oil, which they had consecrated and set aside for the priests who minister in the presence of our God in Jerusalem—things it is not lawful for any of the people even to touch with their hands. Since even the people in Jerusalem have been doing this, they have sent messengers there in order to bring back permission from the council of the elders. When the response reaches them and they act upon it, on that very day they will be handed over to you to be destroyed.

"So when I, your slave, learned all this, I fled from them. God has sent me to accomplish with you things that will astonish the whole world wherever people shall hear about them. Your servant is indeed God-fearing and serves the God of heaven night and day. So, my lord, I will remain with you; but every night your servant will go out into the valley and pray to God. He will tell me when they have committed their sins. Then I will come and tell you, so that you may go out with your whole army, and not one of them will be able to withstand you. Then I will lead you through Judea, until you come to Jerusalem; there I will set your throne. You will drive them like sheep that have no shepherd, and no dog will so much as growl at you. For this was told me to give me foreknowledge; it was announced to me, and I was sent to tell you." *Judith 11:5-19*

"I cannot partake of them, or it will be an offense; but I will have enough with the things I brought with me." Holofernes said to her, "If your supply runs out, where can we get you more of the same? For none of your people are here with us." Judith replied, "As surely as you live, my lord, your servant will not use up the supplies I have with me before the Lord carries out by my hand what he has determined." *Judith 12:2-4*

"Let my lord now give orders to allow your servant to go out and pray." *Judith 12:6*

"Who am I to refuse my lord? Whatever pleases him I will do at once, and it will be a joy to me until the day of my death." *Judith 12:14*

"I will gladly drink, my lord, because today is the greatest day in my whole life." *Judith 12:18*

Then Judith, standing beside his bed, said in her heart, "O Lord God of all might, look in this hour on the work of my hands for the exaltation of Jerusalem. Now indeed is the time to help your heritage and to carry out my design to destroy the enemies who have risen up against us." *Judith 13:4-5*

"Give me strength today, O Lord God of Israel!" *Judith 13:6*

From a distance Judith called out to the sentries at the gates, "Open, open the gate! God, our God, is with us, still showing his power in Israel and his strength against our enemies, as he has done today!" *Judith 13:11*

Then she said to them with a loud voice, "Praise God, O praise him! Praise God, who has not withdrawn his mercy from the house of Israel, but has destroyed our enemies by my hand this very night!" Then she pulled the head out of the bag and showed it to them, and said, "See here, the head of Holofernes, the commander of the Assyrian army, and here is the canopy beneath which he lay in his drunken stupor. The Lord has struck him down by the hand of a woman. As the Lord lives, who has protected me in the way I went, I swear that it was my face that seduced him to his destruction, and that he committed no sin with me, to defile and shame me." *Judith 13:14-16*

"Listen to me, my friends. Take this head and hang it upon the parapet of your wall. As soon as day breaks and the sun rises on the earth, each of you take up your weapons, and let every able-bodied man go out of the town; set a captain over them, as if you were going down to the plain against the Assyrian outpost; only do not go down. Then they will seize their arms and go into the camp and rouse the officers of the Assyrian army. They will rush into the tent of Holofernes and will not find him. Then panic will come over them, and they will flee before you. Then you and all who live within the borders of Israel will pursue them and cut them down in their tracks. But before you do all this, bring Achior the Ammonite to me so that he may see and recognize the man who despised the house of Israel and sent him to us as if to his death." *Judith 14:1-5*

And Judith said, "**Begin a song to my God with tambourines, sing to my Lord with cymbals. Raise to him a new psalm; exalt him, and call upon his name. For the Lord is a God who crushes wars;** he sets up his camp among his people; he delivered me from the hands of my pursuers. The Assyrian came down from the mountains of the north; he came with myriads of his warriors; their numbers blocked up the wadis, and their cavalry covered the hills. He boasted that he would burn up my territory, and kill my young men with the sword, and dash my infants to the ground, and seize my children as booty, and take my virgins as spoil. But the Lord Almighty has foiled them by the hand of a woman. For their mighty one did not fall by the hands of the young men, nor did the sons of the Titans strike him down, nor did tall giants set upon him; but Judith daughter of Merari with the beauty of her countenance undid him." *Judith 16:1-7*

"For she put away her widow's clothing to exalt the oppressed in Israel. She anointed her face with perfume; she fastened her hair with a tiara and put on a linen gown to beguile him. Her sandal ravished his eyes, her beauty captivated his mind, and the sword severed his neck! The Persians trembled at her boldness, the Medes were daunted at her daring." *Judith 16:8-10*

"Then my oppressed people shouted; my weak people cried out, and the enemy trembled; they lifted up their voices, and the enemy were turned back. Sons of slave-girls pierced them through and wounded them like the children of fugitives; they perished before the army of my Lord. I will sing to my God a new song: O Lord, you are great and glorious, wonderful in strength, invincible." *Judith 16:11-13*

"Please, please,
God of my father, God of the heritage of Israel,
Lord of heaven and earth, Creator of the waters,
King of all your creation, hear my prayer!"

"Let all your creatures serve you, for you spoke, and they were made. You sent forth your spirit, and it formed them; there is none that can resist your voice. For the mountains shall be shaken to their foundations with the waters; before your glance the rocks shall melt like wax. But to those who fear you show mercy. For every sacrifice as a fragrant offering is a small thing, and the fat of all whole burnt offerings to you is a very little thing; but whoever fears the Lord is great forever. Woe to the nations that rise up against my people! The Lord Almighty will take vengeance on them in the day of judgment; he will send fire and worms into their flesh; they shall weep in pain forever."
Judith 16:1-17

Judith's story

Do not miss reading this story. Like its heroine, the narrative is bold and confident. In the language of America's Old West, the bad guys are on the move. In this case, it is Holofernes, Nebuchadnezzar's top general, who is advancing across the countryside, conquering town after town. Residents see his vast armies and throw themselves at his feet. Note the fear here: "We, the servants of Nebuchadnezzar, the Great King, lie prostrate before you. Do with us whatever you will. See, our buildings and all our land and all our wheat fields and our flocks and herd and all our encampments lie before you; do with them as you please. Our towns and their inhabitants are also your slaves; come and deal with them as you see fit" (Judith 3:2-4).

Like cornstalks blown down in blizzards, the people are frozen, empty of morale and courage. Holofernes even sees some of them coming toward him "with garlands and dances and tambourines" and moves quickly to demolish their shrines and places of worship (Judith 3:7). Clearly, the enemy is not a man of mercy.

Judith's town, Bethulia (akin to "virgin" in Hebrew), is an especially important site, for it lies directly on the approach to Jerusalem. Take Bethulia and the real prize is within reach. So the little town girds itself for war. Roads and routes are blocked. The town resists until Holofernes cuts off its water supply. The siege lasts for thirty-four days, until the men of Bethulia plead with Uzziah, their leader, to capitulate. Perhaps if they surrender they will not be killed, nor will their daughters be dragged away or their wives raped. Uzziah pleads with them to give him five days, hoping that God will awake from apparent slumber and act to protect them.

Judith, a devout, beautiful, and wealthy widow, hears the news. Pleading with the men of Bethulia, she recounts their sacred history and implores them to stay true to God, not allowing the enemy to advance and conquer. Advising her that he has already cut a deal, Uzziah tells her, rather condescendingly, to go home and pray for rain—for the lack of water threatens to kill the residents even before the enemy can.

Judith prays, but not for raindrops. Rather, in an eloquent and remarkable plea, she asks God to help her destroy the enemy and keep the heart of her people strong.

That night she slips out of town with only her maid, informing fellow residents that she will not tell them her whole plan. Instead, she goes to the enemy camp, acting like one who has thrown in her lot with them and wishes to be saved—unlike her people whom, she says, will soon be destroyed.

Over the course of five days, Judith earns the conquerors' trust. On the last night, she acts as if she is going to seduce Holofernes. She enters his tent, has the door locked from outside, and gets him drunk beyond measure. When he passes out, she grabs his sword, cuts off his head, and returns to her people with the general's head in her food bag. She then instructs them to post his head high on a stake so that the enemy troops will be stunned beyond belief. When they chase after her and find their leader's head looking down on them, they panic and flee.

Consider this

Talk about a powerful woman. Well-respected, prayerful, and articulate, she saves her people from destruction and demonstrates an amazing display of tactical military wisdom.

Yet her story is about more than a battle plan, for Judith also voices profound wisdom about the nature of God and the power of prayer. She warns her people (and, through the ages, us) not to underestimate the power and purposes of God. "Do not try to bind the purposes of the Lord our God; for God is not like a human being, to be threatened, or like a mere mortal to be won over by pleading" (Judith 8:16).

Her words prefigure what will become the doctrines of predestination and providence—and also lay the groundwork of giving thanks no matter the circumstance. "You [O Lord] have designed the things that are now, and those that are to come…. For all your ways are prepared in advance, and your judgment is with foreknowledge" (Judith 9:5-6). A deep sense of ultimate trust pours through in words that have spoken for centuries to people in the midst of difficult situations. "In spite of everything let us give thanks to the Lord… [for] the Lord scourges those who are close to him in order to admonish them" (Judith 8:25, 27).

Many men in scripture, such as Paul and Job and Joseph, have been praised throughout history for similar words of wisdom, but Judith, sadly, has gone (mostly) unacknowledged. She is powerful—and a force not to be missed in a thorough study of scripture.

May the words of Judith roll over us as a song of praise: "I will sing to my God a new song…. Let all your creatures serve you, for you spoke, and they were made. You sent forth your spirit, and it formed them…for every sacrifice as a fragrant offering is a small thing; but whoever fears the Lord is great forever!" (Judith 16:13-16).

JUDITH

There are lessons here about deep prayer, joy, and setting an example for those we love. Do we give up and give in as we age? As we lose those we love? Do we consider our work to be done, even before God does? Or do we give all we have for the survival of future generations? Questions worth considering; a woman worth knowing.

What might we learn from Judith?

▷ Trust in God.

▷ Take that first step; the rest will follow.

▷ Prayer can bring help in troubled times.

▷ Keep yourself in good shape physically.

▷ Acting for the greater good of God's people may involve deceit.

▷ Sometimes older people take risks that younger ones cannot.

For reflection

1. Judith is a remarkably courageous woman who devises a plan to save her people and then acts on it. What do her actions say about her?

2. Judith could have maintained her quiet widow's life but stepped out when God and her community needed her to act. Is it hard to go from routine to something as wild as this?

3. Judith stood up for her beliefs despite all odds. Have you ever done the same? Has someone you known done this? What was the result? Where was God in the process?

CHAPTER 21

WOMEN WHO SPEAK IN ADDITIONS TO THE BOOK OF ESTHER

This book shows a deeper, more contemplative, more faithful Esther than the Esther of the Old Testament, however lovely she is. Prayer and fidelity to God are overt here, and so is a comprehensive understanding of God's hand in creation, and in the life of the Jewish people. The Apocrypha's Esther admits her fear, seems more humble, and prays to God for courage and wisdom.

ESTHER

By the numbers

Words spoken by women in Additions to the Book of Esther: 791

Number of women who speak: One (Esther)

ESTHER

(Greek version containing additional chapters)

PROFILE:
ESTHER- HIGH,
THESE ADDITIONS
- LOW

▷ **READ HER ADDITIONAL STORY:**
The Additions to the Book Esther[73]

▷ **CLASSIC MOMENT/IMPORT:**
Praying fervently to God for her people's deliverance

▷ **LIKELY CHARACTERISTICS:**
(see Esther on page 274) Plus: a woman of prayer and overt faith

▷ **DATA:** 791 words

Who was Esther?

An orphan of the tribe of Benjamin; raised by her cousin Mordecai in Persia (where they were exiled) // A "draftee" into King Ahasuerus's (Xerxes's) harem // A queen // A protector of the Jewish people, saving them from annihilation in Persia // A woman whose actions inspired the Jewish feast of Purim

PLUS: In these texts, a woman of prayer and overt faith

What does Esther say?

And she said to him, "**Go to Mordecai and say, 'All nations of the empire know that if any man or woman goes to the king inside the inner court without being called, there is no escape for that person. Only the one to whom the king stretches out the golden scepter is safe—and it is now thirty days since I was called to go to the king.'**" *Esther (Greek) 4:10-11*

Then Esther gave the messenger this answer to take back to Mordecai: "**Go** and gather all the Jews who are in Susa and fast on my behalf; for three days and nights do not eat or drink, and my maids and I will also go without food. After that I will go to the king, contrary to the law, even if I must die." *Esther (Greek) 4:15-16*

She prayed to the Lord God of Israel, and said: "O my Lord, you only are our king; help me, who am alone and have no helper but you, for my danger is in my hand. Ever since I was born I have heard in the tribe of my family that you, O Lord, took Israel out of all the nations, and our ancestors from among all their forebears, for an everlasting inheritance, and that you did for them all that you promised. And now we have sinned before you, and you have handed us over to our enemies because we glorified their gods. You are righteous, O Lord! And now they are not satisfied that we are in bitter slavery, but they have covenanted with their idols to abolish what your mouth has ordained, and to destroy your inheritance, to stop the mouths of those who praise you and to quench your altar and the glory of your house, to open the mouths of the nations for the praise of vain idols, and to magnify forever a mortal king.

"O Lord, do not surrender your scepter to what has no being; and do not let them laugh at our downfall; but turn their plan against them, and make an example of him who began this against us. Remember, O Lord; make yourself known in this time of our affliction, and give me courage, O King of the gods and Master of all dominion! Put eloquent speech in my mouth before the lion, and turn his heart to hate the man who is fighting against us, so that there may be an end of him and those who agree with him. But save us by your hand, and help me, who am alone and have no helper but you, O Lord.

"You have knowledge of all things, and you know that I hate the splendor of the wicked and abhor the bed of the uncircumcised and of any alien. You know my necessity—that I abhor the sign of my proud position, which is upon my head on days when I appear in public. I abhor it like a filthy rag, and I do not wear it on the days when I am at leisure. And your servant has not eaten at Haman's table, and I have not honored the king's feast or drunk the wine of libations. Your servant has had no joy since the day that I was

ESTHER

brought here until now, except in you, O Lord God of Abraham. O God, whose might is over all, hear the voice of the despairing, and save us from the hands of evildoers. And save me from my fear!" *Esther (Greek)14:3-19 Addition C*

She said to him, "I saw you, my lord, like an angel of God, and my heart was shaken with fear at your glory. For you are wonderful, my lord, and your countenance is full of grace." *Esther (Greek) 15:13-14 Addition D*

And Esther said, "Today is a special day for me. If it pleases the king, let him and Haman come to the dinner that I shall prepare today." *Esther (Greek) 5:4*

She said, "My petition and request is: if I have found favor in the sight of the king, let the king and Haman come to the dinner that I shall prepare them, and tomorrow I will do as I have done today." *Esther (Greek) 5:7-8*

She answered and said, "If I have found favor with the king, let my life be granted me at my petition, and my people at my request. For we have been sold, I and my people, to be destroyed, plundered, and made slaves—we and our children—male and female slaves. This has come to my knowledge. Our antagonist brings shame on the king's court." *Esther (Greek) 7:3-4*

Esther said, "Our enemy is this evil man Haman!" *Esther (Greek) 7:6*

Esther said, "If it pleases you, and if I have found favor, let an order be sent rescinding the letters that Haman wrote and sent to destroy the Jews in your kingdom. How can I look on the ruin of my people? How can I be safe if my ancestral nation is destroyed?" *Esther (Greek) 8:5-6*

And Esther said to the king, "Let the Jews be allowed to do the same tomorrow. Also, hang up the bodies of Haman's ten sons." *Esther (Greek) 9:13*

Esther's story

See the earlier chapter on Esther and review the above comments.

Consider this

In some ways, this edition of Esther makes more sense than its counterpart in the Old Testament. The Bible is, after all, a book about God and faith and prayer, and now those components are present.

Esther also comes across a bit stronger in this version. With God, she pours out her emotions, including speaking of how much she abhors her position as queen and how much she needs God's help to survive and save her people.

In both texts, Esther comes across as a deeply caring person. Yet it would be irresponsible not to point out that when Haman is killed and the people of God are celebrating, Esther also calls for the death of Haman's ten sons—by hanging. There's a bit of vengeance there. It's all part of the Hebrew story but still a bit surprising, coming from this patient and otherwise gentle woman.

What might we learn from these additions to Esther?

- ▷ God is our helper when danger is at hand.
- ▷ Prayer is a conversation with God that sustains and informs our hearts.

ESTHER

For reflection

1. Esther was a young woman when she was brought to the harem. Was God with her when the king made her his queen? What was there about Esther that made her most attractive to the king? Did he look beyond her good looks and discover her spirit and intelligence?

2. Do you think Esther lied to the king to implement her plan or did she just leave out the details? Would you do the same?

3. Was Mordecai's presence a beacon to her while she prayed to God and fasted? Do you have a beacon or anchor in your life?

4. Mordecai brought her up to be a faithful Jew. Do you think Esther questioned her beliefs when asked to help her people?

CHAPTER 22

WOMEN WHO SPEAK IN SUSANNA

The crime of rape, most often directed at women, cares not about affluence or poverty. In this story, which takes place in a seemingly sheltered environment, two villains—ironically, respected judges—have what seems to be a foolproof plan to rape the happily married Susanna. This is a read for the ages and a reminder that the challenges faced by women in the Bible are ones faced by all.[74]

By the numbers

Words spoken by women in Susanna: 112

Number of women who speak: One (Susanna)

SUSANNA

Choosing truth

▷ **READ SUSANNA'S STORY:** The Book of Susanna in the Apocrypha, (Chapter 13 of the Greek Version of Daniel[75])

▷ **CLASSIC MOMENT:** Refusing seduction and entrapment by two elders

▷ **LIKELY CHARACTERISTICS:** Beautiful, Innocent, Virtuous, Brave, Intelligent, Righteous

▷ **DATA:** 112 words

Who was Susanna?

A daughter and wife living in Babylon during the exile // A virtuous woman falsely accused of adultery by two elders who lusted after her // A woman who refuses to sin // A woman humiliated and condemned to death // A woman who entrusts her life to God's justice

---

What did Susanna say?

She said to her maids, "**Bring me olive oil and ointments, and shut the garden doors so that I can bathe.**" *Susanna 1:17*

Susanna groaned and said, "**I am completely trapped. For if I do this, it will mean death for me; if I do not, I cannot escape your hands. I choose not to do it; I will fall into your hands, rather than sin in the sight of the Lord.**" *Susanna 1:22-23*

Then Susanna cried out with a loud voice, and said, "**O eternal God, you know what is secret and are aware of all things before they come to be; you know that these men have given false evidence against me. And now I am to die, though I have done none of the wicked things that they have charged against me!**" *Susanna 1:42-43*

Susanna's story

This story is cited by many as the very first detective story in Western literature.

A beautiful and righteous young wife, Susanna is lusted after by two elders who are also judges of the court. They hide themselves within the garden where she is to bathe, and after she has shut herself in and sent the maids away, they spring out, telling her that they are "burning with desire...so give your consent, and lie with us" (Susanna 1:20). If she does not consent, they inform her that they will publicly accuse her of adultery—saying they saw her with a handsome young man—and that she will get a death sentence.

After Susanna makes her choice to not sin in the sight of the Lord, the wicked elders carry out their threat, painting the picture of her enjoying a young man's attention. Condemned to death, Susanna cries out to God for help, and lo and behold, the world's first detective—Daniel—comes forth to save the day. (This is the same prophet who stars in the biblical Book of Daniel, depicted here as a young man.)

In classic interrogation technique, he separates the two men, asks each what kind of tree they were hiding behind in the garden when they saw the young man, and, when they give different answers, he proves their false witness. The bad guys are executed, and everyone else gives praise to God for Susanna's noble choice to stay faithful both to her husband and to God's law.

SUSANNA

Consider this

Words of praise for Susanna and her story have prevailed for two millennia as one of the best short stories in world literature.

From that day to this, people seem to love good detective stories. And why is that? Perhaps because they remind us of things we deeply want to be true. That while there are indeed devious and evil people in our world—corrupting perhaps even the courts—in the end, truth does come out, and real justice can win the day.

In many ways, this is indeed a happy story. The beautiful and pure woman is saved, due to her smart choice to appeal to God, who stirs up the spirit of Daniel to clear her name. Her honor remains intact.

Yet in the twenty-first century, there remain haunting questions. Susanna maintained her purity, and the whole community celebrated because she had not been sullied. But what if she had been *sullied*? Why should that make her less acceptable? Why should she have to hang if she were caught in adultery? And why should the word of a respected woman not be trusted over that of two elders? Why should a "young lad" have to save her?

Using a contemporary lens, the conclusion leaves one unsettled—for it points to male dominance, and female social vulnerability, still all too common. Throughout the ages, women have often been unfairly accused of inciting sexual violence and have been forced to pay the price, sometimes with their very lives.

Susanna gives contemporary women an important lesson: speak up, loudly, when put in a difficult situation, especially a sexual one. Stand your ground. Scream if need be. And trust in a world that God is creating anew, where women's voices will be heard—and heeded.

What might we learn from Susanna?

 ▷ Life can present us with what look like "damned either way," no-good choices. In those moments, stand firm upon your principles.

 ▷ Doing what is right by God's laws can be painful.

 ▷ Faith and prayer are ways forward.

 ▷ Truth does come out. Justice ultimately wins in the face of evil.

For reflection

1. Susanna was a woman of great strength and wisdom. With her back literally against the wall, she screamed for help because she decided that was the wisest option. In doing so, she risked her life for the truth. Would you have had that courage?

2. How might this story connect to the woman who was to be stoned for committing adultery in the New Testament?

3. How did Susanna find the strength to defy those elders?

4. Why do "good" men sometimes take advantage of women? Why is sexual violence more about power than sex?

5. What contemporary situations resemble this one?

SUSANNA

CHAPTER 23

Women Who Speak in 2 and 4 Maccabees

The woman of seven sons, described both in 2 and 4 Maccabees, tells one of the most heart-wrenching stories in the Bible. Hers is a study in living faith; she is surely worthy of being called a saint. Read her story, and you will not be the same person you are now. If there is someone who deserves to sit next to Jesus in heaven, this would be the soul—yet, no doubt, she would be happiest sitting next to her beloved sons.

By the numbers

Words spoken by women in 2 and 4 Maccabees: 188 and 428, respectively

Number of women who speak: One (the mother of seven sons)

MACCABEES

▷ **READ HER STORY:**
2 Maccabees 7, 4 Maccabees 16-18

▷ **CLASSIC MOMENT:** When she encourages her sons not to give in to torture but to trust that God in his mercy will give life and breath back to them again

▷ **LIKELY CHARACTERISTICS:**
Faithful, Brave, Tough, Resilient, Hope-filled, Righteous

▷ **DATA:** 616 words (188 in 2 Maccabees, 428 in 4 Maccabees)

Who was the mother of seven sons?

A widow under arrest along with her seven sons because they would not violate the laws of their Jewish faith // One of the first people in the Bible to articulate the hope of resurrection // A mother who encouraged her sons to stand firm and die rather than betray God and their faith // A person who died herself rather than betray God and her faith

What did the mother of seven sons say?

"I do not know how you came into being in my womb. It was not I who gave you life and breath, nor I who set in order the elements within each of you. Therefore the Creator of the world, who shaped the beginning of humankind and devised the origin of all things, will in his mercy give life and breath back to you again, since you now forget yourselves for the sake of his laws."
2 Maccabees 7:22-23

MACCABEES

But, leaning close to him, she spoke in their native language as follows, deriding the cruel tyrant: "My son, have pity on me. I carried you nine months in my womb, and nursed you for three years, and have reared you and brought you up to this point in your life, and have taken care of you. I beg you, my child, to look at the heaven and the earth and see everything that is in them, and recognize that God did not make them out of things that existed. And in the same way the human race came into being. Do not fear this butcher, but prove worthy of your brothers. Accept death, so that in God's mercy I may get you back again along with your brothers." *2 Maccabees 7:27-29*

"My sons, noble is the contest to which you are called to bear witness for the nation. Fight zealously for our ancestral law. For it would be shameful if, while an aged man endures such agonies for the sake of religion, you young men were to be terrified by tortures. Remember that it is through God that you have had a share in the world and have enjoyed life, and therefore you ought to endure any suffering for the sake of God. For his sake also our father Abraham was zealous to sacrifice his son Isaac, the ancestor of our nation; and when Isaac saw his father's hand wielding a knife and descending upon him, he did not cower. Daniel the righteous was thrown to the lions, and Hananiah, Azariah, and Mishael were hurled into the fiery furnace and endured it for the sake of God. You too must have the same faith in God and not be grieved. It is unreasonable for people who have religious knowledge not to withstand pain." *4 Maccabees 16:16-23*

The mother of seven sons expressed also these principles to her children: "I was a pure virgin and did not go outside my father's house; but I guarded the rib from which woman was made. No seducer corrupted me on a desert plain, nor did the destroyer, the deceitful serpent, defile the purity of my virginity. In the time of my maturity I remained with my husband, and when these sons had grown up their father died. A happy man was he, who lived out his life with good children, and did not have the grief of bereavement. While he was still with you, he taught you the law and the prophets. He read to you about Abel slain by Cain, and Isaac who was offered as a burnt offering, and about Joseph in prison. He told you of the zeal of Phinehas, and he taught you about Hananiah, Azariah, and Mishael in the fire. He praised Daniel in the den of the lions and blessed him. He reminded you of the scripture of Isaiah, which says, 'Even though you go through the fire, the flame shall not consume you.' He sang to you songs of the psalmist David, who said, 'Many are the afflictions of the righteous.' He recounted to you Solomon's proverb, 'There is a tree of life for those who do his will.' He confirmed the query of Ezekiel, 'Shall these dry bones live?' For he did not forget to teach you the song that Moses taught, which says, 'I kill and I make alive: this is your life and the length of your days.'" *4 Maccabees 18:6-19*

Mother of seven sons' story

Let's be simple. This is a horrendous story. In the second century BCE, the Seleucid king Antiochus IV is working to break the Jewish people of their will and spirit with a reign of terror. A family of seven sons and their mother is brought before the king, who demands they abandon their faith by eating forbidden flesh under the threat of torture and death.

Six of the sons, from oldest to youngest in turn, are horribly and graphically tortured to death before their mother's eyes, as the mother encourages each to "fight zealously for our ancestral law" with their refusal. The king then tells the mother that he will spare, and indeed reward with high position, the final seventh son if she will only convince him to give in.

Thinking that she agrees, Antiochas lets her approach and speak to her son. But leaning in closely, she in fact encourages her boy to stand firm against "this butcher" with an eloquent exposition of faith in God and, more, trust that they will all be reunited and see each other beyond this life in God's great mercy.

The mother herself then dies, throwing herself into the flames "so that no one might touch her body."

MACCABEES

352

Consider this

The Bible is not a book about the basic goodness of human nature. Throughout it, as in the story of the woman cut into pieces, women raped and scorned, and people betrayed, seduced, and abandoned, scripture portrays unflinchingly—and in this case gruesomely—some of the worst of human behavior.

And yet the Bible is a library of hope.

In the story of the mother of seven sons, we see human political leadership at its most despicable apex. And yet this is also a story of nobility, as the mother's strength and faith unite the family and give her sons courage in the midst of a horrendous situation. Moreover, her belief that God created the world and her family out of nothing, and that God has the power to give them life after death, undergirds her bravery.

And in that articulation, she picks up on a new hope in biblical terms: the hope of resurrection. She attests to the promise of new, fuller life beyond the grave, the victory of hope over even the worst that life can dish out. Her story is, then, a significant precursor to the greatest story of God transforming evil into good—the story of the death and resurrection of Jesus.

These books of the Apocrypha, of which 4 Maccabees is the final one, are indeed texts of transition. Written during a period when Greek and Persian scholarship was pushing new boundaries, the books reflect a development in thought about the nature of hope and the possibilities of God's intentions for us all beyond this life. It is most appropriate, then, that the story of the mother of seven sons is our final text before we get to Jesus and the New Testament.

MACCABEES

What might we learn from the mother of seven sons?

▷ The values we give our children are what will sustain them.

▷ A mother's love is very powerful.

▷ Trust in God can help us through horrifying circumstances.

▷ Resurrection is a message of hope in the face of darkest times.

For reflection

1. From where did this mother get her strength? How could she have watched her boys be so tortured and still maintain her sanity and faith?

2. To what extent can this story help guide us through the worst of times?

3. What values did your mother teach you that help you now?

4. Have you known a person who has willingly defied authority for God?

5. What must this woman have been thinking as she threw herself into the flames? And what happened to her after death?

THE WOMEN WHO SPEAK
IN THE NEW TESTAMENT

"I have seen the Lord!" —Mary Magdalene

No one better exemplifies the spirit of the New Testament than Mary Magdalene. Beaten down from intense emotional, spiritual, and physical trauma, she finds healing with Jesus—and helps him transform the world. The same can be said of other New Testament women, especially his mother Mary, who cradles him in her womb and stands by his side as he dies.

Throughout the New Testament, Jesus values women in ways the old order did not. He listens, debates, challenges, heals, honors, redeems, and sanctifies them. He encourages them to talk about their experiences with him in public. He calls on them to be the primary communicators of the day. He frees when others condemn. He accepts respite and hospitality graciously, and encourages women to attend to their souls, rather than just serve. He knows they will accompany him through his bleakest moments and be there when he is restored to life.

Despite moments of pain and suffering, the gospels represent a hope of new life, restored life for women (and men). From the first woman who speaks (a bleeding, chronically ill, untouchable woman in Matthew) to the last (a demon-possessed girl who is being held as a slave in Acts), this much is clear: Jesus deeply values women and their gifts, seeing women of the Bible—and us—as beloved soul mates, partners in mission, and friends.

CHAPTER 24

WOMEN WHO SPEAK IN MATTHEW

In this, the first book of the New Testament, Matthew addresses a primarily Jewish audience, inviting them to share in the wider circle drawn by Jesus while building on the legacy of the past. One of two gospel writers (the other is Luke) to provide a genealogy for Jesus, Matthew provides an extraordinary glimpse into Jesus' maternal ancestors, naming four: Tamar, Rahab, Ruth, Bathsheba (Luke does not name any female ancestors).

Matthew could not have picked four more compelling women, for these are among the most notable in Jewish history. Their words and actions as recorded in the Old Testament influence the Hebrew people, and eventually, Jesus. According to Sister Barbara Reid, "The women's presence in the midst of the male ancestors of Jesus also signals the integral role that women disciples play in the community of Jesus' followers. They remind the reader that women are not marginal to the history of Israel or of Christianity."[76]

In contrast to those four named women in Matthew's genealogy, all of the women who actually speak in this gospel are unnamed. Yet going nameless is not necessarily a negative thing, for anonymity often marks those who were healed by Jesus—thus focusing attention on him and not the individual who was healed. By quoting unnamed women, however, Matthew demonstrates that Jesus' ever-expanding circle includes those without power or lineage. It is a significant witness, then, that the bleeding woman—ostracized, exhausted, and powerless—is the first woman to speak in the New Testament, by order of the writings.

Using one hundred and fourteen words spoken by women, Matthew helps to put the old and new world orders together, paying special attention to the old.

By the numbers

Words spoken by women in the Gospel of Matthew: 114

Number of women who speak: Seven (the bleeding woman, Herodias's daughter, the Syrophoenician woman, mother of the sons of Zebedee (Salome), servant girl #1, servant girl #2, and Pilate's wife)

THE BLEEDING WOMAN

"I will be made well"

▷ **READ HER STORY:** Matthew 9:20-22, Mark 5:25-34, Luke 8:43-48

▷ **CLASSIC MOMENT:** Touching Jesus' cloak and being healed

▷ **LIKELY CHARACTERISTICS:** Purposeful, Fatigued, Downtrodden, Isolated, Faithful, Focused, Hopeful

▷ **DATA:** 22 words (11 in Matthew, 11 in Mark)

Who was the bleeding woman?

The first woman to speak in the New Testament[77] // A woman who, for twelve years, was regarded as unclean // A woman who had used up her money on doctors, hoping for a cure // A woman of strong faith

What did the bleeding woman say?

"If I only touch his cloak, I will be made well." *Matthew 9:21*

"If I but touch his clothes, I will be made well." *Mark 5:28*

The bleeding woman's story

Alone, she stands at the side of the road, watching as the rush of the crowd almost lifts the man in the center off his feet. She, like everyone else in the small town, has heard of Jesus, the Jewish miracle worker, and how he has healed the broken, the lame, and the blind. Something in her has told her that he will heal her, too—if only she can get close.

But it will not be easy. Jairus, the local synagogue's leader, has fallen at Jesus' feet, imploring him to come to his home and heal his dying twelve-year-old daughter. Yet unbeknownst to the swelled-with-purpose crowd, the girl is not the only one who hovers on life's edges—for the woman, too, feels death closing in. Twelve years of uterine hemorrhaging[78] have caused endless suffering. She has spent all her money on doctors but has not found a cure. She has tried everything.

Yet she will not give up. Jesus can heal her! She must reach him. Like a trout from a deep pool watching and then working its way forward through rapid waters, she labors through the crowd, waiting for an opening; then, just as he passes, she dives in and touches the fringe of his cloak.

Energy surges through her. The bleeding stops. She feels warm. Her muscles relax. A lightness goes through her that she has not felt since she was a girl skipping down the street. Bowing her head, she turns to leave.

But Jesus stops—and so does the crowd. "Who touched me?" he wants to know.

Like marionettes, the people shake their heads in unison, all denying an intentional touch. "Master, everyone is pressed up against you," Peter protests. "This whole crowd is touching you."

"No," Jesus says. "Someone deliberately touched me; power has gone out of me."

The woman turns, inching her way back. Falling at his feet, she tells of her twelve-year trauma, and of her immediate healing upon touching his cloak.

Jesus says, "Take heart, daughter; your faith has made you well" (Matthew 9:22).

She watches as the man in the middle of the human caravan disappears down the road, on his way to help another daughter of God.

Consider this

What better woman than this to open the door for women who speak in the New Testament? Poor and marginalized, she is disheartened, laid low by the kind of fatigue that only years of chronic illness can bring. Uterine hemorrhaging has made her ritualistically unclean under Jewish purity laws. Normally a woman would take a *mikvah* (purity bath) to cleanse herself after her period, but with no cessation in her monthly flow, she was prohibited from touching others, cooking for them, or going into the women's court of the temple. (Such rituals may not make sense for contemporary non-Jewish readers, but they were developed over years in the wilderness to keep the people of God strong and healthy.) Yet driven by a certainty that Jesus will heal her, she ignores those rules and dives into the crowd to touch the Messiah. She is healed immediately, and Jesus asks her to step forth, leaving her world of shame behind.

Something stunning—a sea change—is taking place here: Jesus is encouraging, drawing out, prompting a woman's right to proclaim her story of faith in public. Those witnessing the conversation must have been aghast to seen an uprotected women (without a male escort) touching a man without his consent. This wasn't done.[79] To this day, there are those who would deny a woman's right to speak. Google "Bible women who speak" and almost all of the top hits will be articles or semons based on verses such as 1 Timothy 2:11-15 or 1 Corinthians 14:34-35, which question whether women should speak in churches.

Here, Jesus couldn't be more clear: He wants the woman to describe her transformation, he wants her to proclaim her redemption. Jesus wants her to tell her own story of God's healing love, to claim her—and his—story for the good of all.

Jesus insists this broken, untouchable woman speak out. He stops and waits until he hears her voice. There is no higher authority than his. Women's voices are not only welcome but also required as part of the conversation from this point forward.

What might we learn from the bleeding woman?

▷ Faith in God can do surprising things.

▷ Jesus does not intrude; the woman reached out to him.

▷ God does not consider any part of the human body unclean.

▷ Being a daughter of God means sharing personal stories of healing and transformation.

For reflection

1. What driving force inside this woman made her seek healing?

2. When have you experienced God's healing love? To what extent do you share your story, as this woman did? Is it easy? Hard?

3. Have you ever felt shame because of a health issue? How might this story inspire you to find peace and step out of the shadow of illness?

4. Poor health can drain the soul as well as the body, yet it is important not to give up. What do you do to maintain your physical and emotional balance in times of longstanding pain or illness?

5. How did this woman's action affect Jesus' ministry? Why did he turn around once he felt his power leave him?

HERODIAS'S DAUGHTER (AKA SALOME)

"Whatever you say, Mother."

PROFILE: MODERATELY HIGH

▷ **READ HER STORY:** Matthew 14:1-12, Mark 6:17-28

▷ **CLASSIC MOMENT:** Asking for the head of John the Baptist on a platter

▷ **LIKELY CHARACTERISTICS:** Bold, Saucy, Obedient, Insensitive, Shallow

▷ **DATA:** 34 words (12 in Matthew, 22 in Mark)

Who was Herodias's daughter?

The daughter of Herodias and the stepdaughter of Herod // A dancer // The great-granddaughter of Herod the Great (who had ordered the slaughter of the Holy Innocents) // The niece of Herod Agrippa I (who executed James the brother of John) // A force behind the beheading of John the Baptist

What did Herodias's daughter say?

"Give me the head of John the Baptist here on a platter." *Matthew 14:8*

"What should I ask for?" *Mark 6:24*

"I want you to give me at once the head of John the Baptist on a platter." *Mark 6:25*

Herodias's daughter's story

In this, one of the more horrific stories of the New Testament, a mother and daughter unite to bring down one of the Bible's most beloved figures: John the Baptist. To fully understand the girl's story, a bit of family history—some of it quite sordid—is necessary.

Unnamed in Matthew, the girl is briefly called Herodias in Mark (the same as her mother) and is identified as Salome—the name often used in Christian tradition—by the first-century Roman historian Josephus.[80] (For simplicity, the girl is called Salome here.)

Salome's mother, Herodias, is married to Herod Antipas, the ruler of Galilee. Antipas is Salome's stepfather. Her biological father is Herod Philip, Herodias's uncle and first husband. He would still be married to Herodias had not she and Antipas rejected their first spouses for each other.

Enter John the Baptist, criticizing Herod Antipas loudly and publicly for his immoral actions (Matthew 14:4). So incensed is Herodias by John's shaming of Herod (and her) that she wants John dead, ASAP! When Herod throws a birthday party for himself, the perfect opportunity arises.

Suffice it to say that wine flowed freely. And into that den of inebriation floats young Salome, so mesmerizing Herod as she dances for his guests that he promises to give the girl anything she desires. Salome runs to Mama, asking her opinion.

"Get the head of John the Baptist!" hisses Herodias.

Salome concurs. After all, what is he to her, other than a family irritant?

"Give me the head of John the Baptist on a platter."

And so the evil deed is done, causing those who had loved John—perhaps Jesus most of all—to grieve deeply. The one who had lit the way for Jesus was suddenly gone, felled by the murderous desires of a girl and her mother.

Consider this

Tragically, this is the only one-on-one conversation between a mother and daughter in the Bible. Hard to believe, but true.

The Bible itself does not give much detail on Salome: not her age, nor the level of complicity in this gristly tale. Her involvement, then, takes one of three paths:

Possibility #1: Salome is a precocious little girl pleasing her mother, dancing to entertain her stepfather, the king. Obediently doing what her mother instructed, she may have been unaware of the distress between John the Baptist and her parents.

Possibility #2: Salome is older, perhaps an adolescent, and she dances provocatively, shedding one veil after another, playing off Herod's (presumed) attraction to her. This is a disturbing image of budding sexuality misused.

Possibility #3: Mother planned the event and sent her daughter in to dance, accurately gauging what her husband's response would be.

What might we learn from Herodias's daughter?

▷ Mother does not always know best.

▷ Family values, whether moral or immoral, seep into children and young adults more than we know.

▷ A few misspoken words can cause tragedy.

For reflection

1. Do you think Salome helped to plan John's demise, or was she a relative latecomer to her mother's plan to kill him? Does it make a difference?

2. When Salome was presented with John's head on a platter, how do you think she reacted? Horrified? Proud? Would that event have been a lifelong lesson—or a nightmare?

3. What is the most disturbing detail for you in this story?

4. What happens to people who treat human life carelessly?

5. Did your parents ever encourage you to do something you regret? Or have you, as a parent, encouraged your child to do something immoral? What has it been like to live with the consequences? Where is God in the process of overcoming regret?

> **THE SYROPHOENICIAN WOMAN (AKA THE CANAANITE WOMAN[81])**
>
> *Debate team champion*

▷ **READ HER STORY:** Matthew 15:21-28, Mark 7:24-30

▷ **CLASSIC MOMENT:** Coming back at Jesus after he called her a dog

▷ **LIKELY CHARACTERISTICS:** Determined, Passionate, Intelligent, Faithful, Protective, Quick-witted

▷ **DATA:** 44 words (33 in Matthew, 11 in Mark)

Who was the Syrophoenician woman?

A loving mother desperately hoping Jesus would rid her daughter of the demon that possessed her // A Gentile (or pagan) in the eyes of the Israelites // A Phoenician from Syria, thus the name Syrophoenician // A woman bold enough to speak to a man in front of a crowd, rarely done in those times // A woman who identified Jesus as, "Lord, Son of David"

What did the Syrophoenician woman say?

"Have mercy on me, Lord, Son of David; my daughter is tormented by a demon." *Matthew 15:22*

But she came and knelt before him, saying, **"Lord, help me."** *Matthew 15:25*

"Yes, Lord, yet even the dogs eat the crumbs that fall from their masters' table." *Matthew 15:27*

But she answered him, **"Sir, even the dogs under the table eat the children's crumbs."** *Mark 7:28*

The Syrophoenician woman's story

The Syrophoenician woman (pronounced sear-row-pho-nee-shun) loves her demon-possessed daughter so much that she takes Jesus to the mat—and her daughter is healed.

She identifies Jesus as Lord (in Matthew's Gospel) and shouts at him, then kneels at his feet. When Jesus says that it is not fair to give food meant for the children (God's children being the Jews) to dogs (Gentiles being everyone else), she throws his words back at him, saying that even dogs get to eat the crumbs that fall under the table. This suggests her belief that even a wee bit of Jesus' power—even the leftovers—would heal her daughter.

He initially ignores her, reminding her and his disciples that he was sent only to the house of Israel, and that it is not fair for Gentiles to receive Israel's due. Yet, in the end, he heals the girl because of her mother's faith.

Consider this

This story is puzzling and off-putting. Jesus is initially rude and unwilling to share his healing powers with a desperate mother because she is not Jewish. Yikes.

Over the years, this story has been processed in different ways: Jesus was only testing the woman; his ministry was changed because of her; this story symbolizes Jesus' ministry to all the world.

Try this: Jesus was rude, at least initially. Fully divine and fully human, here he expresses human emotions. And yet this story gives Jesus' actions over his lifetime more credibility, rather than less. He gets tired. He was sent to the house of Israel first. And no doubt he is still grieving the recent death of his friend, John the Baptist.

This woman loved her daughter and knew Jesus could cure her. And she knew who Jesus was in relation to Judaism, as evidenced by her statement, "Son of David." When Jesus and the disciples ignored her, she did not back down. When he refused her verbally, she did not flee. Like a judo master, who uses the energy of his/her opponent to direct the opponent's flight path, she engaged Jesus, coming back at him with words he had already used, specifically the word "dog."

Boldly, the woman persevered—and Jesus healed her daughter because of it.

What might we learn from the Syrophoenician woman?

▷ Persistence can bring results.

▷ Faith can play a large part in healing.

▷ Those outside the traditional circle of faith are also God's children.

For reflection

1. Describe your sense of the Syrophoenician woman. What kind of picture emerges?

2. Jesus seems a bit out of character here. Was he surprised by her request? How do you interpret his response? Knowing that Jesus is fully human and fully divine, should it be surprising if, now and then, he shows a more human side?

3. Who in your life would you go to the mat for?

4. Think of the woman's anguished daughter. Do you think Jesus knew who she was? What would it be like to know all people and their ailments?

SALOME, THE MOTHER OF THE SONS OF ZEBEDEE

"I only want the best for my boys."

▷ **READ HER STORY:** Matthew 20:20-23, Matthew 27:55-56, Mark 15:40-16:8

▷ **CLASSIC MOMENT:** Asking for her sons to sit beside Jesus in heaven

▷ **LIKELY CHARACTERISTICS:** Hopeful, Proud, Loyal, Pushy, Faithful, Bold

▷ **DATA:** 22 words

Who was Salome?

The wife of Zebedee, a fisherman in Galilee // The mother of James and John, two of Jesus' closest friends and disciples // An extended family member of Jesus

What did Salome, the mother of James and John, say?

"Declare that these two sons of mine will sit, one at your right hand and one at your left, in your kingdom." *Matthew 20:21*

Salome's story

This tale is a bit of a surprise. Most people remember the woman in the Bible who asks Jesus to seat her two sons on either side of him in paradise, but some do not make the connection that she is the mother of the disciples James and John. Among the first to be called by Jesus into his ministry, her son John is traditionally considered to be the author of the Gospel of John, and James (the Great) was the first apostle to be martyred.

Picture the well-known day when Jesus fished for disciples along the Lake of Galilee's shores. Brothers Simon (later called Peter) and Andrew were called first, then James and John, these sons of Zebedee: "They immediately followed him, leaving the boat and their father behind."[82]

Their mother, however, will not be left behind. There is evidence that she was present for at least some of Jesus' ministry: when she asked her famous question (Matthew 20:21); when Jesus is dying on the cross (Mark 15:40, Matthew 27:56, John 19:25), and when she goes to Jesus' tomb to anoint his body (Mark 16:1).

Clearly she is a woman who does not hold back. If she were only interested in her boys' future welfare, she would not have been with Jesus. (What of her husband Zebedee? We do not know. He might have well stayed behind to keep the family going financially and to provide money for Salome and his sons to support Jesus.)

Consider this

What do we make of her request? One interpretation is simply that she wanted her sons to have a secure future. Let the fog lift here. The woman wanted her sons by Jesus' side in paradise. Contemporary readers will take her request for granted, but paradise was a relatively new concept in first-century Judaism. Given that Jesus had just told the disciples that he would be killed (Matthew 20:19), she may have feared her sons would have shortened life spans—or she just wanted to settle the matter before he died. Soon. By presenting her concern to Jesus, she was entrusting her young men to the Lord, much like Moses' mother had trusted God when floating his little basket in the Nile River.

So yes, she wanted her sons secure. Shocking. What mother doesn't? He had favored them during his lifetime...and why? Perhaps they had become friends, having met as strangers at the Lake of Galilee on that fateful day. Yet there is another possibility here that tends to make the puzzle clear: Jesus was her nephew, the boys were his cousins, and Mary, Jesus' mother, was her sister.

Note who is standing at the cross in John's Gospel: his mother; his mother's sister; Mary the wife of Cleopas; and Mary from Magdala (John 19:25). Scholar William Barclay points out that while the sister was not named in John's gospel, "A study of the parallel passages (Mark 15:40, Matthew 27:56) makes it quite clear that she was Salome, the mother of [the sons of Zebedee] James and John."[83]

Knowing that, she comes more into focus, for Salome would have known Jesus since he was a baby. She knew of his miraculous birth narratives; she may have seen Jesus perform miracles; she knew Elizabeth (her cousin); and she may have traveled with her sister Mary to support both her and the circle of cousins.

That would also explain why, back in Galilee, her sons jumped into the boat so quickly with Jesus: they were cousins; they were family. It may also be why Jesus left his mother in the care of John, her nephew, as he was dying on the cross.

Another interpretation is that she comes from a passionate family. James and John are called the *Boagernes* by Jesus (Mark 3:17), which means "Sons of Thunder." They are not called the Sons of Pastel Colors or the Sons of Fluffy Breezes; their naming by Jesus indicates they were passionate, loud, and quick to anger. One clear example occurs in Luke 9 when, on his way to Jerusalem, Jesus attempts to find lodging for the disciples in Samaria. Refused because the Samaritans and the Jews have been enemies for some seven hundred years[84],

Jesus hears this Mafia-type response from James and John: "Lord, do you want us to command fire from heaven to come down from heaven?" (Luke 9:54).

The boys seem to take after their mother in terms of verbal expression, as Salome, James, and John all tend to say what they are thinking and feeling. And that is part of why this trio is so appealing: they are wonderfully expressive and ready to put their lives on the line.

When the dots are connected here, Salome and Zebedee can be credited with raising remarkable and faithful sons. John, whose eloquent spirit would flow through the gospel penned under his name, is thought to have been the longest-living apostle and, in fact, "the beloved disciple." James, as his mother feared, did give his life for Jesus, and was the first of the twelve to be martyred for his faith (Acts 12:1-2).

We trust that Salome, she of the pushy-but-famous question, is now at peace and that she, Zebedee, James, and John are a family forever united, with all the saints.

What might we learn from Salome?

  ▷   Our family members belong to God, not to us.

  ▷   Know when to act boldly and when to hold back.

  ▷   Don't give only part of yourself to people you love; give all you have.

For reflection

1. How do you understand Salome, the mother of James and John? What motivated her request? In that people of faith are encouraged to share in prayer all that is on their hearts, was it wrong of her to ask her famous question of Jesus? If so, why? If not, why not?

2. What do you think of Jesus' response to her question? (Matthew 20:22-23.)

3. If Jesus was her nephew and Mary was her sister, what might Salome have seen that is not reported in the Bible?

THE SERVANT GIRLS AT THE HIGH PRIEST'S HOUSE

Turf protectors

▷ **READ THEIR STORIES:** Matthew 26:69-75, Mark 14:66-72, Luke 22:54-62

▷ **CLASSIC MOMENT:** Pointing out Peter as a follower of Jesus

▷ **LIKELY CHARACTERISTICS:** Observant, Bold, Confrontational, Accusatory

▷ **DATA:** 35 words

Who were the servant girls?[85]

Older girls and young women of Jerusalem // At least one worked in the household of the high priest // Catalysts and witnesses to Peter's denial of Jesus

What did the girls say?

Maid #1: A servant-girl came to him and said, **"You also were with Jesus the Galilean."** *Matthew 26:69*

Maid #2: When he went out to the porch, another servant-girl saw him, and she said to the bystanders, **"This man was with Jesus of Nazareth."** *Matthew 26:71*

Maid #1: When she saw Peter warming himself, she stared at him and said, **"You also were with Jesus, the man from Nazareth."** *Mark 14:67*

And the servant-girl, on seeing him, began again to say to the bystanders, **"This man is one of them."** *Mark 14:69*

Maid #1: Then a servant-girl, seeing him in the firelight, stared at him and said, **"This man also was with him."** *Luke 22:56*

The girls' story

After Jesus had been arrested at the Garden of Gethsemane, he was taken to the house of Caiaphas, the high priest who had advised the Sanhedrin that it would be better for Jesus to die than "to have the whole nation destroyed" (John 11:50).

No doubt shell-shocked at the quick turn of events, Peter follows the posse at a distance, then sits outside in the courtyard with the other riffraff (called "riffraff" here because those who were of higher rank would have been inside the house).

Alas, he is not left alone for long. A servant girl walks up to him and says, "You were also with Jesus the Galilean."

"I do not know what you are talking about!" he says, and leaves.

On the porch, hoped-for anonymity escapes him as well, as another servant girl identifies him. "This man was with Jesus of Nazareth!" she says.

"Woman, I do not know him!" Peter protests.

And then a bystander comes up. "Of course you are one of them; your accent betrays you."

"I do not know the man!"

And with that angry blast, Peter hears a cock crow. Suddenly weak in the knees, he remembers what Jesus had said, only a few hours before: "...before the cock crows, you will deny me three times" (Matthew 26:34).

Consider this

Sometimes servant girls are helpful and kind, like the girl who assisted Naaman's wife (2 Kings 5:2-3) or the servants who helped Phinehas's wife give birth (1 Samuel 4:19-22). That is not the case here.

Here, the words of the girls are harsh and clipped as they point out Peter, the-guilty-by-association-stranger, in their midst. Only one girl is identified as working for Caiaphas's household, and she may have been trying to protect her job by singling out Peter. Or, like anyone who is generally ignored (and servant girls would have been on that list), they might have enjoyed the momentary power their observations gave them that night.

By their accusations, Jesus' prophecy about the cock crowing proves true. Events were in motion for the death of Jesus; and the servant girls were cogs in the wheels that would not stop grinding until the cursed deed was done.

What might we learn from the servant girls?

▷ Power should be used with discretion.

▷ People's accusations can cause more damage than we know.

▷ God can use even unthinking actions to fulfill prophecies.

For reflection

1. What do these girls have to gain by exposing Peter? Was it their job to do so or were they just overly curious?

2. Put yourself into the place of someone with a thankless and low-paying job. How do you find satisfaction in your work? How do you work off frustrations? Do others get hurt as a result?

3. Have you ever "spoken up" for the hope of a moment of attention or prestige? How did you feel about your actions later?

4. Think of an action in your life that had inadvertent consequences for someone else. How has God used that moment?

PILATE'S WIFE

A rose married to a thorn

▷ **READ PILATE'S WIFE'S STORY:**
Matthew 27:15-24

▷ **CLASSIC MOMENT:** Warning her husband not to condemn Jesus to death

▷ **LIKELY CHARACTERISTICS:** Intuitive, Fearful, Compassionate, Sensitive, Wise

▷ **DATA:** 22 words

Who was Pilate's wife?

The wife of a Roman official // A sensitive soul // A truth-teller

What did Pilate's wife say?

"Have nothing to do with that innocent man, for today I have suffered a great deal because of a dream about him." *Matthew 27:19*

Pilate's wife's story

As the midmorning light spills into her room, Pilate's wife jolts awake, her eyes stretched like saucers. "No! Don't do it! No!"

Hearing her distress, servants tumble into the room. And there they see a strange sight: their disheveled and shaking mistress scrawling words onto a linen napkin used at dinner the night before.[86]

"Here," she says, "Take this to Pilate. Make sure he gets it immediately." As the door closes, she falls back on her bed, haunted by jumbled images from a dream that caused her great pain.

What did that dream include? We do not know. But just possibly: the man they call Jesus—darkness—crowds following him—blackness—crying children—a child without his mother—a cross—a hand from heaven splitting the sky in two. And yes, there is her beloved husband—why is he napping in the town square? Wait...it is only his body; her husband is dead and the ravens are coming for him. Soon they attack her, too, pulling her eyes from her face—tearing into her stomach...

Blocks away, on the judgment seat of Jerusalem, Pilate sits, weighing the fate of one Jesus of Nazareth, a popular rabble-rouser with a divinity complex. Playing to the annual Passover tradition of letting the crowd choose one criminal over another to walk free, he has just asked the mob their opinion: "Is it to be Jesus, who is called the Messiah, or Barabbas, that you want me to release?"

As the crowd starts to roar their response, Pilate takes a closer look. More of a mob than a crowd, he thinks. This could be dangerous. Let Jesus live, and I'd have another riot on my hands. It would be one thing if the idiot would talk to me. But he won't say anything when I ask him who he is.

And then a message is shoved into his hand. "It's from your wife." He unfolds it, and reads: "Have nothing to do with that innocent man, for today I have suffered a great deal because of a dream about him."

Eyeing the advancing mob, Pilate reads the note again, then stands. "Who do you want me to release?" he asks again. "Jesus or Barabbas?"

The resounding reply: "Barabbas! Give us Barabbas!" And with that, Pilate washes his hands before the crowd, saying, "I am innocent of this man's blood. See to it yourselves" (Matthew 27:24).

Consider this

Pilate's wife is remembered for having the courage to speak up, even though her plea was rejected. She could have cast her dream aside as just a bad nightmare. But she listened and acted.

Given the history of powerful dreams in the Bible (e.g., God telling Joseph to go ahead and wed Mary, then telling him to leave Bethlehem for Egypt), perhaps her dream was God-inspired, a direct message from the top to stop the crucifixion. Perhaps she had watched Jesus from her window as he helped the blind to see and the lame to walk, and she knew him to be a good and decent man.

Either way, she was a woman who did the right thing—so much so that she is remembered as a saint in the Greek Orthodox Church. Later non-biblical writings suggest that she might even have been a secret follower of Jesus.

One thing is clear: she spoke the truth about what might happen. After Jesus was crucified, Pilate was reportedly banished to the south of France, where he committed suicide.[87]

What might we learn from Pilate's wife?

- ▷ Stand up for the innocent.
- ▷ Do not hesitate to act against injustice.
- ▷ Communicate with our families.
- ▷ Pay attention to dreams and intuition.

For reflection

1. Pilate's wife trusted her dream enough to act on it. Was the dream inspired by the Holy Spirit? Had she a sense that Jesus was the son of God? Was she a woman who worked from intuition, or did she have a feeling that Pilate's life would be in danger?

2. What would you have done in this situation?

3. To what extent have you used images, dreams, and intuition to guide your decision making? How do you rate the value of such gifts? What instance in your life might this story remind you of?

CHAPTER 25

WOMEN WHO SPEAK IN MARK

Fewer women speak in this gospel than any other—but that is not surprising, given that it is the shortest one. Like a journalist, Mark is brief, and to the point; one of his oft-used words is "immediately." His favorite themes are service and leadership, and he clearly sees women active in those roles, such as when Peter's quiet mother-in-law serves the disciples (Mark 1:31) right after Jesus heals her (no time to rest!).

By the numbers

Words spoken by women in Mark: 79

Number of women who speak: Five individuals (the bleeding woman, Herodias [daughter], Herodias [mother], the Syrophoenician woman, and the servant girl of the high priest #1) and one group of three women at the tomb (Mary Magdalene, Mary, the mother of James, and Salome)

HERODIAS

Bad Mama

PROFILE:
MODERATE

▷ **READ HER STORY:** Matthew 14:1-11, Mark 6:17-28, Luke 3:19

▷ **CLASSIC MOMENT:** Prompting her daughter to ask for John the Baptist's head on a platter

▷ **LIKELY CHARACTERISTICS:** Manipulative, Vengeful, Selfish, Bloodthirsty, Ruthless

▷ **DATA:** 6 words

Who was Herodias?

Wife of King Herod Antipas when John is beheaded // Ex-wife of Herod Philip (her half-uncle and Antipas's half brother) // Mother of Salome (Herod Philip is the biological father) // A woman greatly irritated by John the Baptist // Wife to Antipas when Pilate sent Jesus to Herod to decide his fate (Herod sent Jesus back to Pilate instead of freeing him)

What did Herodias say?

"The head of John the baptizer." *Mark 6:24*

Herodias's story

It is hard to know exactly what went through Herodias's mind. Raised in a family that seemed to value evil deeds, beheadings, and power grabs, she probably wasn't praying or planning tea parties for her servants. Perhaps her thoughts went something like this:

I want that man dead. Yet it won't be easy. If I have a guard run a sword through his side then everyone would blame me. Have Herod throw him to the lions and there would be riots. Everybody likes this John-man, even though he's crazy. He quotes God. Big deal. The only real god is Baal.

Plus, that shaggy creep is telling everyone that God says Herod can't have me. Well, he's already got me! We're married, for heaven's sake. So what if I threw my old husband away? He's happy now, married to old what's-her-name.

How can I get rid of the Baptist? Oh, I know!

There's that birthday party coming up for Herod. Let's see, Herod likes my girl. Too much, methinks, but that's a problem for another day. I'll have her dance at the party, that's it! And I'll make sure Big H gets very merry. With any luck, the tide will turn. Herod will be so drunk that he'll give her whatever she wants. And I'll make sure that she knows exactly what to ask for.

Consider this

Presented above is only one scenario. While impossible to tell exactly what went through Herodias's mind, the point is this: she was not a passive bystander to the demise of John the Baptist.

Possibly one of the most evil women in biblical history, it appears she was indeed an active force in separating John's head from his body. And it remains staggering to ponder that this is the only full mother-daughter conversation in the entire Bible.

Enough said.

What might we learn from Herodias?

▷ Grudges can result in murderous actions.

▷ Sometimes it is better to leave young people alone.

▷ The role of a parent is not to manipulate their children into taking certain actions; the role is to help the child grow in love, wisdom, and maturity.

▷ Parents always have power; the question is how best to use it.

For reflection

1. We know how Herodias regarded John the Baptist, but how do you think she regarded her daughter and her husband? If there was some attraction to Salome on Herod's part, what does it say about Herodias that she capitalized on it? What does it say about her understanding of motherhood?

2. Exodus 20:5 says, "...I the LORD your God am a jealous God, punishing children for the iniquity of parents, to the third and the fourth generation of those who reject me." While Salome comes from a destructive and faithless family, her mother's iniquity causes problems here. Does such iniquity carry through generations and how so?

3. Does revenge ever improve a situation? How does God take evil and turn it to good?

4. How does one enlist God's help in turning away from generations of learned negative behavior?

THE WOMEN AT THE TOMB: MARY MAGDALENE; MARY, THE MOTHER OF JAMES; SALOME, THE MOTHER OF THE SONS OF ZEBEDEE

PROFILE: HIGH

▷ **READ THEIR STORY:** Mark 16:1-8

▷ **CLASSIC MOMENT:** Discovering Jesus' empty tomb

▷ **LIKELY CHARACTERISTICS:** Loyal, Compassionate, Attentive, Diligent, Grief-stricken, Devoted

▷ **DATA:** 14 words

Who were these women at the tomb?

Mary Magdalene was one of Jesus' closest friends and followers // Mary was the mother of the apostle James (the Less) // Salome was the mother of the sons of Zebedee, James (the Great) and John // They were all closely connected to Jesus' life and work

What did the women at the tomb say?

"Who will roll away the stone for us from the entrance to the tomb?" *Mark 16:3*

The women at the tomb's story

Harrowing might best describe the last two days for these women, for they had watched Jesus suffer and die and were now on their way to prepare his body for its final rest. Two were mothers of apostles; the other was Jesus' unique and loyal companion Mary from Magdala.

Unlike the disciples who were too scared to stay with Jesus at Golgotha (except John), these women would see Jesus and his mortal shell through to the end. Even while grief-stricken, they discussed what would await them: a heavy stone blocking the tomb's entrance. Imagine their surprise, then, as they turned the corner. The stone had been moved, the tomb was open, and a young man dressed in white stood to greet them. "Jesus is not here," he said. "He is risen. You will see him again, for he is in Galilee. Go now. Tell the disciples and Peter."

One would think they would be thrilled; perhaps they were. But Mark, in his blunt journalistic style, describes their reaction as one of fear: "They went out and fled from the tomb, for terror and amazement had seized them; and they said nothing to anyone, for they were afraid."

Consider this

Who knew? The women thought they had been through the worst already when they stood at the crucifixion. Such a move took great courage, for armed Roman soldiers were surely lurking about. Some commentators have said that women in those biblical days were so insignificant that they were in no danger. Hmmm...not so.

It is always dangerous to align oneself against authority, especially in matters of heresy, writes William Barclay. "The presence of these women at the Cross was not due to the fact that they were so unimportant that no one would notice them; their presence was due to the fact that perfect love casts out fear."[88]

Providers of perfect love. No other title fits these women better.

MARK

What might we learn from the women at the tomb?

- ▷ Good friends and true relatives continue to honor a friendship even after death.

- ▷ Fear, death, and heavy stones might block our path, but God will overcome them to reach us.

- ▷ God's overwhelming glory can frighten us because we do not know how to react to something beyond our understanding.

For reflection

1. Focus on these words (Mark 16:8): "And [the women] went out and fled from the tomb; for terror and amazement had seized them; and they said nothing to anyone, for they were afraid." What must it have been like to be present in that moment, so afraid that you were trembling?

2. Do you blame these women for being too afraid to tell anyone at first? What might they have been risking? What do you think persuaded them to move past that fear?

3. Have you ever run from something because you were afraid? Was it the right move? Has God helped move the heavy weight of that experience, or does it still frighten you?

4. Many women are responsible for seeing tasks through in their faith communities and have reached a certain level of fatigue because of it. How do you keep your spiritual life balanced while attending to the many details of your personal and/or professional life?

Women at Jesus' tomb: A study in differences

The gospel accounts vary regarding women at the empty tomb, but keep in mind these common denominators:

- Women were the first to approach the tomb after the sabbath.

- Women were the first to be addressed by the angels and/or Jesus.

- Women were the first to see Jesus after the Resurrection.

- Women were the first to spread the news about his Resurrection.

- "Woman" was the first word spoken by the angels (in John) after the Resurrection.

- "Woman" was the first word spoken by Jesus (in John) after the Resurrection.

- The disciples did not believe the women, except for Peter and John (initially), who ran to the tomb after Mary Magdalene had sought them out.

MATTHEW: Mary Magdalene and the "other Mary" find the tomb empty, hear an angel say that Jesus has risen, run to tell the disciples, and are met by Jesus (Matthew 28:1-10).

MARK has two endings: 1) Mary the mother of James, Salome the mother of James and John, and Mary Magdalene find the tomb empty. They are told by a messenger that Jesus has risen and are so stunned they say nothing to anyone. 2) Jesus appears to Mary Magdalene; she goes to his distraught companions and tells them he is alive and well, but they do not believe her (Mark 16).

LUKE: The women go to the tomb and cannot find Jesus' body. Two angels, full of light, ask them why they seek the living among the dead; they return empty-handed. Luke names the women as Mary Magdalene, Joanna, Mary the mother of James, and the "other women with them." The words seemed to the disciples "an idle tale," and they initially did not believe them (Luke 24:1-12).

JOHN: Mary Magdalene goes to the tomb and sees the stone moved away. She runs to tell Peter and "the beloved disciple," who run to the tomb, go inside, find nothing, and return home. Jesus appears to Mary Magdalene, who tells the disciples (John 20:1-10).

CHAPTER 26

WOMEN WHO SPEAK IN LUKE

Luke is a physician and the compiler of both the Gospel of Luke and the Book of Acts, thought originally to be one book. The only gospel writer who is not Jewish, he directs his writings to the Gentile community, writes in Greek, and uses historical details to help paint the scene. Women speak almost as much here (327 words) as they do in John, but most of Luke's energy for women who speak is in the opening pages.

By the numbers

Words spoken by women in Luke: 327

Number of women who speak: Five (Elizabeth, Mary the mother of Jesus, Martha of Bethany, woman in the crowd, and servant girl #2)

ELIZABETH

The mother of John the Baptist

PROFILE:
MODERATELY
HIGH

▷ **READ HER STORY:** Luke 1

▷ **CLASSIC MOMENT:** When Mary visited Elizabeth, her child leaped in her womb and she recognized Mary as "the mother of my Lord"

▷ **LIKELY CHARACTERISTICS:** Jubilant, Magnanimous, Open-hearted, Principled, Prophetic, Loving, Grateful

▷ **DATA:** 102 words

Who was Elizabeth?

A descendent of Aaron; daughter of a family of priests // Wife of Zechariah, who was a member of the priestly order of Abijah // Childless and past childbearing age // Cousin of Mary, the mother of Jesus // Blessed by God in her old age with the birth of her son John the Baptist // The first to greet Mary as the mother of the Messiah // A woman of great faith

What did Elizabeth say?

"This is what the Lord has done for me when he looked favorably on me and took away the disgrace I have endured among my people." *Luke 1:25*

When Elizabeth heard Mary's greeting, the child leaped in her womb. And Elizabeth was filled with the Holy Spirit and exclaimed with a loud cry, **"Blessed are you among women, and blessed is the fruit of your womb. And why has this happened to me, that the mother of my Lord comes to me? For** as soon as I heard the sound of your greeting, the child in my womb leaped for joy. And blessed is she who believed that there would be a fulfillment of what was spoken to her by the Lord." *Luke 1:42-45*

But his mother said, **"No; he is to be called John."** *Luke 1:60*

Elizabeth's story

An older woman, Elizabeth is married to a priest named Zechariah. Neither of them is mentioned in the Bible until Luke 1, when sacred clues—smoke, infertility, an angel—point to An Important Event About to Happen.

Zechariah and Elizabeth have a AAA rating: they both descend from the priestly caste of Aaron, Moses' brother. Well-behaved on all counts, they are neither rabble-rousers nor whiners. They go about their work year after year until one special day, when Zechariah is chosen by lot for the lifetime honor of burning incense in the temple on behalf of his people.

Luke does not say where Elizabeth is when Zechariah disappears into the inner sanctum. She may be in the Court of Women, praying. She might be at home making dinner, sewing vestments, or resting. Little does she, or anyone else, know that her husband is about to have the surprise of his life—for in that smoky space emerges God's holy messenger, Gabriel.

Imagine the flourish, and Zechariah's surprise, when Gabriel appears. He most likely suspects the form is a heavenly being, but knows nothing more.

The angel is blunt. "Your wife will bear a child," he says.

Zechariah stands speechless. Such a thought has been his lifelong dream, but who is this strange creature?

"His name will be John, and he will point his people to the Lord their God," Gabriel explains. "You shall raise him as one set apart by God. He will be a holy man."

The priest does not believe what he is hearing and has much the same reaction that Abraham did when God's messengers said Sarah would bear a child in her old age.

"I am an old man," he protests, "and my wife is getting on in years!"

"Fine," says Gabriel. "Don't believe me. I'm making you mute until after the baby is born because of your unbelief. That way you won't have any trouble keeping your thoughts to yourself."

Despite being in God's penalty zone, Zechariah is able to communicate to Elizabeth the good news that they will be parents. Elizabeth, God bless her (and this is probably why God chose her), rejoices without question, in full trust.

Several months later, she hears a knock at her door. It is her cousin, young Mary of Nazareth, breathless because of the long trek. Fleeing from her home, she has come "with haste" to see Elizabeth. Upon hearing Mary's voice, baby John leaps in Elizabeth's womb—and instantly Elizabeth understands.

"Blessed are you among women, and blessed is the fruit of your womb!" cries Elizabeth. "And why has this happened, that the mother of my Lord comes to me?"

Imagine Mary's joy. Finally she is with someone who rejoices in her pregnancy and understands it not as problematic, but as good and holy. So content is Mary that she recites the *Magnificat*, a glorious spoken hymn praising God. And then she stays with Elizabeth for three months, no doubt a time of both rejoicing and sharing for both mothers-to-be: one young, one old.

When John is eight days of age, his parents bring him to the temple for the traditional rite of circumcision. Those gathered round begin to name the child Zechariah, after his father.

Elizabeth speaks up, saying: "No; he is to be called John." But her word is not enough; they check with Zechariah, still mute. Grabbing for a tablet, he confirms her statement, writing, "His name is John."

Later known as John the Baptist, their son would spend his adult life preparing the way for his cousin Jesus: baptizing, teaching, and preaching. In his early thirties, he was beheaded for criticizing Herod.

One hopes his mother and father had passed away by then.

Consider this

Imagine the surprise Elizabeth felt when she opened her door to find Mary on her threshold. Unlike Sarah, who laughed skeptically when she was told she would bear a child in old age, Elizabeth rejoiced in the whole process: hearing the news, anticipating the birth, and sharing in Mary's joy.

And imagine the thump in her stomach as baby John leaped in her womb upon hearing Mary's voice. Called to prepare the way of Jesus, his work had already started.

Over thirty years later, Jesus would ask Simon Peter, "...who do you say that I am?" Peter would answer, "You are the Messiah, the Son of the living God" (Matthew 16:15-16) And in Luke 9:20: "The Messiah of God." The woman at the well would ask almost the same thing: "Come, see a man who told me all that I ever did. He cannot be the Messiah, can he?" (John 4:29).

This, then, is the earliest confession in the New Testament—initiated by wee John and spoken by Elizabeth: "Blessed are you among women, and blessed is the fruit of your womb...the mother of my Lord comes to me..."

We do not know anything of John's childhood, other than that he was raised a nazirite, one commissioned by God for a sacred role. But we do know his mother loved him dearly and was delighted to be such a key part of God's unfolding plan.

What might we learn from Elizabeth?

▷ Calls to serve God can come at any age.

▷ Patience can be rewarding; miracles can happen.

▷ Virtues such as faith, joy, and bravery can indeed be passed onto a child.

▷ Joy is contagious.

For reflection

1. Elizabeth had been waiting on God for most of her adult life, hoping to have a child. Such attentive waiting was perhaps one reason why God chose her to bear John. What other traits did she have that caused God to call her, late in life, to the vocation of motherhood?

2. Elizabeth and Mary were cousins but also seemed to be soul mates. Have you known such women in your life? What traits would you use to describe them?

3. C.S. Lewis titled his autobiography *Surprised by Joy*. What joys has God surprised you with in your life?

4. Consider how you have been able to let go of your children, or other loved ones, into God's hands when the time is right. What has God done with their lives that you might not have envisioned?

MARY

The mother of Jesus

PROFILE: HIGH

▷ **READ HER STORY:** Matthew 1:16-23, 2:11, 12:46-50, 13:54-58; Mark 3:31-35, 6:1-6, Luke 1:26-56, 2:1-52, 8:19-21; John 2:1-12, 19:25-27; Acts 1:12-14

▷ **CLASSIC MOMENT:** Saying yes to God and giving birth to Jesus

▷ **LIKELY CHARACTERISTICS:** Brave, Humble, Thoughtful, Practical, Trusting, Resilient, Faithful

▷ **DATA:** 191 words (182 in Luke, 9 in John)

Who was Mary?

The mother of Jesus, initially single when called to motherhood // A girl, most likely fourteen to sixteen years of age, engaged to a carpenter named Joseph // A native of Nazareth in Galilee // The daughter of Anna and Joachim, a descendent of Leah and a member of the tribe of Judah // The *Theotokos* (Greek: God-bearer, a traditional title)

What did Mary say?

Mary said to the angel, **"How can this be, since I am a virgin?"** *Luke 1:34*

Then Mary said, **"Here am I, the servant of the Lord; let it be with me according to your word."** *Luke 1:38*

And Mary said,

"My soul magnifies the Lord,
  and my spirit rejoices in God my Savior,
    for he has looked with favor on the lowliness of his servant.
Surely, from now on all generations will call me blessed;
  for the Mighty One has done great things for me,
    and holy is his name.
His mercy is for those who fear him
  from generation to generation.
He has shown strength with his arm;
  he has scattered the proud in the thoughts of their hearts.
He has brought down the powerful from their thrones,
  and lifted up the lowly;
he has filled the hungry with good things,
  and sent the rich away empty.
He has helped his servant Israel,
  in remembrance of his mercy,
    according to the promise he made to our ancestors,
    to Abraham and to his descendants forever." *Luke 1:46-56*

When his parents saw him they were astonished; and his mother said to him, **"Child, why have you treated us like this? Look, your father and I have been searching for you in great anxiety."** *Luke 2:48*

When the wine gave out, the mother of Jesus said to him, **"They have no wine."** *John 2:3*

His mother said to the servants, **"Do whatever he tells you."** *John 2:5*

Mary's story

She is Jesus' mother. Everything we know about her springs from that relationship. Loved and revered by millions over the centuries, especially in the Roman Catholic and Orthodox churches, she still manages to be, like her son, transformative and accessible.

Her major life events are well-known: The encounter with the angel Gabriel and her embrace of God's plan, the haste with which she flees to see Elizabeth, the birth of Jesus in a stable far from her home, the visit of the wise men, the holy family's flight to Egypt, the mad search for Jesus when he was twelve, the miracle of the wedding in Cana, the perplexity Mary faces when Jesus seems to reject his original family, and finally, her grief at his death.

Events, however, are only one aspect of learning about Bible women. With an inquiring and discerning heart, consider Mary's words, spoken and unspoken.

When Gabriel approaches Mary, he tells her, "Hail, O favored one, the Lord is with you!" The gospel says that her unspoken response (which is as important as any spoken response) is to be "much perplexed by his words" as she wonders "what sort of greeting this might be" (Luke 1:28-29).

She's a smart girl. Most people do not wish to be high on the radar of cosmic forces, oncologists, or fire departments. Mary knows that she is on God's radar. Of course she is troubled. Of course she considers in her mind what sort of greeting "this might be."

She knows the scriptures: how the Angel of Death went through King Sennacherib's camp, causing 185,000 Assyrian soldiers to die (2 Kings 19:35); how Jacob fought with an angel and was disabled (Genesis 32:24-30); how an angel had issued a call to war by causing a fire to spring up in front of Gideon (Judges 6:11-21).

Such knowledge makes it hard not to be afraid, especially because she is a virgin and is only betrothed to be married, not yet married—and punishment for adultery is stoning. Neither Joseph nor her parents will understand. And yet somehow, she finds the strength and faith to tell Gabriel, "Let it be to me according to your word."

After her visit to Elizabeth (which seems like more of an escape, away from prying eyes and ears), and after the birth of Jesus in a stable because the young couple could not find shelter in Bethlehem, Mary is visited by shepherds and wise men alike. Luke says, "Mary treasured all these words and pondered them in her heart."

That phrase will again be used by Luke when Mary and Joseph lose track of Jesus on their caravan (many families traveling together) home from Jerusalem. Unbeknownst to them, he has stayed behind to teach in the temple. When, after three days, they finally locate him, Mary is beside herself. "Why have you treated us like this? We have been in great anxiety!" And although Mary does not understand her son, Luke says, again, that she "treasured these things in her heart."

About eighteen years later, Mary is at a wedding with Jesus at Cana in Galilee, and the host runs out of wine. This would have been a terribly embarrassing problem for first-century hosts, whose celebrations would last for days. In classic mother style, she volunteers her son Jesus to fix the problem. Bringing him to the servants, she says, "Do whatever he tells you."

Jesus, in classic grown-son style, refuses, saying, "My time has not yet come!" But eventually he does what his mother tells him to do, and all are happy. Perhaps she has seen him practice miracles around the house and knows it is his time. Clearly, the fruit of "pondering things" in her heart is taking shape. Such mother-privilege, however, does not seem to count later in Jesus' ministry when he refuses to see her. He is too busy healing people, saying, "all who believe" are now his family members. Again, probable consternation for Mary.

Finally, the day comes that will be the hardest of all: Jesus' death. Mary stands at the cross and watches the life drain from her beloved son. That grief-filled day, too, must have found her pondering her son's life and death in her heart.

In selecting Mary, God made a wise choice. And Mary made a courageous choice in affirming God's plan.

Consider this

Mary could have refused Gabriel's request. God would not have demanded she bear his son—after all, God is the primary believer in free will and designed this world to have it. What might have happened had she said no or run away? The Jesus we know would not have been born.

Some would say that God needed Mary's cooperation. Others would say God does not need human beings, and, rather, deeply desired Mary's cooperation. Each statement holds truth, as does this: God invited Mary into a radical, life-transforming experience. She agreed and opened herself to love, self-sacrifice, and divine intervention in world affairs.

There can be no greater evidence of God's love for women. Christ was born of a woman, Christ was first confessed by a woman, and Christ first revealed his risen self to a woman.

What might we learn from Mary?

▷ Honor the young among us, for God often gives them huge tasks.

▷ Ponder and ask questions, and then give ourselves freely to God's work.

▷ Devote ourselves to God out of love rather than a desire for reward.

▷ Direct credit we receive back to God.

For reflection

1. How much do you think Mary understood about Jesus' life when he was a baby? A boy? A man?

2. Out of the millions of souls on earth, why do you think God chose Mary to be Jesus' mother? Was it that the time was right? Was it that she was right?

3. If an angel came to you from God, how easily would you believe whatever s/he said?

4. What emotions might you have struggled with if you had been in Mary's place? Fear? Pride? Love? Desire?

5. Do you know anyone whose inner strength seems unshakable? How do they approach life?

MARTHA OF BETHANY

Hospitality personified

PROFILE: HIGH

▷ **READ HER STORY:** Luke 10:38-42, John 11:1-44, John 12:2

▷ **CLASSIC MOMENT:** Complaining that her sister is not helping her prepare dinner

▷ **LIKELY CHARACTERISTICS:** Practical, Hardworking, Outspoken, Domestic, Hospitable, Faithful, Loving, Tenacious

▷ **DATA:** 106 words (24 in Luke, 82 in John)

Who was Martha of Bethany?

A woman living with her sister Mary and brother Lazarus in the village of Bethany // A homemaker // A friend and follower of Jesus // A minister of hospitality, creating a warm, loving place for Jesus to visit

What did Martha of Bethany say?

But Martha was distracted by her many tasks; so she came to him and asked, **"Lord, do you not care that my sister has left me to do all the work by myself? Tell her then to help me."** *Luke 10:40*

Martha said to Jesus, **"Lord, if you had been here, my brother would not have died. But even now I know that God will give you whatever you ask of him."** *John 11:21-22*

Martha said to him, **"I know that he will rise again in the resurrection on the last day."** *John 11:24*

She said to him, **"Yes, Lord, I believe that you are the Messiah, the Son of God, the one coming into the world."** When she had said this, she went back and called her sister Mary, and told her privately, **"The Teacher is here and is calling for you."** *John 11:27-28*

Martha, the sister of the dead man, said to him, **"Lord, already there is a stench because he has been dead four days."** *John 11:39*

Martha's story

Even more than Mary, action defines Martha. We see her personality most clearly during the "I need some help!" dinner conflict, and when Lazarus dies.

Act 1: Put yourself in Martha's place. You are making dinner for Jesus and his friends, over a dozen people. You were the one who invited them, but it's a large group, larger than you had thought.

You can tell they haven't had a good meal in weeks. They're ravenous. Andrew and Bartholomew are already nodding off in the corner. Let's see...food for fifteen. Fish would be good...we'll have to get that, and lots of water at the well. Maybe some pickled herring and pletzels.[89] Wine? Someone will have to run and get it. Jesus turned wine into water once, but his mother isn't here to make him do it now. Figs. Figs would be good after dinner.

Soon the floor becomes more crowded, for in first-century Palestine, it is normal to stretch out on one's side to eat. You need help. Where is Mary?

Ah, of course: at Jesus' feet. You tilt your head, showing Mary that you need her. Nothing. You gesture with your hand. No response. So you ask for someone to be the bad cop. "Jesus, tell Mary to help me, would you?"

"Martha, Martha," Jesus replies. "Your distractions overpower you. One thing for dinner is enough; one stew pot is plenty. Mary has chosen the better part."

Act 2: Lazarus is terribly sick, almost to the point of death. You send a messenger for Jesus, sure that he will heal your beloved brother. No response; Lazarus dies. With tears and precious oils, you anoint his body and place it in the burial caves.

Four days later, Jesus finally arrives.

"Lazarus would not have died if you had been here!" you berate him. "And even now, I know God will give you whatever you ask."

Jesus says, "Lazarus will be raised up."

"I know," you sigh. "On the last day."

But he is thinking of something else. "You don't have to wait. I am the resurrection and the life. The one who believes in me, even though he or she dies, will live. Do you believe this?"

"Yes," you say. "All along I have believed that you are the Messiah, the Son of God who comes into the world."

Soon there is a mad rush to the tomb with townspeople, neighbors, and your sister Mary. "Lazarus, come out!" Jesus says.

You recoil. "But Lord, the smell!" (What? The smell? Did I really say that?)

Lazarus stumbles out, his eyes blinded by the light. And you were right; there is a horrible smell of decaying flesh.

But it doesn't matter. Nothing matters right then. Except for Lazarus. Except for Jesus. Except this: What you had long suspected—that Jesus is the Messiah— has been confirmed. And it couldn't have happened in happier circumstances.

Consider this

Traditionally, Martha has been seen as inferior, not as spiritually developed as Mary. She is neither. In her sometimes-harried life, she simply takes on too much. Like most of us.

Jesus and his friends might have gone to that little house in Bethany once, at Martha's initial invitation. But would they have returned if it was not such a place of transformation? Most of what made their renewal possible was due to Martha, the ultimate minister of hospitality.

By declaring that Jesus is Lord, especially before Lazarus is raised, Martha offers up one of the most magnificent confessions of faith in the New Testament.

One final note: Tradition has it that Martha went on to become a missionary, traveling as far as modern-day France, intent on spreading the word about Jesus and protecting his people. Often pictured with a dragon at her feet and an asperges (a container used to splash holy water), she is credited with saving the people of Aix from a dragon hiding on the banks of the Rhone River.

Ah, Martha, Martha. For Jesus, she would do whatever needed to be done: make meals, sweep the floor, shelter the disciples, proclaim Jesus as Lord—even kill dragons!

Sounds like many women of faith throughout the centuries, doing what needs to be done.

What might we learn from Martha of Bethany?

▷ A balance between work and reflection is elusive but important.

▷ Hospitality is indeed a ministry and vocation.

▷ Slaying dragons and providing hospitality are both part of life in Christ.

▷ Death is on God's time, not ours.

For reflection

1. What were Martha's gifts and how did others depend on them?

2. When have you felt particularly welcome at someone's house? What did the host do to help that happen? If you were to picture Martha, would she look like that person?

3. When have you, in your personal life, or in your faith community, done too much when less would have sufficed?

4. What one "pot" do you believe Jesus would want you to keep filled that others might draw from—that would be sufficient for them and give you some balance?

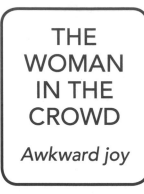

THE WOMAN IN THE CROWD

Awkward joy

PROFILE: VERY LOW

▷ **READ HER STORY:** Luke 11:27-28

▷ **CLASSIC MOMENT:** In an emotional outburst after listening to Jesus, she praises the womb that bore him and the breasts that nursed him

▷ **LIKELY CHARACTERISTICS:** Exuberant, Emotional, Bold, Impulsive, Positive, Inept

▷ **DATA:** 13 words

Who was the woman in the crowd?

A spectator listening to Jesus and witnessing him cast a mute demon out of a man // Probably a resident of Bethany or the surrounding towns

What did the woman in the crowd say?

While he was saying this, a woman in the crowd raised her voice and said to him, **"Blessed is the womb that bore you and the breasts that nursed you!"** But he said, "Blessed rather are those who hear the word of God and obey it!" *Luke 11:27-28*

The woman in the crowd's story

This tale is a bit awkward, inserted into an already uneasy situation. Jesus has just cast a "deaf demon" out of a man, and the man was able to speak. While many are awed, some are skeptical. Soon statements such as these are flying around about Jesus: "He's consorting with Beelzebub! Make him give us a sign from heaven to prove his worth!"

Yikes. In the midst of demon talk, the woman rises up and affirms Jesus by praising the female body parts that bore and nurtured him. Odd phrasing, but Jesus turns it to good use, transforming her awkward statement into a teaching moment. "Blessed, rather, are those who hear the word of God and obey it!"

Consider this

Statements by women, especially in the New Testament, are never without value. Yes, these words might strike the reader as odd. (Imagine if someone loudly blessed your mother's womb and breasts while you were speaking). But think about this: in this section of Luke, Jesus redeems three women—validating them, healing them, and in two cases, soliciting their participation as part of the public conversation.

First there was the bleeding woman who broke through the crowd, convinced that she would be healed if only she touched Jesus. When he felt his power leave him, he could have kept on walking—but instead invited her to tell her story (Luke 8:43-48).

Second was the crippled, bent-over woman who apparently had been forced to stare at the ground for eighteen years because of her infirmity. When Jesus laid his hands on her, she stood up straight and began praising God. Even though temple leaders condemned Jesus for "working" on the sabbath, he was adamant that she be set free from bondage, and that the sabbath was a most appropriate day for her release[90] (Luke 13:10-14).

Third, this woman in the crowd, who speaks out on her own, is validated by Jesus. He could have condemned her or ignored her. Instead, he took her words and turned them outward, saying that all who hear the word of God and obey it are blessed (Luke 11:27-28).

Ironically this incident contrasts with an earlier event, when Jesus appeared to be dismissive of his mother, at least temporarily. Mary and his brothers came to see Jesus, but could not reach him because of the crowds (Luke 8:19-21). Told they were waiting outside, he replied, "My mother and my brothers are those who hear the word of God and do it." The woman in the crowd could have been sticking up for Mary. More likely, however, she was expressing simple joy and admiration for the chain of creation that had produced this wonderful healer.

In short, Jesus uses one woman's words as a teaching platform; he calls upon another to proclaim her divine healing; and he heals another upon discovery, knowing that she would praise and glorify God. In a time when women's voices were not normally welcomed as part of the public conversation, Jesus embraced, used, and raised up what women had to say, awkward or not.

What might we learn from the woman in the crowd?

▷ There is nothing that cannot be shared with God.

▷ Being with Jesus is cause for spontaneous outbursts.

▷ Jesus clearly welcomes the voice and contributions of women.

▷ Sometimes just being near God will bring healing.

For reflection

1. How do you see the woman in the crowd? What might have made her utter the words she did? What might have been her (back) story?

2. In later years, several New Testament writers proclaimed that women should be silent in churches. How does that statement compare to Jesus' words here?

3. Emotion often drives a knowledge and love of God. To what extent has that been the case in your spiritual journey?

4. In seeking to include all believers into his family, Jesus seems a bit cold to his mother and brothers. How do you think Mary reconciled his actions?

CHAPTER 27

WOMEN WHO SPEAK IN JOHN

The spirit, eloquence, and faith of John flow through this gospel. Symbols, relationships, and dialogue are key. A powerful writer, the author presents the fullest picture of women in the Bible, both editorially and numerically (at 336 words). Here, we hear the longest conversation that anyone had with Jesus, through Jesus' lively banter with the woman at the well. We see a fuller picture of Mary and Martha of Bethany, both close friends of Jesus. And of course, we witness the penultimate moment when Mary Magdalene discovers that Jesus has not abandoned her.

JOHN

By the numbers

Words spoken by women in John: 336

Number of women who speak: Seven (Mary the mother of Jesus, the Samaritan woman, the woman caught in adultery, Martha of Bethany, Mary of Bethany, the woman guarding the gate, and Mary Magdalene)

THE SAMARITAN WOMAN

Prosecutor and evangelist

PROFILE: MODERATELY HIGH

▷ **READ HER STORY:** John 4:1-42

▷ **CLASSIC MOMENT:** Debating Jesus nonstop, then becoming convinced that he is the Messiah

▷ **LIKELY CHARACTERISTICS:** Scandalous, Spirited, Curious, Careworn, Intelligent, Gutsy, Analytical

▷ **DATA:** 151 words

Who was the Samaritan woman?

An unnamed woman from Sychar, a city near Jacob's well in Samaria // A woman married five times and living with a man who is not her husband // A woman who was considered an outcast in her own town // A woman with whom Jesus had the longest recorded conversation in the Bible // A woman who had her world turned upside down after she met Jesus and learned of his "living water"

What did the Samaritan woman say?

The Samaritan woman said to him, **"How is it that you, a Jew, ask a drink of me, a woman of Samaria?"** *John 4:9*

The woman said to him, **"Sir, you have no bucket, and the well is deep. Where do you get that living water? Are you greater than our ancestor Jacob, who gave us the well, and with his sons and his flocks drank from it?"** *John 4:11-12*

The woman said to him, **"Sir, give me this water, so that I may never be thirsty or have to keep coming here to draw water."** *John 4:15*

The woman answered him, **"I have no husband."** *John 4:17*

The woman said to him, **"Sir, I see that you are a prophet. Our ancestors worshiped on this mountain, but you say that the place where people must worship is in Jerusalem."** *John 4:19-20*

The woman said to him, **"I know that Messiah is coming (who is called Christ). When he comes, he will proclaim all things to us."** *John 4:25*

"Come and see a man who told me everything I have ever done! He cannot be the Messiah, can he?" *John 4:29*

The Samaritan woman's story

Picture the scene: Jesus, tired and dusty, is journeying north with his disciples from Jerusalem to Galilee, taking the "short cut" through Samaria (which requires about three days of walking rather than six). A friendly place it is not—for although Jews and Samaritans carry many of the same genes, they are age-old enemies.

Under the hot midday sun, the group stops for rest and water. The apostles go into town for food; Jesus waits, alone and resting, but his solitude is soon broken as a middle-aged, careworn woman carrying an empty water jug approaches. She ignores him, and expects he will do the same, as is the custom.

But Jesus says, "Give me a drink of water."

The woman is surprised. "What? Why is it that you, a Jew, talk to me, a woman of Samaria?"

From the start, they pound each other with words and thoughts. She would be a good prosecuting attorney, for she is bright, does not flinch, and looks for the truth. One senses good humor from Jesus' parrying: "You say you want water? I'll give you living water!"

The woman snaps back with, "Sir, you don't even have a bucket! Are you a better man than Jacob, who dug this well and deeded it to us?" (Note that she moves in with authority. Jacob is her ancestor. Of course he was Jesus', too, and she knows that, but he is not in Kansas anymore—he is in her stomping grounds, not his.)

Jesus is enigmatic. "Anyone who drinks the living water will never thirst."

The woman baits Jesus with a dose of sarcasm. "Give me that water, so I'll never have to come back here again!"

One gets the feeling that Jesus is enjoying himself with this comment: "Go get your husband and bring him back here."

Ouch. The ground is shifting, and he has gained the upper hand.

The woman tells him, "I have no husband." And it's the truth, at least technically, but one wonders if she would pass a lie detector test.

Zinger from Jesus: "That's right! You do not have a husband—you've had five, and the man you're living with now isn't your husband!"

Boom. Game over. Or so it appears. But she comes back. "Oh! So you're a prophet, are you?"

Like a ping-pong match, the conversation continues. She questions him, parries with him, searches for answers. Her people, the Samaritans, believe the Messiah will come, but the primary place for worship is Mount Gerazim (in view from where they stand), not Jerusalem. The Samaritans believe that the Messiah will come, but not yet.

The woman finally concedes, "When the Messiah comes, he'll straighten all this out."

Then she gets the surprise of her life when Jesus says, "You don't have to look for him to come. He's here. Right in front of you."

Eyes wide open, she gets it. Shaken, overjoyed, and a bit confused, she races back to town, leaving her water jug behind. Knowing that her word might be discredited because she is viewed as immoral, she invites others to see for themselves.

"I've just met a man by the well who knows everything I've ever done! Do you think this could be the Messiah? Come and see for yourselves!"

Much like how Jesus had met the woman on her ground, she invites the townspeople to come to know Jesus on their terms.

And they do, asking Jesus to stay for two days, during which time many people entrust their lives to him. We can't ignore the townspeople's comment to the woman after those two days, though: "We're believing on our own now, because we've seen the Messiah—not because of what you said!"

Consider this

Surprisingly, many commonalities existed between Jesus and the Samaritan woman. They shared the same bloodlines: Samaritans lived in what had been the northern kingdom of Israel, but their bloodline was a mixture of both Jewish and pagan ancestry. Both Samaritans and Jews were children of Abraham. Both held Mosaic law in common. Both believed in the Torah (the first five books of the Bible). They knew their sacred history. They were both people of story, people of God, people of the Law.

Yet enmity abounded on both sides, with rancor and hatred present for centuries. In 720 BCE, when the Assyrians invaded the northern kingdom of Samaria, most of the Hebrew people were carried off to Media as slaves, and never returned to their home (this group is known as the "lost ten tribes of Israel.") The few Hebrew people left behind married people of other races and belief systems. Racial impurity was deeply compromised and seen as a betrayal.

Jewish pilgrims would often avoid Samaria while walking south to Jerusalem, adding days on to their journey. Jesus and his disciples were an exception, explaining why the Samaritan woman was aghast that Jesus, a rabbi, would speak to her. Jesus and the woman were both outside the mainstream in their cultures. Jesus had just come from difficult times with the Pharisees. Of late, the Pharisees had been keeping score between who was baptizing more people—John the Baptist or Jesus. Tiresome. Irritating. And because of the many men in her life, the woman was a societal castoff. This explains why she was going to the well at midday, long after other women and girls had collected their water in the cool morning hours.

Both the Samaritan woman and Jesus invited people to enter into conversation rather than remain silent or push themselves on others. Trademarks of Jesus' ministry—inviting others to be in relationship with him, to drink of God's eternal living water, and to live a life reflecting God's abundance—were shared by the woman when she said, "Can this be the Messiah? Come and see."

That "come and see" and "experience for yourself" framework was particularly emphasized in John's Gospel, points out scholar Mary Ann Getty-Sullivan: "The Samaritan woman represents all the Gospel is about. She believes on her own experience, and she tells others so they can 'see' for themselves and 'believe.'"[91]

The woman at the well was an evangelist, one of the first. She was bright and smart and outspoken; she was a woman of humor. Most of all, Jesus considered her worthy—worthy of the abundant life which God had promised. Whether she knew it or not, she had indeed herself been dunked in God's well of living water—and transformed.

What might we learn from the Samaritan woman?

▷ Don't be shy about engaging some strangers in conversation; you never know what you may learn.

▷ God may be present in unexpected places.

▷ Intellect is a powerful asset in discerning answers to faith questions.

▷ The right words can give you insight and change your future.

For reflection

1. The Samaritan woman was not afraid to argue—and it would appear that Jesus enjoyed the verbal jousting as well. What might have motivated her to respond as she did? What did she gain from the conversation? What did Jesus gain?

2. This is the longest conversation that Jesus had with anyone in scripture, male or female. What does this say about the woman? What does it say about Jesus?

3. The woman at the well knew the history of her people. What steps might you take to help others, especially children, know their spiritual history?

THE WOMAN CAUGHT IN ADULTERY

"No one, sir."

PROFILE: MODERATELY HIGH

▷ **READ HER STORY:** John 8:1-11

▷ **CLASSIC MOMENT:** Being let off the hook by her accusers after Jesus tells them to go ahead and stone her, but only if they are without sin themselves

▷ **LIKELY CHARACTERISTICS:** Scared, Resigned, Relieved

▷ **DATA:** 3 words

Who was the woman caught in adultery?

Probably a citizen of Galilee // A married or betrothed woman

---

What did woman caught in adultery say?

Jesus straightened up and said to her, "Woman, where are they? Has no one condemned you?" She said, **"No one, sir."** *John 8:10-11*

Woman caught in adultery's story

This woman's story is short and one-sided. The man who was presumably caught with the woman is not present—and the accused says little, neither confirming nor denying the charges.

Under first-century Jewish law, adultery was punishable by death, usually by stoning or strangulation. Roman law, however, said that Jews could not mete out the death penalty on their own, as it was reserved to Roman authority (which is why Jesus himself was turned over to Herod and Pilate by the Jewish Sanhedrin).

The accusers apparently intend to circumvent Roman law and stone the accused woman on the spot. Resigned, she awaits her fate in silence. No apologies, no weeping, no trembling, no trying to flee. It is almost as if, while the accusers are picking out the stones with which to murder her, she has given up. Perhaps she loved the man with whom she was caught. Perhaps he had forced himself upon her. Her secrets would stay her own.

Surprisingly, Jesus crouches down and writes with his finger in the dirt. And then he stands, saying, "Go ahead. Whoever is without sin should be the one to throw the first stone." One by one, the men disappear, leaving Jesus alone with the woman. And then Jesus crouches down again, continuing to write in the dust.

Finally he looks at her, saying, "Woman, what happened to your accusers? Has no one condemned you?"

"No one, sir."

"Neither do I condemn you. Go—and sin no more."

Consider this

The woman says little; the men say they caught her red-handed in the act of adultery—having intercourse with someone other than her husband. A woman of few words, her silence could well be taken as an indicator of guilt.

Yet none of her accusers are without guilt, either. Although the axiom, "Let the one who is without sin cast the first stone," has become a classic warning against over-judging others, there is a foul wind abroad here: a potential triple Pharisaic trap for Jesus.

First, had Jesus said yes to the stoning, he could well have been accused of being a liar and a hypocrite, in contrast to his stated mission about love and mercy.[92] Second, since rabbis were not allowed to authorize or oversee punishments, he would have become bait for the Roman authorities. Third, if he had said no, he would have appeared indifferent to Jewish law, or even opposed to it, as the seventh commandment condemns adultery.

A loving and brilliant strategy by Jesus saves the woman's life and sets her free, while honoring the commandments with the admonition to sin no more. He also proclaims a new, deeper vision of grace and forgiveness in telling her accusers to look at their own transgressions before condemning hers.

What was Jesus writing in that dirt? Hypotheses have come and gone through the years. No one except Jesus and those close enough to read his writing know for sure. Scholar William Barclay suggests this intriguing possibility: that Jesus was writing the sins of the accusers on the ground.[93] Given that the words "without sin" translate in Aramaic to "without a sinful desire," Jesus may have been saying, "Go ahead and stone her, but only if you have never wanted to commit the same sin yourselves." He may have listed the sins of the men first; they saw them and dispersed. Then he listed the woman's sins.

And what about love? There is a possibility here that the woman was found with a man she loved, and that such love—not a prerequisite for or an expectation of marriage—was breaking through. Jesus may have seen something here that no one else did. And perhaps that is why he ultimately freed her, giving her another chance at life while commanding her to sin no more.

In the end what matters is the relief, joy, and opportunity for new life encapsulated in this woman's words: that no one was condemning her. By the grace and love of Christ, she has been freed from deadly punishment and given another chance at love and life.

What might we learn from the woman caught in adultery?

▷ Do not commit adultery.

▷ Do not be over-quick to judge others.

▷ We are all fallen and in need of grace.

▷ God is merciful.

▷ Christ's love redeems people; it does not condemn them.

For reflection

1. It is not clear if the woman was found with a man other than her husband, or if she was being sexually assaulted (which would, unfortunately count as adultery), or if the Pharisees were just trying to trick Jesus. Given those uncertainties, what can be learned from Jesus' response?

2. What do you think Jesus might have been writing in the dirt? Why do you think the woman said so little?

3. As stoning for adultery is still permitted in some countries, how might Jesus' action be relevant for today's world?

4. What does this story say about forgiveness? About forgiving others? About living with forgiveness?

MARY OF BETHANY

Soul mate to Jesus

PROFILE: HIGH

▷ **READ HER STORY:** Luke 10:38-42, John 11:1-45, John 12:1-8

▷ **CLASSIC MOMENT:**
Anointing Jesus' feet

▷ **LIKELY CHARACTERISTICS:**
Quiet, Contemplative, Sensual, Generous, Intuitive, Passionate, Hyper-focused

▷ **DATA:** 12 words

Who was Mary of Bethany?

A woman of great spiritual depth and contemplation // The sister of Martha and Lazarus // A sorrowful, heartbroken woman after her brother Lazarus dies

What did Mary of Bethany say?

"Lord, if you had been here, my brother would not have died." *John 11:32*

Together with her sister Martha: "**Lord, he whom you love is ill.**" *John 11:3*

Mary of Bethany's story

Mary and her sister Martha are standout figures in the New Testament, for they provide Jesus with a place of healing and respite, one to which he and the disciples return to regularly. Although Mary seems to get more positive press than Martha, they are both indisputably valuable to Jesus.

The setting for this story is Martha's small home in Bethany, shared by the sisters. A scant two miles from Jerusalem, the dirt-floor house was probably two stories high, part of a square block of dwellings that shared an inner courtyard for cooking and socializing, fronting onto a hard-packed street. Light and laughter would have spilled out both front and back, especially when Jesus and his friends were in residence.

Along with providing extraordinary hospitality, the sisters are remembered for three events: Martha's fuming at Mary because she would not help her make dinner; Jesus' raising of Lazarus from the dead (see Martha of Bethany's story for details); and Mary's anointing of Jesus with a costly jar of spikenard.

Luke describes the first event: As Martha prepares food for Jesus and his disciples, Mary sits at Jesus' feet, soaking up his presence. Soon, Martha is simmering as much as the vegetables (and with good reason). Boiling over, she demands that Jesus tell Mary to help her, only to hear him respond that Mary has chosen "the better part."

"Sitting at Jesus' feet" perfectly describes Mary. Contemplative by nature, she has found her bliss in simply being with him, focusing on his teachings and learning all she can. When Jesus gently tells Martha that she is distracted by many things, he praises Mary for focusing her attention and finding a spiritual respite at his feet.

Soon it becomes obvious that their soul connection is a two-way street. When Jesus raises Lazarus from the dead, for example, he is approached first by Martha, but is "deeply moved" only after Mary falls at his feet, weeping.

That deep connection is symbolized further when, at a later dinner, Mary takes Jesus' feet, washes them (as a host normally would), and then pours an exotic and costly ointment on Jesus' feet. Using spikenard, a precious oil that would cost about a year's salary, she lovingly moistens his calluses, treats blisters, wipes away the dust, and them dries them with her long hair.

The disciples become outraged. Their anger is not altogether a surprise, for some say that the evocative scent of spikenard could be smelled up to half a mile away. Judas, especially, gets angry and reminds the others how that money could have been better used to serve the poor.

"Let her alone," says Jesus. "Let her alone. Let her keep it for the day of my burial. The poor you will always have with you; you will not always have me."

Consider this

Anointing took place for several reasons, including setting apart and consecrating royalty (e.g., Samuel anointing Saul and David long before they were crowned); marking God's presence and consecrating worship space; healing (Mark 6:13); preparing one's body for love (Song of Solomon 1:2-4); and symbolizing the abundance of God's blessings.

By placing this story at the little house in Bethany six days before the Passover and less than two weeks before the crucifixion, John demonstrates Mary's attentiveness to Jesus in a time of crisis. Somewhere in her soul, Mary sensed the end was drawing near. She didn't talk about it; she didn't share it with the others, but Jesus would have understood—and most likely, her actions gave him strength to face the days ahead.

Truth be told, this narrative is classic Mary of Bethany with Jesus: offering the very best she has, shutting out others in the room, concentrating fully, and offering healing to one whose body will soon be bruised and cast aside.

What might we learn from Mary of Bethany?

▷ Value your teachers and mentors.

▷ Be generous with your gifts.

▷ Pay attention to your friendships.

▷ Trust your instincts.

For reflection

1. Mary of Bethany was intent on listening to Jesus. She also had a sister who probably did most of the day-to-day work around the house. Where are you on this spectrum and how do you find balance?

2. Mary's gift of spikenard was considered extravagant, even though Jesus would all too soon extravagantly give his body and blood for the human race. Why were gifts from the wise men gratefully accepted at Jesus' birth, but the gift of oil criticized near the end?

3. Mary and Martha believed their brother would not have died if Jesus had only shown up earlier. Is there a moment in your life that might have gone differently if God had only shown up sooner? In hindsight, how did it work out?

THE WOMAN GUARDING THE GATE

The bouncer

PROFILE: LOW

▷ **READ HER STORY:** John 18:1-18

▷ **CLASSIC MOMENT:** Asking if Peter was a disciple of Jesus

▷ **LIKELY CHARACTERISTICS:** Curious, Suspicious

▷ **DATA:** 11 words

Who was the woman guarding the gate?

A servant who worked for the high priest // A woman who accused Peter of being a disciple of Jesus // A woman whose comment spurred Peter to lie

What did the woman guarding the gate say?

The woman said to Peter, **"You are not also one of this man's disciples, are you?"** *John 18:17*

Woman guarding the gate's story

Like the servant girls who accused Peter of being with Jesus, this woman is present on one of the saddest nights in sacred history. Her job is to keep enemies and friends of the accused criminals on the other side of the door.

Jesus is inside, having been surrounded by Roman soldiers at the Garden of Gethsemane. One of the disciples is inside as well (although not named, he is most likely John) because he is known to the high priest. Peter, however, is left standing at the gate. John speaks to the woman guarding the gate, and she brings Peter inside.

And it is there her fateful words occur: "You're not one of this man's disciples, are you?" Peter replies, "I am not."

And she is not heard from again.

Consider this

In all likelihood, the woman was just doing her job. She could have spoken casually, or she could have queried Peter because that was why she was at the gate—to keep the "wrong" people out. Given the brevity of her story, it is hard to tell. Compare her story to that of the servant girls, for they are similar (See page 377).

Somehow, whether by observation or instinct, they knew the truth about Peter, and proclaimed it. Unlike the women in the Old Testament who gracefully help people through transitions, this woman almost sells Peter down the river by identifying him.

Such is the power of spoken words. They affirm; they condemn; they teach; they spar. In this case, they make true Jesus' conviction that before the cock crowed, Peter would deny Jesus three times.

What can we learn from the woman guarding the gate?

▷ You never know who is on the other side of the wall.

▷ Doing a job sometimes requires discretion.

▷ We can make transitions difficult or easy for people.

For reflection

1. Consider this woman and her possible motives for identifying Peter. What do you think made her link him to Jesus?

2. Do you think she later regretted her question? Do you think she cared?

3. Sometimes people "just doing their job" can be the most difficult colleagues of all. How do you incorporate your spiritual values into the workplace? Does it help?

MARY MAGDALENE

"I have seen the Lord!"

PROFILE: HIGH

▷ **READ HER STORY:** Matthew 27:55-61, 28:1-10; Mark 15:40-47, 16:1-11; Luke 8:1-3, 24:1-12; John 19:25, 20:1-18

▷ **CLASSIC MOMENT:** Encountering the risen Christ after discovering the empty tomb

▷ **LIKELY CHARACTERISTICS:** Lionhearted, Loyal, Intrepid, Loving, Resilient, Faithful, Tenacious

▷ **DATA:** 61 words

Who was Mary Magdalene?

A woman from Magdala (thus her name) in Galilee // A follower of Jesus // A woman inhabited by seven demons that were cast out by Jesus // A witness to both the Crucifixion and the Resurrection // The first person to whom Jesus appeared after he rose from the dead, and the first to proclaim Jesus' Resurrection in Matthew and John (she is also named in Luke and John as doing so, but is joined by "other women") // Contrary to popular thought, there is no evidence in the gospels that she was a prostitute

What did Mary Magdalene say?

So she ran and went to Simon Peter and the other disciple, the one whom Jesus loved, and said to them, **"They have taken the Lord out of the tomb, and we do not know where they have laid him."** *John 20:2*

[Two angels] said to her, "Woman, why are you weeping?" She said to them, **"They have taken away my Lord, and I do not know where they have laid him."** *John 20:13*

Jesus said to her, "Woman, why are you weeping? Whom are you looking for?" Supposing him to be the gardener, she said to him, **"Sir, if you have carried him away, tell me where you have laid him, and I will take him away."** Jesus said to her, "Mary!" She turned and said to him in Hebrew, **"Rabbouni!"** *John 20:15-16*

Mary Magdalene went and announced to the disciples, **"I have seen the Lord";** and she told them that he had said these things to her. *John 20:18*

Mary Magdalene's story

The story of Mary Magdalene is one of unabashed love for the one who healed her: Jesus.

Surprisingly—because she is such a key woman in the New Testament—her only recorded words come after Jesus' death.

What, then, do we know about her from scripture? This is a question not asked enough over the last two thousand years, as most of what we do hear about her—that she was a prostitute—has no scriptural basis.

Here is what the Bible says about Mary Magdalene: She was healed by Jesus from seven demons (Mark 16:9; Luke 8:1-3); she traveled on the road with Jesus' disciples at least some of the time (Mark 15:40-41; Luke 8:1-3); she stood at the foot of the cross (Matthew 27:56; Mark 15:40-41; John 25:19); she was the first to see and talk with Jesus after the resurrection (Matthew 28:9; John 20:14); and she proclaimed him as the Christ (John 20:18).

What about those demons? This book is not about contradicting Jesus. If Jesus healed people from demons, then demons they were. Today we might define such afflictions as panic attacks, schizophrenia, obsessive compulsive disorder, bipolar disorder, epilepsy, substance abuse, etc. Whatever the illness, whatever the deficiency, whatever the cause, Jesus healed those whose lives were shattered and torn apart by outside and/or inner forces—overpowering the forces that kept people from living whole and integrated lives.

Mary Magdalene was one of those broken people. Suffering from seven— count 'em, seven—maladies, her distress would have been overpowering, her isolation unbearable. It did not matter if the bars that surrounded her were invisible, for she had indeed known solitary confinement. During that time of disease and terror, perhaps she did support herself by prostitution, for there would have been few other ways to buy food. True or not, the Bible does not mention it. Neither does it mention the possibility that she might have been married, though she does have the finances to help support Jesus (Luke 8:3).

What mattered was that upon meeting Jesus, her long sentence of turmoil-filled heartbreak was ended. With a word and touch, Jesus healed her. Completely. For the first time in many years, she was a free, fully integrated person—with a new group of people to love and a reason to live: Jesus. No wonder she was so loyal to him.

She traveled with the group at his request (Luke 8:2), along with other women who had been healed and were providing needed funds. Coed travel was taboo in those days, but Jesus made room.

She was a leader among women. When she is named with other women in the gospels, her name is consistently at the top of the list. One senses that because of her life experiences, she was able to guide the other women through the tensions of living away from their families and camping outdoors. She may also have acted as a bridge to the men in the group, who most likely found it frustrating that women were taking on key roles. Such bridgework was evident when, from the empty tomb, she ran to Peter's house first.

She stood at the foot of the cross and saw her friend through until the end. She may have been scared; she may have worried; she may have been filled with anticipatory grief and more—but she was there, risking all.

She was the first to see and talk with Jesus after the Resurrection. There were many reasons why Mary Magdalene might not have gone to the tomb that morning, but one overarching reason why she did: she loved Jesus and wanted to make sure he was properly cared for, even in death. Imagine her surprise and delight upon recognizing him. Imagine her wanting to throw her arms around him. Imagine her heart soaring when he called her by name. Many had disappointed her in life; Jesus had not.

She was the first to proclaim that he was risen, that he had overcome death and the grave. With the simple words, "I have seen the Lord," history was rocked forever.

Consider this

Jesus chose a once-broken woman to carry the most important news of all time to the world: that the powers of darkness had been beaten back. Mary Magdalene had seen the risen Jesus, the one who had overcome death and the grave, the one who would make eternal life possible for all who believe.

And this is where commentary fails. Perhaps the words of Mary, Jesus' mother, are best invoked: "Let it be to me according to your word." Like her, Mary Magdalene gave her heart and soul to Jesus—and suffered greatly because of it. As Jesus took care of his mother from the cross by appointing her a "new" son, Jesus also reached out to Mary Magdalene after his Resurrection, assuring her that he had overcome death and the grave—and would always be accessible to her and to others who believe.

What might we learn from Mary Magdalene?

- ▷ Jesus calls surprising people into relationship with him.

- ▷ Give all you have to Jesus.

- ▷ True healing gathers and integrates the whole self.

- ▷ Real ministry comes from deep love, not obligation.

- ▷ Communicating God's presence with others, from what we know, is essential.

For reflection

1. Even though Mary Magdalene was quite wounded before Jesus healed her, she must have had qualities that were clearly important to him, for she was one of his closest friends. What might those qualities have been?

2. Mary Magdalene had known spiritual warfare in her soul. To what extent could that have made her more aware of Jesus' power and more loyal to him for healing her? How does brokenness contribute to discipleship?

3. What must Mary Magdalene have felt when she realized that Jesus had risen from the grave? How would you feel if someone you loved had died, and then reappeared?

4. After personal distress and injury, some people remain guarded, unable to break free from trauma. What made Mary Magdalene so trusting? To what extent have you been able to use painful moments from your past to bring others closer to God?

CHAPTER 28

WOMEN WHO SPEAK IN ACTS

In just thirty-nine words, Luke tells of three distinct women: a new Christian gone bad; a new Christian who supports the growing church; and a girl who badgers Paul until he frees her from demons. Sapphira, the first, speaks just five words, while the others use seventeen words each to get their points across.

ACTS

By the numbers

Words spoken by women in Acts: 39

Number of women who speak: Three (Sapphira, Lydia, and the fortune-telling slave girl)

SAPPHIRA

Holding back, unwisely

▷ **READ HER STORY:** Acts 5:1-11

▷ **CLASSIC MOMENT:** Lying to the apostles and dying immediately thereafter

▷ **LIKELY CHARACTERISTICS:** Initially well-intentioned, Committed; Eventually, Duplicitous, Deceitful, Selfish

▷ **DATA:** 5 words

Who was Sapphira?

The wife and co-conspirator of Ananias // A citizen of first-century Jerusalem // A member of one of the first faith communities // A coworker of Peter and other apostles

What did Sapphira say?

Peter said to her, "Tell me whether you and your husband sold the land for such and such a price." And she said, **"Yes, that was the price."** *Acts 5:9*

Sapphira's story

Sapphira and her husband, Ananias, were part of the early Christian community at Jerusalem after Jesus' death and resurrection. Committed to the risen Christ and to changing the world with God's love, their eyes and ears must have been full, listening to firsthand accounts of those who traveled with Jesus.

The ones who had lived with Jesus were used to life in community—sharing out of one's abundance, giving freely to those who had little. They had seen the miracles Jesus performed, including the feeding of the five thousand. They knew that all human life would, one day, turn to dust. They had seen Jesus encourage others to join the movement, then watched as people, for one reason or another, did not commit. In the new faith community, no one was hungry or needy, says Luke, the author of Acts. Believers gave freely, yet those who gave were not forced to sell everything.

Into this group come the husband and wife team of Ananias and Sapphira who, apparently, intend to emulate the generosity of Barnabas, Paul's traveling companion, who sold his land holdings and laid all the money at the disciples' feet. Such gifts made possible the extraordinary work of this community—to share God's Good News.

Sapphira and Ananias mean to show their enthusiasm with their own similar gift from the proceeds of the sale of their land.

But Peter somehow knows the truth: that the couple have lied to the group regarding the sale price and kept some money back for themselves. It could have been 1 percent, it could have been 10 or 50 percent. It doesn't matter. The important point is that with their lie, deceit is entering the community.

Peter demands, "How did Satan tempt you this way, Ananias? Why did you lie about the price of the field? The land was yours to do with as you wanted; so was the money. You didn't have to give any of it to us, but you did need to be honest!"

Upon hearing these words, Ananias falls down dead.

About three hours later, Sapphira comes home, without a notion of what has just happened. "Tell me, Sapphira," Peter asks, "Were you given this price for your field?"

Sapphira answers, "Yes, that's right! That was the price."

"What is going on here that has made you connive against the Holy Spirit?" Peter fumes. "The young men who buried Ananias are at the door. You're next!"

And then Sapphira falls down dead. Like her husband, she has been struck dead by God, for they have grieved the Holy Spirit, the deep Spirit of truth in the new Jerusalem.

Consider this

Ananias and Sapphira may well have joined the group with the best of intentions, wanting to do their part to belong and to support the community. Their sin, then, was not in holding back some of the money from the disciples but in lying about the sale price.

In this first deceitful act in the new faith community, Peter recognized the work of the old adversary, Satan, and called the couple on it. It was as if the serpent was sneaking back into the garden to undermine God's new work.

Sapphira had a chance to redeem herself: she could have told the truth when asked. Yet the only thing she went on record for was a lie. She put her relationship with Ananias before her relationship with God, and in that choice, she lost all.

In their quest to belong, Sapphira and Ananias demonstrated an important point. Whereas all people of faith are constantly tempted, it is often the newer believers who may be more vulnerable to spiritual warfare. They might have benefitted from teachings such as these: "Discipline yourselves, keep alert. Like a roaring lion your adversary the devil prowls around, looking for someone to devour. Resist him, steadfast in your faith" (1 Peter 5:8-9).

God wanted to communicate that living as part of the Body of Christ demands honesty and an upright character. And apparently that message came across loud and strong, for right after Sapphira's death, Luke writes, "And great fear seized the whole church and all who heard of these things" (Acts 5:11). They knew God was not to be trifled with. [94]

What can we learn from Sapphira?

▷ Be truthful.

▷ Give so that others may live.

▷ Stay transparent in your business dealings.

▷ Remember the classic Bible verse from Matthew 6:24: "No one can serve two masters…You cannot serve God and wealth."

For reflection

1. Do you think Sapphira's punishment fit her crime? The story implies that God struck down Sapphira and Ananias, but they could have died from shock. What do you think was the cause of death? And why was Peter so angry with them?

2. What does this story say about marriage and the concept of speaking honestly, even if your spouse does not? What might that mean for you?

3. What did Sapphira's actions have to do with the goal of seeking praise? Have you ever been in a situation where you sought praise but didn't deserve it—and you were the only one who knew?

4. How do you avoid temptation? How are you helping others avoid it? How does being in community with other people of faith help with that goal?

LYDIA

The woman of purple

PROFILE: MODERATE

▷ **READ HER STORY:** Acts 16:13-15

▷ **CLASSIC MOMENT:** Hosting Paul

▷ **LIKELY CHARACTERISTICS:**
Enterprising, Compelling, Faithful, Hospitable, Generous, Evangelistic

▷ **DATA:** 17 words

Who was Lydia?

The first Christian convert in Europe // A businesswoman // A minister of hospitality

What did Lydia say?

When she and her household were baptized, she urged us, saying, **"If you have judged me to be faithful to the Lord, come and stay at my home."** And she prevailed upon us. *Acts 16:15*

Lydia's story

Lydia's story begins near water, where she has gone to pray. A merchant with a flourishing business in purple cloth, she greets women friends on the riverbank outside the little town of Philippi. From there (now modern-day Greece), she keeps up with personal relationships and hears news from travelers near and far.

She is peaceful, yet attentive—good traits for a successful merchant—and she has learned to quickly assess potential buyers and suppliers.

In business, one must make quick judgments and synthesize information. Is this man an honest supplier? Can I trust him? Does this woman have the money to pay me for what she is ordering? Why does that man have shifty eyes? The woman wonders if I need an associate. I do, but is she a hard worker? Wait, look at the stitches in her veil: painstakingly minute. She cares about details; she'll be fine.

And indeed, Lydia's instincts are on high alert this morning, for the women are soon approached by a man named Paul and his friends. He tells her how he once persecuted Christians to the death, was transformed by seeing Jesus in a vision, came to know Jesus as the fulfillment of the ancient scriptures, and now works as a missionary, building communities of faith in Jesus' name. Communities of faith that reach out, that speak of eternal life, of purpose, of God.

Heart and mind tug at Lydia. There is something so real about this man, about what he is saying. He speaks the truth. He knows God. I can see it in his face, in his eyes. This Jesus of which he speaks...he loves me? He knows me? He was there when I was made? He was there at creation?

Within hours, Lydia is the first convert to Christianity on European soil. Baptized at the river with her household (perhaps she went back to get them; perhaps they had walked with her to the river), she invites Paul and his friends to stay with her while they are in Philippi—making her home one of the first faith communities on distant shores.

Her commitment to her new friends will soon be tested. Shortly, Paul and Silas will be arrested and imprisoned, survive an earthquake in jail, maintain their faith by singing and praying, convert the jailer and his family—and happily head back to Lydia's home dusty, bruised, starving, and exhausted.

Consider this

Lydia seems to be a fairly problem-free kind of woman. No demons, no physical issues, no poverty. She runs a prosperous business, she is able to make quick decisions (for example, she heard Paul preach and was baptized the same day), she is well-respected around the region, and she is quick to open her home and purse for the work of God's people.

She gives Paul a heart to trust within the faith community at Philippi—the recipient of one of Paul's most beautiful letters, still read regularly in congregations today. In that letter, he says that the Philippians were the only ones who gave him "financial help when he brought the good news and then traveled on..."[95] Given Lydia's character and generosity, the reader might have an inkling of just who Paul meant.

What might we learn from Lydia?

▷ Heart, mind, and soul are all worthy and necessary in a life of faith.

▷ Sharing our talents, time, and treasure can change the world.

▷ Setting aside time for prayer and spiritual companionship opens doors for the Holy Spirit to find us.

For reflection

1. What about Lydia was so helpful to the emerging faith community? What happened first with her that made all the difference?

2. How would you compare your stewardship of time, talent, and treasure to hers?

3. Lydia was responsible for helping God's mission be successful in the world. Often, we think of missions as specific projects to be accomplished in distant places. How did she see mission, and how do you see it?

THE FORTUNE-TELLING SLAVE GIRL

Demon-possessed

▷ **READ HER STORY:** Acts 16:16-19

▷ **CLASSIC MOMENT:** Shouting at and haranguing Paul, Silas, and most likely Luke

▷ **LIKELY CHARACTERISTICS:** Sad, Persistent, Perceptive, Annoying, Mission-minded

▷ **DATA:** 17 words

Who was the fortune-telling slave girl?

A slave girl, living in Philippi, who was owned by several men // A girl possessed by a spirit that supposedly gave her the ability to tell fortunes // A money maker for her owners // The last female to speak in the Bible[96]

What did the fortune-telling slave girl say?

While she followed Paul and us, she would cry out, "**These men are slaves of the Most High God, who proclaim to you a way of salvation.**" *Acts 16:17*

The fortune-telling slave girl's story

Imagine you are a girl who can tell fortunes—or sort of. Your mind is not your own; it seems to be controlled by other forces. Before it happened, you were just like everyone else, living at home. But no longer. Several men bought you from your parents, and now you travel, telling fortunes like a gypsy, day after day, hour after hour. The men never let you alone. One is always there to "interpret" your words, for sometimes your thoughts sound like incoherent babbling.

You do seem to have the gift of clairvoyance, ever since your mind went crazy. You sometimes see things. You sometimes understand what is in people's hearts. And you also listen, intently. Part of you enjoys knowing secrets, but most of you longs to be normal.

And what's with those three guys, the ones who have been hanging around the town square the last few days? You smile, but they ignore you. You wave, but they look the other way. Yet something about them sets off a clanging bell in your head. And then you know. Like you, they are also slaves, but to God.

You prance around them, "These men are slaves of God! They proclaim to you a way of salvation!" Over and over, you say it. "These men are slaves of God! They proclaim to you a way of salvation!" Day after day, you shout whenever you see them. You know you are annoying the men, but what do you have to lose? The world has already turned against you.

Finally the one who seems to be in charge cannot take it anymore. He turns to you and shouts, "I order you in the name of Jesus Christ to come out of her!"

And within the hour, you are acting like your old self. You are calm, happy, breathing deeply, thankful to the man who has healed you, and to Jesus, although you're not sure who he is. Yet your owners are upset. You have lost the ability to babble and can't see into the future. Leaving you alone, they run and drag Paul and the others into the town square, beating and mauling them.

There is nothing you can do but run. Slipping behind buildings, weaving in and out of the shadows, you flee, thankful for the one who set you free.

Consider this

The fortune-telling slave girl is the last female to have her words recorded in the Bible. Most people then didn't know her and wouldn't have cared if she had vanished. Likewise, most people now have not heard of her.

Unbeknownst to her, and unnoticed by most of history, is the fact that her soul was clamoring for freedom. Whether that longing was God-inspired or self-generated, this girl was knocking on doors, looking to be released from her chains, both external (the men) and internal (the demon).

Who else in the Bible is like this girl, knocking to be let loose from physical or spiritual constraints? Some good examples include Hannah, in her prayerful request that God would unlock her womb; the bleeding woman, in her pursuit of Jesus after twelve years of uterine bleeding; and Mary Magdalene finding release from her own demons.

One more example that's too important to be overlooked is Eve, the first woman in the Bible to speak. Like the fortune-telling slave girl, Eve sought to be free, to step outside constraints, to know more, to be more. Like the fortune-telling girl whose actions were judged inappropriate by Paul, Eve, too, was told she was out of bounds. And yet both are part of God's story.

Women's first and last words inscripture indicate the search for freedom and the use of free will. All the way through the Bible, women knock on doors. Searching. Yearning. Reaching out. Restless.

Free will, freedom of thought, freedom of movement, freedom to know the world on one's own terms. Such is the nature of women throughout the Bible—and notice that all parts of the Trinity, all sides of God, support women in that quest. God is angry with Eve but protects her future path. Jesus reveals himself to Mary Magdalene after the Crucifixion, giving her the most precious job of all: to proclaim to the others that he has risen. And the Holy Spirit moves between Paul's surprise visit to Philippi (the course of his travels having been changed through a dream) and his annoyance at the slave girl's repeated calls to him. There does comes a time, after all, when a coincidence is no longer a coincidence.

What might we learn from the fortune-telling slave girl?

▷ Persistence or dogging someone can lead to unexpected consequences.

▷ God works in mysterious ways in spreading the word of salvation.

▷ Freedom is worth fighting for.

▷ Free will is a gift from God.

For reflection

1. What caused the fortune-telling slave girl to keep shouting at Paul and Silas? Could she have seen something in them, being naturally intuitive? Or couldn't the demon help itself from bothering men of God?

2. How did her owners use her fortune-telling skills to make money? Do you think she really could tell fortunes, or did the men just interpret her incoherent sounds as prophecies?

3. How might the term "spiritual warfare" describe what was happening inside and around the girl? How can women who are trapped in harmful situations also find their way out? What part does the Holy Spirit play?

AND ALL SHALL BE WELL

I hope and pray that this is the way things have worked out:

Sarah and Hagar are now friends.

The mother of the tortured seven sons has been reunited with her boys, and all are pulled up around God's heavenly table.

Mary and Jesus and Joseph are infinitely close and no longer does Mary have to stand outside in the crowds, only to have Jesus say, "Who is my mother?"

The woman who was caught in adultery has found true love.

The Samaritan woman at the well was able to settle on a husband.

Someone has made dinner for Martha of Bethany.

Pilate has learned to listen to his wife.

Young Tamar has children and is happy.

Leah is finally loved—passionately—for who she is.

The Samaritan woman at the well has passed the bar exam. Without studying.

Bathsheba can take a bath and just have it be a bath.

Jephthah's daughter is frolicking in heaven.

Lot's daughter is convinced she had a really bad dream.

and...

The concubine who was raped and then divided into pieces has been made whole...and when Jesus died, he searched for her, found her, brushed his hand against her forehead to heal her memories, then offered her his arm... and entered heaven with her at his side.

ACKNOWLEDGMENTS

With thanks to...

The Episcopal Church Women (ECW), for a research grant to accomplish this work, and for their companionship in the process.

Forward Movement, for its longtime ministry of communications in The Episcopal Church and for its support in publishing these findings.

Researchers Susan Webster and Christy Stang of Trinity Episcopal Church in Excelsior, Minnesota, for their four-year commitment to this project, for their love of all things biblical, for maintaining our database of who spoke and what they said, and for their help in all facets of this book. When you see the term "we," these are my research partners.

Joyce White, of Trinity, Excelsior, for her extensive proofreading and encouragement.

Sis Coenan, of St. John's Episcopal Church in Ketchikan, Alaska, who provided the first draft of study questions and set up our initial database.

The Rev. Devon Anderson, Trinity's rector, for her vibrant support and hospitality.

Robert Larner, PhD, our Roman Catholic Boston-based consultant, for his extensive scope of biblical and theological knowledge.

Missionary Carol Erickson (Kenya), Lelia Mizer (Florida), Kami Pohl (Minnesota), and Shirley Erickson (Washington) for their expertise in all things biblical and for their participation in our online study/discovery group.

Cordelia Burt and the women of St. Jude's Episcopal Church, Ocean View, Hawaii, for their prayers, Kona coffee, and chocolate-covered macadamia nuts that sustained this writer at all hours.

Sheryl Kujawa-Holbrook, vice president for academic affairs and dean of the faculty at Claremont School of Theology in Claremont, California, and Cynthia Briggs Kittredge, president and dean of the Seminary of the Southwest in Austin, Texas, for thirty years of friendship and support.

Nancy Crawford, president of the Episcopal Church Women, for her leadership skills and energy around this project.

Scott Gunn, Richelle Thompson, Rachel Tjornehoj, and Miriam McKenney of Forward Movement, for their considerable expertise and ability to make things happen—and for the rest of the Forward Movement staff who turn words into magic.

Jana Riess, editor, for her love of language, knowledge of scripture, and phenomenal biblical humor.

Leonard Freeman, my loving and talented husband, who is both blessed and cursed in hearing the opinion, several times over, of every Bible woman who has ever spoken. A poet and priest, he manages to keep his sanity, faith, and humor, and is my primary theological consultant, numbers-cruncher, and beloved soul mate.

Lindsay Hardin Freeman

SUGGESTIONS FOR USE

Written for both individual and group use, this book may be read cover to cover or studied thematically. While not an exhaustive list in each area, here are some ideas for retreats or weekly study:

Advent Studies (three weeks)

Samson's Mother   Elizabeth
Mary, the Mother of Jesus

Witches and Prophets (four weeks)

Deborah   The witch of Endor
Huldah   The Syrophoenecian woman

Lenten Studies (five weeks)

Martha of Bethany   Mary of Bethany
Pilate's wife   Mary Magdalene
Mary Magdalene, Mary the mother of James, and Salome

The Power of Love (six weeks)

The real mother   The widow of Zarephath
The Shulammite woman   Esther
Edna   Mary Magdalene

Healing from Rape, Incest, and Prostitution (six weeks)

Lot's older daughter   Young Tamar
Tamar   The real mother and the false mother
Rahab   Susanna

Prayer and Sacrifice (seven weeks)

Hannah

Esther

Mother of seven sons

Salome, mother of the sons of Zebedee

Jephthah's daughter

Sarah, wife to seven husbands

Mary the mother of Jesus

Wicked and Wily Women (seven weeks)

Potiphar's wife

The false mother

Athaliah

Sapphira

Delilah

Jezebel

Herodias (the mother)

Diplomats and Survivors (seven weeks)

Tamar

Jael

Naomi

The wise woman of Tekoa

Rahab

Ruth

Abigail

Women and War (eight weeks)

Deborah

Servant girl of Namaan's wife

The woman of Bahurim

The wives and women of Pathros

Jael

The woman who ate her son

The wise woman of Abel

Judith

Sorrow and Anguish (eight weeks)

Hagar

Phinehas's wife

Job's wife

Mary Magdalene

Rachel

The mother of seven sons

The woman caught in adultery

Mary the mother of Jesus

Healing and hospitality (nine weeks)

Sarah

Edna

The servant girl of Namaan's wife

The bleeding woman

Martha of Bethany

The widow of Zarephath

The Shunammite woman

The Syrophoenician woman

Mary of Bethany

Faith and Business Issues (nine weeks)

Shiprah and Puah

Achsah

Wise woman of Baharim

Susanna

Lydia

Daughters of Zelophehad

The queen of Sheba

The Syrophoenician woman

Sapphira

Girls in the Bible (ten weeks)

Rebekah

Jephthah's daughter

Young Tamar

Herodias (the daughter)

Mary

Miriam

Girls fetching water

The servant girl of Namaan's wife

Servant girls

The fortune-telling slave girl

The Original Team: The Women of Genesis (eleven weeks)

Eve

Hagar

Rebekah

Rachel

Tamar

Potiphar's wife

Sarah

Lot's older daughter

Leah

Rachel's midwife

Tamar's midwife

Mothers in the Bible (twenty weeks)

Sarah

Rebekah

Rachel

Hannah

The wise woman of Tekoa

The widow of Zarephath

The woman who ate her son

King Belshazzar's mother

Herodias

Mary the mother of James and Salome

Hagar

Leah

Samson's mother

Bathsheba

The real mother and the false mother

The Shunammite woman

Job's wife

The mother of seven sons

The Syrophoenician woman

Mary the mother of Jesus

STATISTICS

No women speak in:

Leviticus

Deuteronomy

Ezra

Nehemiah

The Book of Psalms

The Book of Proverbs

Ecclesiastes

Isaiah

Lamentations

Ezekiel

Hosea

Amos

Obadiah

Jonah

Micah

Nahum

Habakkuk

Zephaniah

Haggai

Zechariah

Malachi

In the Apocrypha:

Wisdom of Solomon

Ecclesiasticus

Baruch

The Letter of Jeremiah

The Additions to the Greek Book
  of Daniel

The Prayer of Azariah & the Song
  of the Three Jews

1 and 3 Maccabees

1,2,3, and 4 Esdras

Prayer of Manasseh

Psalm 151

In the New Testament

Romans	Titus
1 & 2 Corinthians	Philemon
Galatians	Hebrews
Ephesians	James
Philippians	1 & 2 Peter
Colossians	1,2, & 3 John
1 & 2 Thessalonians	Jude
1 & 2 Timothy	Revelation

Word Totals for All Women: most to fewest

Total Word Count for All Bible Women=14,056
Women in the Apocrypha are listed in italics.
*Esther speaks in the Old Testament and the Apocrypha.

Woman	Number of Words
Judith	2,689
Shulammite woman	1,425
Esther*	1207 (416 words in OT, 791 words in Apocrypha)
Mother of seven sons	616
Hannah	474
Woman of Tekoa	437
Huldah	416
Naomi	411
Abigail	316
Rebekah	293

Rahab	255
Queen of Sheba	228
Ruth	212
Sarah, wife of seven husbands	208
Bathsheba	192
Mary, mother of Jesus	191
Real mother	165
Anna	151
Samaritan woman	151
Shunammite woman	150
Sarah	141
Leah	137
Samson's mother	129
Witch of Endor	126
Delilah	123
Edna	120
Deborah	114
Rachel	112
Susanna	112
Jezebel	108
Martha	106
Widow of Zarephath	104
King Belshazzar's mother	104
Elizabeth	102
Potiphar's wife	99

Wise woman of Abel	86
Young Tamar, David's daughter	82
Lot's older daughter	80
Girls fetching water	77 (group)
Eve	74
Jephthah's daughter	65
Rachel and Leah	64 (group)
Daughters of Zelophehad	64 (group)
Women of Bethlehem	64 (group)
Mary Magdalene	61
Tamar	60
Woman who ate her son	55
Michal	54
Maid of Raguel	52
Syrophoenician/Canaanite woman	44
Wife of a member of the company of prophets	43
Women of Pathros	42 (group)
Achsah	41
Miriam	36
Herodias's daughter	34
Hagar	33
Pharoah's daughter	32
Micah's mother	28
Samson's wife	25

Shiphrah and Puah	23 (group)
Jael	23
Bleeding woman	22
Salome, mother of sons of Zebedee	22
Servant girl 1	22
Pilate's wife	22
False mother	21
Servant girl of Naaman's wife	19
Priest of Midian's daughters	17 (group)
Lydia	17
Fortune-telling slave girl	17
Zipporah	15
Phinehas's wife	14
Mary Magdalene, Mary mother of James, and Salome	14 (group)
Tamar's midwife	13
Servant girl 2	13
Woman in the crowd	13
Mary of Bethany	12
Rachel's midwife	11
Job's wife	11
Woman guarding the gate	11
Women attending wife of Phinehas	10 (group)

Women of Israel	10 (group)
Ruth and Orpah	9 (group)
Woman at Bahurim	8
Martha and Mary of Bethany	7 (group)
Mother of Jabez	6
Herodias (mother)	6
Sapphira	5
Athaliah	4
Woman caught in adultery	3

NOTES

[1] Roman Catholic and Orthodox Christian Bibles include the books of Apocrypha as part of the Old Testament, for forty-nine and fifty-one total books respectively, while Jewish Bibles do not include the Apocrypha texts.

[2] Although consciously limited, the pronoun "he" is used a handful of times in this book to refer to God. Some readers may find that offensive; however, many find the use of no pronouns or gender-neutral pronouns to be even more awkward, especially when it comes to sacred storytelling. I have also come to believe that helping others to develop a relationship with God—and with these ancient women of faith—is more important than strict gender protocol in every instance.

[3] http://www.presidency.ucsb.edu/sou_words.php

[4] http://www.crossway.org/blog/2007/11/bible-text-stats, using the *New American Bible* as a general reference.

[5] For some of the women of the Bible (the Shulammite woman, or Zilphah), different translations have variant spellings. We have followed the conventions of the New Revised Standard Version.

[6] Naomi Harris Rosenblatt, *After the Apple: Women in the Bible—Timeless Stories of Love, Lust and Longing.* (New York: Miramax Books, 2005), 25.

[7] Charlotte Gordon, *The Woman Who Named God: Abraham's Dilemma and the Birth of Three Faiths.* (Boston: Little, Brown and Company, 2009), 138.

[8] The others are Eve and Rebekah.

[9] Various biblical traditions have suggested that it was Ishmael who wept. He may have wept, and most likely did, but the original Hebrew says it is Hagar who wept. See vs. 21:16. Phyllis Trible, *Texts of Terror: Literary-Feminist Readings of Biblical Narratives* (Philadelphia: Fortress Press, 1984), 24-25. For consistency's sake with biblical usage, however, this book uses the New Revised Standard Version translation where God responded first to Ishmael's voice.

[10] The other woman was her younger sister.

[11] Some Bible translations say the women were married; others say they were engaged (virginity was the primary issue).

[12] The other was Salome, asking for John the Baptist's head on a platter (Mark 6:24-25).

[13] Miki Raver, *Listen to Her Voice: Women of the Hebrew Bible* (San Francisco: Chronicle Books, 1998), 63.

[14] *The Hymnal* according to the use of The Episcopal Church (New York: The Church Hymnal Corporation, 1982), Ora Labora, 541.

[15] Tikva Frymer-Kensky, *Reading the Women of the Bible: A New Interpretation of their Stories.* (New York: Schocken Books, 200). See pages 266-271 for a brilliant interpretation of the levirate laws.

[16] *The New Oxford Annotated Bible,* New Revised Standard Version with the Apocrypha (New York: Oxford University Press, 2010), 85.

[17] Uncle Wiggily Longears was an elderly, lop-eared, rabbit created by author Howard R. Garis in 1910. Often in danger, he was usually saved by little woodland creatures for whom he had once done a favor. Moral underdogs saving God's people is a favorite biblical theme as well.

[18] Noted here because of importance; not included in word count as Miriam is speaking with a male.

[19] Carol L. Meyers, Toni Craven, and Ross Shepard Kraemer, eds., *Women in Scripture: A Dictionary of Named and Unnamed Women in the Hebrew Bible, the Apocryphal/Deuterocanonical Books, and the New Testament.* (Grand Rapids, Michigan: William B. Eerdmans Publishing Company, 2000), 187. Though Zipporah, Moses' pedigree is enhanced, given that Levites were the priestly caste.

[20] Carol A. Newsom and Sharon H. Ringe, eds., *Women's Bible Commentary.* (Louisville, Kentucky: Westminster John Knox Press, 1988), 88. In ancient Hebrew, the word "feet" was sometimes substituted as a euphemism for genitalia.

[21] Edith Deen, *All the Women of the Bible.* (New York: Harper and Row, 1955), 54-56.

[22] Tikva Frymer-Kensky, "Zipporah," *Women in Scripture,* 171.

[23] http://www.jta.org/2013/06/28/news-opinion/politics/edie-windsors-lawyer-and-the-daughters-of-zelophehad

[24] Deen, *All the Women of the Bible,* 63.

[25] This is an estimate; some say up to a million.

[26] Numbers 13. Caleb is righteous in both accounts, Joshua in one.

[27] Numbers 14:3.

[28] The copy in Joshua 2 is sexually ambiguous.

[29] Holy war means that everything is destroyed but no plunder is taken. Everything goes to God.

[30] There is some debate about this, but 1 Chronicles 2:49 seems to indicate it.

[31] Read Numbers 13-14 for background.

[32] Numbers 32:16-17 contradicts earlier biblical tradition a bit in terms of who was allowed to settle in the Promised Land, but the point is that Caleb was a brave man; his daughter inherited that trait.

[33] Frymer-Kensky, *Reading the Women of the Bible: A New Interpretation of their Stories,* 53.

[34] http://jwa.org/encyclopedia/article/jael-wife-of-heber-kenite-midrash-and-aggadah

[35] Note the tone of Samson's parents' voices above: Is not there a woman anywhere who would please you besides THAT ONE? Similar parent/child conflict occurs in the twenty-first century; sometimes it seems as though not much has changed.

[36] *The New Oxford Annotated Bible,* 380.

[37] *The New Oxford Annotated Bible,* 323. Living in the Valley of Sorek, Delilah could have been either a Philistine or an Israelite.

[38] Whether they had sexual intercourse is something scholars have disagreed on; after much research, this author believes they did not, as Boaz was an honorable man and, most likely, would not have taken advantage of Ruth, even though she presented herself in a sexual manner. Curling up with a happy and probably drunk man was not normal advice...but then, Naomi was not a normal mother-in-law.

[39] Although Ruth speaks separately elsewhere, she and Orpah comprise a subgroup of named women who speak together.

[40] In the Book of Ruth, there are three instances where an unnamed group of women speaks. They may be composed of the same women, or they may not. Erring on the side of accuracy, here these groups are designated as separate bodies.

[41] The Ark of the Covenant contained the stone tablets on which the Ten Commandments were inscribed; it was a symbol of God's presence.

[42] Samuel did not want the people of Israel to have a king because he saw God as the king. In taking his case to God, however, God said, "Listen to their voice and set a king over them" (1 Samuel 8:22).

[43] Rosenblatt, *After the Apple: Women in the Bible: Timeless Stories of Love, Lust and Longing*, 148.

[44] 1 Kings 1:30. This is more of a feat than it appears, for usually the crown would go to the oldest son. Solomon was the second son of the Bathsheba union, conceived immediately after the illegitimate infant son who died (2 Samuel 12:24). But in 1 Chronicles 3, Solomon is listed as the fourth living son of the Bathsheba-David union. Despite this apparent discrepancy, the main point is that God's desires outweigh traditional lines of succession. God does new things.

[45] When David was close to death, the beautiful young Abishag had been sent in to keep the old king "warm." When David was not sexually aroused, word traveled fast: death really was approaching. With David's death, she would have been "passed on" to Solomon, not Adonijah.

[46] Phyllis Trible. 1984. *Texts of Terror: Literary-Feminist Readings of Biblical Narratives*. Philadelphia: Fortress Press. She names four such heart-wrenching stories, including Tamar; the concubine who was gang-raped, divided into twelve pieces, and sent to the twelve tribes of Israel (Judges 19:22-29); Jephthah's daughter (Judges 11:29-40); and Hagar (Genesis 16, 21:9-20).

[47] Absalom had fled after killing Amnon. His exile lasted about three years.

[48] Claudia V. Camp, "Wise Woman of Abel-Beth Maacah: Bible" *The Jewish Women's Archives*, http://jwa.org/encyclopedia/article/wise-woman-of-abel-beth-maacah-bible.

[49] There is no equivalent word for "kingdom," like "queendom," or else we would use it.

[50] One talent is roughly the equivalent of seventy-five pounds, so 120 talents of gold equals roughly 9,000 pounds or 94.5 US tons. With the price of gold at circa $1255 per troy ounce in early 2014 (one ounce equals 0.91145833 troy ounces), the figure used in the Bible works out to just about $164,718,750. Bottom line: The Queen of Sheba is very wealthy. And Solomon notices.

[51] *The Book of Common Prayer*, An Outline of the Faith, 854.

[52] Some scholars consider this story to be an analogy of God's love for Israel: although the kingdoms had become divided, there still lingered a flicker of hope for unity and redemption.

[53] Athaliah is mentioned as being from the house of Omri (2 Kings 8:26) but she is clearly Ahab's

relative (some say sister but most commentators say daughter, as does the Bible). Ahab was a descendant of King David.

54 Meyers, *Women in Scripture*, 277.

55 The word "prophetess" is used in some Bible translations, but is a rather lackluster word; thus the choice to use the word "prophet."

56 The keeper of the wardrobe's job was to protect, mend, organize, and keep priestly garments clean for use in the temple.

57 2 Kings 22:8. Many scholars think that this discovery was either the entire Pentateuch (the first five books of the Bible) or just the book of Deuteronomy.

58 The Second Quarter refers to a new quarter to the north of the temple, most likely built for temple workers.

59 No women speak in 2 Chronicles, Ezra, or Nehemiah.

60 *The New Oxford Annotated Bible*, 581.

61 *The New American Standard Bible* translates fifty cubits as seventy-five feet high.

62 Deen, *All the Women of the Bible*, 146.

63 Meyers, *Women in Scripture*, 293.

64 No women speak in Psalms, Proverbs, or Ecclesiastes. Some readers may wonder why Lady Wisdom is not included here, since she figures prominently in the wisdom books of the Bible and speaks a significant amount of words. Our parameters for this book include only those women who are real flesh and blood women and who speak for themselves.

65 http://jewishencyclopedia.com/articles/13916-song-of-songs.

66 Lindsay Hardin Freeman, *The Scarlet Cord: Conversations with God's Chosen Women* (London: John Hunt Publishing, 2010), 82.

67 No women speak in Isaiah.

68 Gordon D. Fee and Robert L. Hubbard, Jr., eds., *The Eerdmans Companion to the Bible* (Grand Rapids, Michigan: William B. Eerdmans Publishing Company, 2011), 415.

69 Kathleen M. O'Connor, *Women's Bible Commentary*. (Louisville, KY: Westminster John Knox Press, 1988), 183.

70 http://www.biblegateway.com/blog/2011/03/did-god-have-a-wife, March 25, 2013.

71 No women speak in Lamentations, Ezekiel, Hosea, Amos, Obadiah, Jonah, Micah, Nahum, Habakkuk, Zephaniah, Haggai, Zechariah, or Malachi.

72 In ancient days, demons were understood to be the cause of emotional and physical ailments. We understand both differently today, but even Jesus seemed to place the blame for many ailments on actual demons, and once he called them out, people were healed. Truth be told, emotional and physical illness are often the work of outside influences—from cancer-causing environments, trauma suffered as a child or as an adult, poverty, genetic imbalances, or the work of the Adversary—all of which separate us from God.

73 No women speak in Wisdom of Solomon, Ecclesiasticus, Baruch, or The Letter of Jeremiah.

74 Susanna is included in Roman Catholic and Orthodox Bibles as Chapter 13 of the Book of Daniel.

[75] No women speak in 1 and 3 Maccabees; 1, 2, 3 and 4 Esdras; Prayer of Manasseh; or Psalm 151.

[76] Barbara Reid, O.P., *The Gospel According to Matthew* (Collegeville, MN: Liturgical Press, 2005), 14.

[77] She is listed here as the first woman to speak because, although Matthew says, "she spoke to herself," Mark simply says, "she spoke."

[78] The text does not name the body part from which the woman was bleeding, but twenty centuries of oral history have defined her disorder as uterine bleeding.

[79] Newsom, *Women's Bible Commentary with Apocrypha*, 355.

[80] Josephus, *Antiquities* 18.5.137-38.

[81] Matthew refers to this woman as the "Canaanite woman." Mark, more accurately, calls her the "Syrophoenician woman," because Tyre (on the coast of the Mediterranean) was in Syria, once a part of ancient Phoenicia (a wealthy, seafaring territory on the Mediterranean Sea, whose residents worshiped Baal). Both Matthew and Mark are emphasizing that this woman is an outsider, both religiously and geographically.

[82] Mark is kinder, saying Zebedee was left "with the hired men" (Mark 1:20).

[83] William Barclay, *The Gospel of John, volume 2.* (Philadelphia, Westminster Press, 1975), 256.

[84] See more about the conflict between Jews and Samaritans on page 258.

[85] Because their story is the same but they speak individually, these girls are presented together, but counted separately.

[86] The napkin and the details of the dream are expansions upon the actual Bible text.

[87] Deen 1955. 208.

[88] William Barclay, *The Gospel of John.* (Philadelphia, Westminster Press, 1975), 255.

[89] Pletzels are small pieces of onion bread enjoyed in Jesus' time. Anthony F. Chiffolo and Rayner W. Hesse Jr. *Cooking with the Bible* (Westport, CT: Greenwood Press, 2006).

[90] Anthony F. Chiffolo and Rayner W. Hesse Jr., *Cooking with the Bible.* (Westport, CT: Greenwood Press, 2006). Pletzels are small pieces of onion bread enjoyed in Jesus' time. [89] She is not profiled here because her exact words are not reported.

[91] Mary Ann Getty-Sullivan, *Women in the New Testament.* (Collegeville, MN: The Liturgical Press, 2001), 96 ff.

[92] Barclay, *The Gospel of John, 2.* 2.

[93] Barclay, *The Gospel of John, 4.*

[94] Eugene H. Peterson, *The Message.* (Colorado Springs, CO: NavPress Publishing Group, 2005), 1980.

[95] Paul's letter to the Philippians 4:15.

[96] No women speak in the remaining books of the New Testament: Romans; 1 and 2 Corinthians; Galatians; Ephesians; Philippians; Colossians; 1 and 2 Thessalonians; 1 and 2 Timothy; Titus; Philemon; Hebrews; James; 1 and 2 Peter; 1, 2, and 3 John; Jude; and Revelation.

SOURCES AND FURTHER READING

Barclay, William. *The Gospel of John,* Volume 1. Philadelphia: The Westminster Press, 1975.

Bauckham, Richard. *Gospel Women: Studies of the Named Women in the Gospels.* Grand Rapids, Michigan: William B. Eerdmans Publishing Company, 2002.

Bellis, Alice Ogden. *Helpmates, Harlots, and Heroes: Women's Stories in the Hebrew Bible.* Louisville, Kentucky: Westminster/John Knox Press, 1994.

Brueggemann, Walter. *The Land: Place as Gift, Promise, and Challenge in Biblical Faith.* Minneapolis: Fortress Press, 2002.

Bushnell, Katharine C. *God's Word to Women.* Minneapolis, Minnesota: Christians for Biblical Equality, 1930, 2003.

Carter, Jimmy. *A Call to Action: Women, Religion, Violence and Power.* New York: Simon and Schuster, 2014.

Chiffolo, Anthony F., and Rayner, W. Hesse, Jr. *Cooking with the Bible: Biblical Food, Feasts, and Lore.* Westport, Connecticut: Greenwood Press, 2006.

Chittister, Joan. *The Friendship of Women: The Hidden Tradition of the Bible.* New York: BlueBridge, 2006.

Davis, Ellen F. *Who Are You, My Daughter?: Reading Ruth Through Image and Text.* Louisville, KY: Westminster John Knox Press, 2003.

Deen, Edith. *All of the Women of the Bible.* San Francisco: Harper and Row, 1955.

Essex, Barbara J. *More Bad Girls of the Bible.* Cleveland, Ohio: The Pilgrim Press, 2009.

Fee, Gordon D., and Robert L. Hubbard, Jr. *The Eerdmans Companion to the Bible.* Grand Rapids, Michigan, William B. Eerdmans Publishing Company, 2011.

Freeman, Lindsay Hardin and Karen N. Canton. *The Scarlet Cord: Conversations with God's Chosen Women.* London: Circle Books, 2010.

Feiler, Bruce. *Abraham: A Journey to the Heart of Three Faiths.* New York: William Morrow, 2002.

Frymer-Kensky, Tikva. *Reading the Women of the Bible: A New Interpretation of their Stories.* New York: Schocken Books, 2002.

Getty-Sullivan, Mary Ann. *Women in the New Testament.* Collegeville, Minnesota: The Liturgical Press, 2001.

Gordon, Charlotte. *The Woman who Named God: Abraham's Dilemma and the Birth of Three Faiths.* Boston: Little, Brown and Company, 2009.

Kalas, J. Ellsworth. *Strong Was her Faith: Women of the New Testament.* Nashville, Tennessee: Abingdon Press, 2007.

Kam, Rose Sallberg. *Their Stories, Our Stories: Women of the Bible.* New York: Continuum, 1995.

Klein, Lillian R. *From Deborah to Esther: Sexual Politics in the Hebrew Bible.* Minneapolis: Fortress Press, 2003.

Levine, Amy-Jill and Marc Zvi Brettler. *The Jewish Annotated New Testament.* New York: Oxford University Press, 2011.

McKenna, Megan. *Leave Her Alone.* Maryknoll, New York: Orbis Books, 2000.

Metzer, Bruce M., and Michael D. Coogan. *The Oxford Guide to People and Places of the Bible.* New York: Oxford University Press, 2001.

Meyers, Carol. Toni Craven, and Ross Kraemer, eds. *Women in Scripture: A Dictionary of Named and Unnamed Women in the Hebrew Bible, the Apocryphal/Deuterocanonical Books, and the New Testament.* Grand Rapids, Michigan: William B. Eerdmans Publishing Company, 2000.

Mirkin, Marsha. *The Women Who Danced by the Sea: Finding Ourselves in the Stories of our Biblical Foremothers.* Rhinebeck, New York: Monkfish Book Publishing Company, 2004.

Moltmann-Wendell, Elizabeth. *The Women Around Jesus.* Translated by John Bowden. New York: Crossroad, 1980.

Newsom, Carol A. and Sharon H. Ringe, eds. *Women's Bible Commentary: Expanded Edition with Apocrypha.* Louisville, Kentucky: Westminster John Knox Press, 1998.

Nowell, Irene, OSB. *Women in the Old Testament.* Collegeville, Minnesota: The Liturgical Press, 1997.

Ochs, Vanessa L. *Sarah Laughed: Modern Lessons from the Wisdom and Stories of Biblical Women.* New York: McGraw-Hill, 2004.

Odelain, O. and R. Seguineau. *The Dictionary of Proper Names and Places in the Bible.* Garden City, New York: Doubleday and Company, 1981.

Raver, Miki. *Listen to Her Voice: Women of the Hebrew Bible.* San Francisco: Chronicle Books, 1998.

Reid, Barbara E., O.P. *The Gospel According to Matthew.* Volume 1. Collegeville, Minnesota: Liturgical Press, 2005.

Rivers, Francine. *Unashamed: Rahab.* Carol Stream, Illinois: Tyndale House Publishers, 2001.

Ritley, M.R. *God of Our Mothers, Face to Face with Powerful Women of the Old Testament.* Harrisburg, Pennsylvania: Morehouse Publishing, 2006.

Rosenblatt, Naomi Harris. *After the Apple: Women in the Bible—Timeless Stories of Love, Lust, and Longing.* New York: Miramax Books, 2005.

Schoemperlen, Diane. *Our Lady of the Lost and Found: A Novel of Mary, Faith, and Friendship.* New York: Viking, 2001.

Soelle, Dorothee and Joe H. Kirchberger. *Great Women of the Bible in Art and Literature.* Minneapolis: Fortress Press, 2006.

Spencer, F. Scott. *Dancing Girls, Loose Ladies, and Women of the Cloth: The Women in Jesus' Life.* New York: The Continuum Publishing Group, 2004.

Spina, Frank Anthony. *The Faith of the Outsider: Exclusion and Inclusion in the Biblical Story.* Grand Rapids, Michigan: William B. Eerdmans Publishing Company, 2005.

Taylor, Marion Ann and Heather E. Weir. *Let Her Speak for Herself: Nineteenth-century Women Writing on Women in Genesis.* Waco, Texas: Baylor University Press, 2006.

Telushkin, Joseph. *Biblical Literacy: The Most Important People, Events and Ideas of the Hebrew Bible.* New York: William Morrow and Company, 1997.

Trible, Phyllis. *Texts of Terror: Literary-Feminist Readings of Biblical Narratives.* Philadelphia: Fortress Press, 1984.

Trigilio, John and Kenneth Brighenti. *Women in the Bible for Dummies.* Hoboken, New Jersey: Wiley, 2005.

Ulanov, Ann Belford. *The Female Ancestors of Christ.* Boston: Shambhala, 1993.

Wray, T.J. *Good Girls, Bad Girls: The Enduring Lessons of Twelve Women of the Old Testament.* Lanham, Connecticut: Rowman and Littlefield Publishers, 2008.

ABOUT THE AUTHOR

Lindsay Hardin Freeman is a Minnesota-based Episcopal priest, author, and mother. She is the author and/or editor of five books, including *The Scarlet Cord: Conversation with God's Chosen Women* and *The Spy on Noah's Ark and Other Bible Stories from the Inside Out.*

A popular speaker and retreat leader, she enjoys finding humor and grace in the Bible, and sharing it fully—and often irreverently. Her work takes her around the country, speaking to groups large and small about the accomplishments and struggles of Bible women as models for contemporary spirituality.

The longtime editor of *Vestry Papers* (2001 - 2010), she has won more than thirty awards for journalistic excellence. She serves as a ministry developer for the Episcopal Church in Minnesota and as adjunct clergy for St. David's, Minnetonka.

She is married to the Rev. Leonard Freeman (a poet, priest, and teacher) and has two sons and four stepchildren.

Bible Women: All Their Words and Why They Matter is the culmination of four years of work with a research team to explore the words of every woman who spoke in the Bible and what they have to say for us today.

To learn more about workshops, retreats, preaching, or conference speaking, visit www.LindsayHardinFreeman.com